On This Day In

INDIANAPOLIS HISTORY

DAWN E. BAKKEN

THE History PRESS

Published by The History Press
Charleston, SC
www.historypress.net

Front cover: City Market, 1908. *Courtesy Library of Congress, Prints and Photographs Division (LOC)*; Kurt Vonnegut Jr. *Courtesy Vonnegut Family Archives*; Soldiers and Sailors Monument, 1904. *Courtesy LOC*; World War I Farewell Parade, 1918. *Courtesy LOC*; Indiana State Fair Poster, 1886. *Courtesy LOC.*

Back cover, top: Dinosphere. *Courtesy Children's Museum of Indianapolis.*

First published 2016

Manufactured in the United States

ISBN 978.1.62619.757.2

Library of Congress Control Number: 2015954745

CONTENTS

ACKNOWLEDGEMENTS

Thank you to my parents, Darrell Bakken and Ruth Partridge Bakken, for teaching me a love of history and a love of reading. Both have led me to the job I am thankful to hold. Thanks to all of my colleagues—faculty and graduate students—at the *Indiana Magazine of History*, who have taught me so much about the process of researching, writing and revising history that is pleasurable to read, interesting and academically sound.

The new generation of technically proficient librarians has saved me countless hours of work. Thanks especially to the wonderful people at the Digital Library Program at Indiana University–Bloomington who digitized the *Indiana Magazine of History*, to the librarians at the Indiana State Library who have worked with the Library of Congress to digitize historic newspapers from all over the state and to the librarians at Indiana University–Purdue University Indianapolis for their digital collections relating to the history of Indianapolis.

Finally, thanks to Leslie Olsen of the Children's Museum of Indianapolis and to Julia Whitehead of the Kurt Vonnegut Memorial Library and members of the Vonnegut family for their generosity in providing two of my cover illustrations.

INTRODUCTION

In the summer of 1965, just before I entered first grade, my family moved to Indianapolis. We moved into a ranch-style house on the city's west side, and if the wind was coming in the right direction on race day, you could listen to the Indianapolis 500 on the radio from our driveway and hear the sound of the cars in the air. I attended Indianapolis Public Schools until we moved a little farther west—still within the bounds of the city, thanks to Unigov—where I attended Ben Davis High School. Many of my memories of Indianapolis are from the city of the mid-1960s to late 1970s: Pacers games when the team was still in the ABA; the Indianapolis Indians at Bush Stadium; fireworks downtown on the Fourth of July; the Indianapolis 500 (with my father, from high seats just into the first turn); a bus trip downtown with my mother every December for a day's shopping (and lunch at the Tea Room) at L.S. Ayres. The city today is vastly different from the one in which I grew up. But then Indianapolis, in its almost-two-hundred-year history, has undergone much greater changes than those of the last few decades.

Indianapolis was a town invented by the state legislature, and it grew slowly from its frontier origins. Until the 1850s, growth was held back by inadequate roads, a failed canal system and an unnavigable river. Railroads began to transform Indianapolis; the technological progress of post–Civil War America furthered the city's growth. By the turn of the twentieth century, Indianapolis was a bustling city that was home to three of the nation's most popular authors and to more than sixty factories manufacturing that new sensation, the automobile.

The city, like others in the Midwest, saw urban decay threaten in the 1960s and 1970s. Renewal came about from the work of mayors and local business leaders, members of neighborhood associations, historic preservationists and the owners, promoters and fans of a wide variety of sports. Indianapolis, when it was known for little else, was famous for the Indianapolis Motor Speedway and the Indy 500. By the end of the twentieth century, it was home to major league NFL and NBA teams, its longtime professional baseball team had a wonderful new downtown home, it had become a perennial host for Olympic trials and NCAA tournaments and the Speedway was hosting NASCAR and Formula One races.

The stories in this book are not presented in chronological order. I begin in 1970 and end in 1823. I have written about men and women who played major roles in the life of the city and the state (and sometimes the nation) and people whose names have been lost to history. You will find entries about a statehouse styled after a Greek temple and a roadhouse where John Dillinger and his gang went to drink. I have inevitably left out people, places and events that will be remarked on by some readers. The content, including errors and omissions, may be attributed solely to the author.

JANUARY

January 1, 1970

In one day, Indianapolis went from the twenty-sixth-largest city in the nation to the eleventh, when it became incorporated with Marion County into the political entity known as Unigov. By the 1960s, the county encompassed Indianapolis and a number of independent cities with their own mayors and councils, local ordinances, schools and police and fire forces. Indianapolis mayor Richard G. Lugar proposed a consolidation intended to streamline government, cut costs, improve efficiency and help revitalize the urban center of Indianapolis. The city would be governed by a city-county council, with an executive branch that oversaw administration of the county, and a city-county court system. Some cities, including Speedway and Beech Grove, retained much of their autonomy; schools remained divided between city and township; and many county offices mandated by the state constitution were retained. Urban planners, inside and outside the state, praised the move as a bold rethinking of city government. Within the city and throughout Indiana, reaction differed widely, but decades later, Unigov's basic structure remains in place.

January 2, 1910

"Electric Cars Collide in Dense New Year's Fog" read the *Indianapolis Star* headline. An interurban car leaving downtown Indianapolis headed to Martinsville had been struck by a "city" car carrying residents home.

Passengers escaped the wreckage of the smaller car, although the driver later died from injuries. The city's first interurban line—from Indianapolis to Greenwood to Franklin and back—had begun on January 1, 1900. Three weeks later, the Board of Public Works set the ticket price at six for twenty-five cents, with transfers included. By 1904, so many lines and so many cars were coming into and going out of the city that the interurban companies built the Indianapolis Traction Terminal downtown. By 1910, every city within a 120-mile distance from Indianapolis could be reached via a low-priced ticket on a comfortable electric interurban car. Most lines ran ten to twelve trains per day from early in the morning until late at night, and interurban transportation quickly became a preferred mode of travel within central Indiana. Ten thousand people passed through the Traction Terminal on an average day.

January 3, 1922

"Dry City Is Shank's Pledge!" exclaimed the *Indianapolis Star*. Thanks to the efforts of tens of thousands of temperance crusaders, the Woman's Christian Temperance Union and the Anti-Saloon League, Prohibition had finally been introduced in the United States in January 1920. In Indianapolis, the crime rate dropped for several months. But all too many citizens were unwilling to remain dry, and by the time Lew Shank was sworn in as the new mayor in January 1922, city jails and courts were clogged with bootleggers and those arrested for serving and consuming alcohol. In his inaugural speech, Shank took a hard line: "I've pledged myself to strict enforcement of the laws, and I'm going to enforce them. I don't care if you wear a high silk hat or overalls. If you're a bootlegger, I'm going to get you. So, boys, beware." Shank admitted, "I wasn't in favor of prohibition when the law was passed…but it's the law now." He also promised that there would be "no public gambling, and that is meant for crap-shooters as well as poker players."

January 4, 1934

Until the early 1930s, Indianapolis, like most of the nation, offered assistance to the poor, the unemployed, the sick and the hungry at the local level, often through private groups working with the city government or township trustees. The Depression overwhelmed social welfare networks, and in 1933, President Franklin D. Roosevelt began a series of federal programs supported by Indiana's new Democratic governor, Paul McNutt. From the statehouse and from the Indianapolis office of the Governor's Commission on Unemployment Relief, federal funds flowed into Indiana—more than $71 million in two years through the Federal Emergency Relief Administration alone. In 1934, FDR rolled out even more relief programs. Many Hoosiers opposed an increasingly powerful federal government, but their objections went largely unheard. "Roosevelt Wins Congress Acclaim," the *Indianapolis Star* headline read one day before the president had even presented the specifics of his new proposals. "Heavy majorities prepare to ratify recover moves. Practically no organized opposition indicated after president personally appeals for continued co-operation."

January 5, 1958

By the late 1950s, the nation was at the height of the Cold War. Politically conservative Hoosiers feared anything that suggested communism, a term that appeared frequently in editorials and letters to the editor in Indianapolis newspapers. The connection between the topic under consideration and the political philosophy was sometimes less than direct, but the vehemence of the authors was real. In January 1958, the chairman of the education committee of the Indianapolis Chamber of Commerce expressed his opposition to progressive education: "Child-centered programs stand revealed as soft and aimless when national survival is itself in question… Indianapolis escaped the worst idiocies of progressivism. Moreover we began the return to sanity long before Mr. Khrushchev made such a course of action seem highly desirable." But Chairman Burkhart was still worried, charging that most parents seemed to prefer driver education to foreign language education and "by similar reasoning, band gets more votes than algebra and extra-curricular activities are somehow seen as more valuable than the homework they have replaced…In the Sputnik age we can no longer afford such indulgences."

January 6, 1821

How do you choose the name of a new town, especially if that town is to become the state capital? In 1813, Corydon, along the Ohio River, became the capital of the Indiana Territory; in 1816, it became the first state capital. As Indiana's population grew and extended northward, state legislators began to debate the need for a new capital. After choosing a site in central Indiana, in January 1821 the legislature appointed three commissioners to oversee laying out the town and selling lots. One group of lawmakers wanted to name the town "Tecumseh," and another faction supported "Suwarrow." State Supreme Court justice Jeremiah Sullivan and Governor Jonathan Jennings supported the winning choice—Indianapolis. The Vincennes *Indiana Centinel* proclaimed the choice "one of the most ludicrous acts…of the sojourners at Corydon…Pronounce it as you please, gentle readers—you can do it as you wish—there is no danger in violating any system or rule." The "ludicrous" name stuck, and on January 10, 1825, Indianapolis (literally, "Indiana city") became the permanent capital.

January 7, 1862

Much of the history of the Civil War can be told, as filmmaker Ken Burns discovered, through the letters and diaries of soldiers. Men wrote private letters to their families and friends; many also wrote letters to their hometown newspapers, sharing their war experiences with a larger audience. The *Indianapolis Daily State Sentinel* printed a long letter from Lieutenant Jerome Beals, titled simply "Out on Picket." "Bang! *Down, boys*, there comes a rebel bullet," Beals began, describing how it felt "lying on one's back or side for twenty-four hours, not daring hardly to raise one's head, if you did, a bullet was sure to follow, is anything but pleasant." Beals wrote about the volleys that would go back and forth after one side fired a single shot at the other; he also tried to explain to readers back home how quickly death could come: "One of company G's men got a little too high up and received a ball through both lungs, he lingered a few days and finally died."

January 8, 1830

Had the predictions of Indiana state representative Alexander Morrison come true, the United States would have set aside January 8 as a national holiday celebrating the final major battle of the War of 1812. During a legislative session in January 1830, Morrison took the floor to commemorate the Battle of New Orleans: "Second only to the day of our national Jubilee, the birth-day of our independence, will the Eighth of January, 1815, be registered in the annals of our country's fame. On this day was asserted and defended what was proclaimed and demanded on the Fourth of July, 1776." The House's Committee on Arrangements organized "a procession comprised of the military, members of the Senate and House of Representatives, citizens, and many…visitors," which formed on Washington Street and marched to the courthouse to hear speeches. The day ended with a dinner that included forty-two toasts. The *Indianapolis Journal* reported a few days later that "at half past 2 o'clock, the company retired."

January 9, 1827

The *Indianapolis Journal* carried notice of the death of Alexander Ralston, remembering him as "skillful in his profession, honest in his dealings…a liberal and hospitable citizen." The Scottish emigrant made his name in the United States through his survey work for the federal government but made his mark on Indianapolis more directly—by laying out the town. In 1820, Ralston, who by then had moved westward, was hired to survey the site for Indiana's new state capital. In 1821, he developed a plat for a one-square-mile city with a circle at its center. The governor's home would sit within the circle; four streets radiated out diagonally from the circle, and the remaining streets were laid out north/south and east/west. Ralston's design was a triumph of optimism over reality: log cabins sat in the middle of some proposed streets, and 120-foot-wide Washington Street, designed to become an avenue for businesses and government buildings, was full of tree stumps that protruded from the ground. But Ralston's vision can still be seen in downtown Indianapolis—especially on Monument Circle.

January 10, 1943

By the beginning of 1943, the war was affecting life on the homefront, and businesses responded to and reflected those changes, even in their advertising. An ad in the *Indianapolis Star* for clothing detergent evoked the need to conserve and re-use: "I'm jealous," proclaimed a glamorous blonde, "my negligee is a washout, so streaked…but your pajamas look almost new after 29 washings!" "Sure," replied the pajama-clad brunette, "they're washed with gentle Ivory Flakes." Omar Bakeries advertised its bread delivery service with a testimonial from Mrs. George Alter, whose husband drove the family's only car to his war job every weekday: "You can't buy a week's supply of bread all at once. We depend on Omar Service." The ad also featured delivery driver Jack Kafold: "If you could talk to the folks in the 428 homes he served, you would learn that he's saving a lot of miles on their family cars…Now with gasoline and tire rationing in effect, his customers depend on him to keep them supplied with a basic food."

January 11, 1897

The *Indianapolis Sun* opened the debate on January 1: "It Is Dangerous: Football Under Present Rules Is a Menace to Life." Baseball manager W.H. Watkins offered his opinion that football should "hardly be classed as sport" and would never rival baseball because it was simply "too brutal" for spectators on a regular basis. On January 5, an editorial praised a University of Michigan professor for his denunciation of college athletics ("of little if any value") and his attempt to reform the school's athletic programs under faculty control. On January 6, the president of Franklin College weighed in: "[Football] seems to me brutal, dangerous and almost without an apology. The true philosophy of physical exercise is that it be moderate and at regular intervals." On January 11, the president of Butler College pronounced that the call to legislate an end to football was unnecessary: "Football is fast declining. There is not much life left in it—in this state, at any rate." On March 31, 1906, sixty-two colleges formed the Intercollegiate Athletic Association to regulate college sports—in particular, the game of football.

January 12, 1882

On March 3, 1880, Wabash, Indiana, became the first city in the world to have its streets lighted with electricity. In 1881, the Brush Electric Light Company approached the Indianapolis City Council with a similar offer. After months of rejection, the council granted a franchise to the company but refused the offer of streetlights. So in January 1882, the company displayed its technology in Union Station. "The Electric Light…The Experiment a Gratifying Success," reported the *Indianapolis Journal*. The company placed sixteen electric lights inside and around the building to be turned on at twilight and to stay on until 11:00 p.m. "Many who had not seen the light," wrote the reporter, "visited the depot, so that the building was full of people during the evening. When the trains came in at 10 o'clock, the light attracted much attention." But not until 1892 did the city council grant a local company a contract for electric lights on the city's streets.

January 13, 1828

On this day in 1828, Isaiah Osborn went to the printing office in Indianapolis to mail a letter to his brother John, who lived in Ohio. Isaiah wrote that he had just received John's last letter, dated December 9, 1827, one day earlier, because the mail "had been detained by high water till this time." Of Indianapolis itself, he wrote: "This town is situated on the east side of White river in a high-dry bottom, the court house three-fourths of a mile from the river. The place begins to look like a town. There are about a thousand acres cut smooth, ten stores, six taverns, a court house which cost $15,000, many fine houses, and six weeks back had in it 1,066 inhabitants, lots worth $100, and the place somewhat sickly but improving." Although Isaiah was earning "from three to four dollars a week clear," he intended to leave Indianapolis soon—there were few fellow Quakers in the city, and he preferred to return to the Richmond area to "work on my land or teach a school."

January 14, 1911

The twentieth century brought a revolution in public health as scientists began to understand the microscopic causes behind common illnesses. One Sunday *Indianapolis Star* devoted a dramatically illustrated page to the small metal drinking cups attached to public water fountains. "Death Lurks on Brim of Public Cup" read the headline, next to a pictured gentleman offering a cup of water to a lady. Issuing from the cup was a black cloud; in the cloud, hovering behind the woman's head, was a skeletal figure reaching toward her. The point of the article was very real: according to studies conducted by the Kansas State Board of Health, now under review by the Indiana Board of Health, public drinking cups had been found to be laden with a variety of germs, many of which were related to infectious diseases, including diphtheria. One of the proposed solutions was a new type of fountain, from which a bubbling stream of water continuously issued, allowing people to drink directly from the water source without touching anything.

January 15, 1915

In the first decades of the twentieth century, a plan to erect a ten-story building in downtown Indianapolis was front-page news. The *Indianapolis Star* reported that a "huge" edifice "devoted especially to shops...the first of its kind in Indianapolis" was planned for the corner of Washington and Meridian Streets. The building, like so many other important buildings in

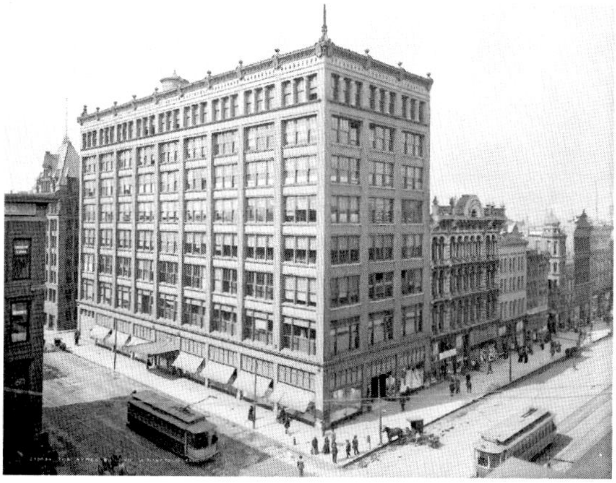

The L.S. Ayres building, designed by Vonnegut & Bohn. *Author's collection.*

the city, was designed by Vonnegut & Bohn. In 1888, German immigrants Bernard Vonnegut and Arthur Bohn began a twenty-year partnership that produced, among other city landmarks, Das Deutsche Haus, the Herron School of Art and the L.S. Ayres department store. After Bernard's death, Vonnegut's son replaced him at the firm, which continued to design public buildings and private homes, including the William H. Block building and the American Fletcher National Bank building.

January 16, 2014

As Indiana celebrated the legacy of Dr. Martin Luther King Jr., members of the General Assembly and representatives of state history organizations gathered in the statehouse to unveil two bronze busts. One portrayed Congresswoman Julia Carson, the first black woman from Indianapolis to serve in the U.S. Congress; the other bust commemorated James Sidney Hinton, the first African American to serve in the Indiana General Assembly. Hinton was born in 1834 to free black parents and moved with his family to Terre Haute, Indiana, at age fourteen. Hinton served in the Union army, recruiting other African Americans for the U.S. Colored Troops, including the Indiana Twenty-eighth Regiment of Colored Troops. After the war, Hinton settled in Indianapolis and became active in the Republican Party. From 1873 to 1877, he served the state as a trustee of the Wabash and Erie Canal, and in 1880, he was elected to the House of Representatives. The *Indianapolis Journal* described him as "a man of decided force and ability, with a lively interest in the welfare of Marion county." Hinton served one term, sponsoring a variety of legislation to benefit his constituents and to promote the civil rights of black Hoosiers.

January 17, 1944

Putting out newspapers that were daily filled with war news, it must have amused the editors of the *Indianapolis News* to offer some old-fashioned news on the front page. "Old Bootleg Days Recalled by Raid" was the headline for a story out of the 1920s. Police had raided the home of Mr. and Mrs. Claude Hawkins, arresting the couple and three other people in the house when they discovered a still, fashioned out of a fifteen-gallon auto gasoline tank. The officer representing the Bureau of Internal Revenue, Alcohol Tax Unit, told the reporter that "a dead rat had been found in the mash." The agent and the police conducted four other raids, arresting several people, including those gathered at a "gaming house" kept by Lawrence Bradley. The results of the Bradley raid were distinctly unimpressive, yielding only "a deck of cards, 50 cents and a bottle of whisky."

January 18, 1942

In 1925, the first Hoosier Salon showcased members of the Hoosier Group—including T.C. Steele, J. Ottis Adams and Will Vawter—as well as works by other artists born in or working across the state. Success prompted the sponsoring Daughters of Indiana to make the salon an annual event. For many years, the exhibition was held at Marshall Fields in downtown Chicago. In 1942, the salon finally arrived in Indianapolis, in the auditorium of the William H. Block department store. Among the painters shown that year was Brown County artist Edward K. Williams. Interviewed by the *Milwaukee Journal* about his painting of a winter scene in Door County, Wisconsin, Williams explained, "You can't get good snow for a winter landscape anywhere else, certainly not in southern Indiana," even if he did have to work "with my easel set up on a snowbank." The salon was a feature of downtown Indianapolis culture for decades. Today, the salon continues its support "for both visual art and its public appreciation" in the Arts and Design District of Carmel, Indiana.

January 19, 1859

A crowd filled the main chamber of the statehouse to listen to three women plead the cause of women's rights to a joint gathering of the General Assembly. Mary F. Thomas spoke in favor of a petition—signed by more than one thousand men and women from Wayne County—that the legislators "grant to women the same rights in property as men, and also the right of suffrage." In 1844, the legislature had rejected a petition to allow married women to own property, advising instead that women adopt "the good old mode of a loving and abiding confidence" in their husbands. In 1846, Indiana women gained the right to make their own wills, but thirteen years later little else had changed. After listening to the speeches, the legislators retired to their deliberations. Representative R.J. Ryan, the clerk of the House, offered "some wholesome advice" to the women—"everything was conceded to the ladies" already, and he offered as proof his new suit of clothing, purchased "because he had lately to step so often in the gutters, to let the ladies have the clean dry side-walk." The petition failed; the next petition for women's suffrage did not reach the General Assembly until 1871, when it was also defeated.

January 20, 2015

As more Americans have begun to conduct genealogical research, local and state libraries have responded by offering special programs, creating research guides to the libraries' holdings and hiring and training library staff with expertise in historical records research. Many libraries have also developed sophisticated websites that allow remote users to access holdings in an easy-to-navigate digital environment. When Family Tree software makers released their 2015 list of the best genealogical websites in the nation, Indiana was represented by the Indiana Historical Society. The society began in 1830; in 1886, led by historian Jacob Piatt Dunn, the society was reorganized and revitalized. The society's library opened in 1934; during the same period, the IHS began to publish documentary collections of state history and distinguished monographs. Challenged by a lack of space, the society moved into its own downtown building in 1999. Historical and genealogical researchers can now make extensive use of the William H. Smith Memorial Library and its collections both in person and online.

January 21, 1899

In 1895, William Porter and George Stewart began publishing the weekly *Indianapolis Recorder*, "a Negro newspaper" that "solicit[ed] news, contributions, opinions and in fact all matter affecting the Race." The editors offered their opinions on important matters of the day—"Rumor has it that there is a movement on foot among our Republican friends in Marion county to quietly but steadily 'unload' the Negro," began the lead editorial on January 21, 1899. Readers could keep abreast of legal, political and business news that affected the African American community; they could read about events at local churches and social clubs; they could follow the progress of black sports teams; and they could find out what movies, plays and musical concerts were being offered that week in black-owned theaters and clubs. The owners of all types of black-owned businesses could advertise to their customer base in the highly segregated business conditions of Indianapolis. By the early 1900s, while other local newspapers offered back-page columns of "Negro news," the *Recorder* enjoyed a weekly circulation of fifteen thousand.

January 22, 1822

One of the first marriages in Indianapolis took place on this day, according to Sarah Fletcher's diary: "Mr. [Uriah] Gates was to-day wedded to Miss Patsy Chinn, both of Indianapolis. I attended the wedding. It was a very disagreeable day, but notwithstanding there was a great concourse of people present." The next day, Wilkes Reagan, a butcher who also served as the local justice of the peace, gave a party for the couple. Fletcher recalled that guests "danced till a bout 1 o clock." John Nowland, in his account of early Indianapolis, added that the centerpiece of the meal that night was a whole roasted pig, prominently displayed with an apple in its mouth. Six days later, the first issue of the town's first newspaper, the *Indianapolis Gazette*, announced the wedding and, in honor of the event, printed what must have been the first poem to contain the town's name: "Come Hymen, now, and bear thy sway / In Indianapolis, / And hasten on the wished-for day / That crowns the nuptial bliss."

January 23, 1879

The *Indianapolis Journal* printed a story of the death of farmer Leonidas Grover. Grover had lived an ordinary, peaceable life with his daughter and her husband until one winter morning. Going to awake her father for breakfast, the woman found him "lying upon his shattered bed, a mutilated corpse." There was "a ragged opening in the roof directly over the breast of the unfortunate man, which was torn through as if by cannon shot." Searchers discovered "a meteoric stone…weighing twenty pounds…and stained with blood" lodged five feet down in the ground, "thus showing the fearful impetus with which it struck the dwelling." Grover was reported to have been asleep when the meteor crashed through the ceiling, and his death had been "painless." Alas for the editors of the *Journal*, the story turned out to be a hoax. A few days later, the *Journal* announced: "We take it back in its totality…[Grover] didn't die. He didn't get hurt. He didn't even get frightened. He wasn't there. He isn't anywhere now…If Mr. Leonidas Grover ever should come into existence, and get killed by an aerolite, he will have to get someone else to write his obituary."

January 24, 1921

At the end of the nineteenth century and during the early twentieth century, Indiana authors were producing a remarkable stream of popular, best-selling literature. This "golden age" included authors Lew Wallace, George Barr McCutcheon, George Ade, Gene Stratton-Porter and Kin Hubbard; Indianapolis boasted three of the best-known writers of the group—poet James Whitcomb Riley and novelists Booth Tarkington and Meredith Nicholson. When East Coast society looked askance at Midwest culture, Indianapolis residents could offer up their city's literature as proof of sophistication, as did the wife of Indiana's former governor James Goodrich to women's groups in New York City. "Culture Exists West of Hudson," announced a front-page headline of the *Indianapolis Star*. "Culture in America today is the same the country over. People who think otherwise do not know this country of ours," Cora Goodrich proclaimed to her New York listeners. "Why, Booth Tarkington, who is a personal friend of mine, is almost better known in New York than at home."

January 25, 1935

In the early days of his second term in the Indiana General Assembly, Henry Richardson Jr. introduced two resolutions—one in support of federal anti-lynching legislation—which were passed unanimously. This kind of legislative business rarely merited notice, but the *Chicago Defender* printed the news because Richardson was one of the few black men elected to the Indiana state legislature in the early twentieth century. During his first term, he wrote and worked for the passage of the "Richardson Labor Discrimination Bill," among the earliest fair employment practices legislation in the nation. In his second term, he introduced legislation to ensure equal access to public accommodations, but with strong opposition from the Klan, the bill was defeated. During a career that lasted until his death at age eighty-one in 1983, Richardson worked on a broad spectrum of civil rights issues, including the 1949 state school desegregation law. In the 1960s, he organized and founded the Indianapolis branch of the Urban League and voiced opposition to the proposed Unigov consolidation as a Republican attempt to lessen black political influence in the city.

January 26, 1978

On January 25, 1978, five inches of snow fell in Indianapolis. Local newspapers and television stations forecast a major winter storm the next day. The system hit Illinois, Indiana and Ohio. In Indianapolis, fifteen inches of snowfall combined with winds gusting up to one hundred miles per hour and temperatures that dropped precipitously as the front passed through. Less than two feet of snow turned into drifts up to ten feet high, and roads became impassable. Snow, and then ice, piled up at the front and back doors of homes and businesses. Snow continued to fall the next day, and wind chills dipped to fifty degrees below zero. For three days, the city shut down, as National Guard units tried to rescue drivers stranded on the interstate. Photographs of downtown Indianapolis reveal streets filled with deserted cars, visible only by their roofs emerging from snowdrifts. The city spent days digging out from the Great Blizzard of '78, as it came to be called. To date, no other winter storm has had a greater impact on the city.

January 27, 1863

On January 23, renowned philosopher and author Ralph Waldo Emerson arrived in Indianapolis to speak at the city's Masonic Hall. Emerson was on a lecture tour that had begun in New York and taken him through Ohio, Michigan, Wisconsin and Illinois. After disembarking from his Chicago train, Emerson was informed by his local booking agent that no one had booked the hall for his lecture that night and the venue was unavailable until January 27. Reluctantly remaining in the city for the needed lecture fees, Emerson checked into the Bates House for a stay that he later described in a letter to his daughter Ellen as "imprisonment in dingy hotel & muddy town"; he spent some time touring the Indianapolis Blind School, observing classes and speaking to the pupils. On the evening of January 27, he addressed an "appreciative" crowd on "Clubs, or Conversation," a commentary on "what conversation is, and its value in teaching men or bringing out their characters, and the importance of 'clubs' or social gatherings…to produce and cultivate genuine conversation." Emerson's lecture, according to a reporter, "overflowed with anecdote and erudition."

January 28, 1969

In 1968, Mayor Richard Lugar called for "a great state university in Indianapolis." The city had established liberal arts colleges, including Butler and Marian, and was home to schools of nursing, medicine and dentistry, as well as the Herron School of Art. Both Indiana University and Purdue University had extension offices in Indianapolis that offered a variety of credit and non-credit courses (IU since 1916, Purdue since 1943). In January 1969, a new downtown, urban university began when IU and Purdue joined together to form Indiana University–Purdue University at Indianapolis, more commonly known by the acronym IUPUI. By the beginning of the twenty-first century, more than thirty thousand students were enrolled in the university's 185 degree programs. IUPUI alumni make up 85 percent of the state's dentists, 50 percent of its physicians, nearly 50 percent of its lawyers and more than one-third of its nurses. The university also draws on its urban resources, offering, for example, degrees in philanthropic studies and professional certifications in fundraising through the Lilly Family School of Philanthropy.

January 29, 1859

On this date, Otto Stark was born in Indianapolis. Although he worked with his father as a young boy in the cabinetmaking business, Otto became interested in lithography and apprenticed in Cincinnati; while there, however, he began to study painting. Stark eventually studied in New York and Paris and gained recognition for his impressionist style. He returned to the United States with his wife and children, and after his wife's death in 1893, he brought his family back to Indianapolis. Stark became known as part of the Hoosier Group of artists and was recognized particularly for his landscapes. He also exercised great influence on the artistic life of Indianapolis. In 1899, he became supervisor of art at Manual High School and went on to become an instructor at the city's Herron School in 1905. Stark retired from both positions in 1919 and devoted the years until his death in 1926 to his painting, often working with friend and fellow Hoosier Group artist J. Ottis Adams. In 1977, the Indianapolis Museum of Art held a retrospective exhibition of his work.

January 30, 1906

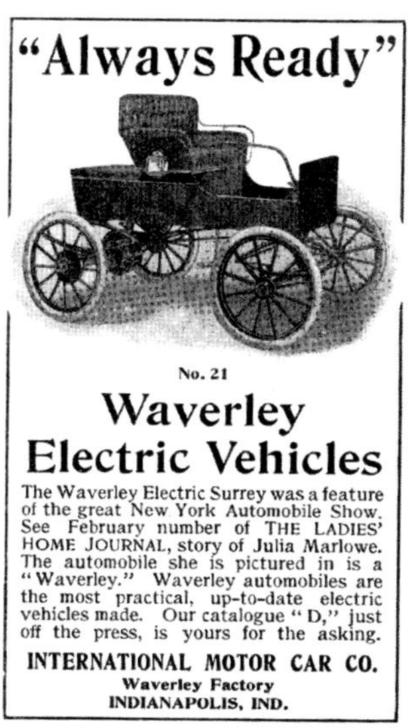

A 1903 Waverley advertisement for the electric surrey. *Author's collection.*

"Hoosier Machines Will Take a Big Part in Chicago Show," announced the *Indianapolis Sun*. The automobile show featured cars made by six Indianapolis firms: National, Premier, Nordyke-Marmon, Marion, American and Waverley. "All of the cars," the *Sun* noted, "will be gasoline, with the exception of the Waverley exhibit. This company has an electric car that will no doubt attract much attention." Waverley began as a bicycle manufacturer and made its first electric car in 1898. Most of the early models were two-person runabouts, but the company was soon making larger luxury vehicles, often marketed to female drivers as "always ready, noiseless, clean, stylish, and dependable." Waverley electric cars were driven by many celebrities—Hoosier owners included beauty-product manufacturer Madame C.J. Walker and author Lew Wallace. Waverley produced its last automobiles in 1916.

January 31, 1852

Reporting on the day's business in the state legislature, the *Indiana State Sentinel* recorded that the Senate Committee on the State Library had adopted a resolution to consider buying "thirty-eight bound volumes of the 'Western Sun and General Advertiser,' published at Vincennes by Elihu Stout for the use of the State Library." The Indiana State Library was begun in 1825 for the use of government officials and employees, acting as the state's historical repository and acquiring historical documents of interest, such as copies of the *Western Sun*, the earliest newspaper in the Indiana Territory. In its early years, the secretary of state served as the head librarian; in 1841, the library became a separate institution with its own director. It was not until 1934 that the State Library moved from the crowded statehouse into its own building downtown. Today's State Library offers students and the general public "Indiana's virtual online library" through INSPIRE; among its most prized collections are those in genealogy and Indiana history.

FEBRUARY

February 1, 1923

As the number of automobiles increased on Indianapolis streets, so did the number of injuries and deaths caused by automobiles hitting pedestrians. The issue was the focus of an *Indianapolis Star* story with the headline "Movie Thrills Surpassed Hourly in Traffic Center of City by Reckless Pedestrians." The city had installed downtown traffic towers staffed by policemen—the tower at the corner of Washington and Meridian was the focus of the article. From his vantage point, the reporter described the steady stream of automobiles and streetcars moving and stopping according to the relatively new technology of traffic lights. The glitch in the system was the jaywalker: "Look! There, a bundled up lady with one arm entwined around a package and the other dragging a child. Steps in front of an oncoming auto in the middle of the block. The driver jams on his brakes and turns aside just in time to miss them by a hair's breadth. Then, in her excitement at the narrow escape, she plunges toward a moving street car [*sic*], but draws up just in time to prevent skidding into it full speed ahead."

February 2, 1923

In 1893, Erwin George Baker and his family moved to Indianapolis. The young man apprenticed as a machinist, but his passion was his motorcycle. He won his first race on July 3, 1908, and rose to fame the next year, winning a motorcycle race at the new Indianapolis Motor Speedway. In 1915, Baker accepted a challenge from carmaker Harry Stutz to set a cross-country record driving a Stutz Bearcat; Baker drove from San Diego to New York City in eleven days, seven hours and fifteen minutes, claiming the record and the Bearcat. In 1923, "Cannon Ball" (a nickname given by a reporter and adopted by Baker) planned two cross-country races by car and one by motorcycle, and he continued to earn fame throughout the 1920s for driving a variety of vehicles (in 1926, a Ford Model T; in 1927, a General Motors truck) across the country. In 1933, he set the last of his records driving cross-country in fifty-three hours and thirty minutes. In 1947, Baker became the first commissioner of NASCAR and held the post until his death in 1960. His 1909 Indian Motorcycle can be seen at the Indianapolis Motor Speedway Museum; his tombstone at Crown Hill Cemetery reads simply "Cannon Ball Baker."

February 3, 1904

Before American women had the vote, many middle- and upper-class women banded together in women's clubs to pursue social reforms as well as personal improvement. One of the most influential clubs in the capital city was the Indianapolis Woman's Club. In April 1888, a committee of clubwomen began to look for a permanent headquarters. Chair May Wright Sewall suggested a wider plan: forming a joint stock company to purchase a building to be used by a variety of women's clubs. In June 1888, the Indianapolis Propylaeum was incorporated, and it became an important gathering place for influential women. In February 1904, when Sewall had become the chair of the International Council of Women, the National Council of Women met in Indianapolis at the Propylaeum. In 1923, the Propylaeum's original home was torn down to make room for the World War Memorial Plaza. The new home, a stately Victorian mansion on North Delaware Street, remains as the modern Propylaeum.

February 4, 1904

"State Museum Groundhog Sets Up Wail of Discontent: Little Stuffed Animal Objects to Being Photographed," ran the satiric headline in the

Indianapolis Journal. It is scarcely surprising that its collections were held up for ridicule, as the Indiana State Museum had an inauspicious beginning. The museum began in the 1860s as a small geology collection held by the state librarian and displayed in a few cabinets in the statehouse. In the 1880s, a larger set of display cabinets held various natural history items. In 1899, the collections were moved to the basement, where they languished until 1966, as politicians repeatedly denied funding. The museum finally moved in 1967 to the old city hall, where professional staff organized and expanded its holdings and displayed some of its treasures—including the Selma N. Steele collection of more than three hundred paintings and drawings by T.C. Steele, as well as Selma's collection of decorative arts. Curators continued to acquire works by Hoosier artists (including painters J. Ottis Adams, William Forsyth and Adolph Shulz) and built a major collection of historical and contemporary Indiana art.

February 5, 2012

New York Giants 21–New England Patriots 17. When Super Bowl XLVI ended, Indianapolis residents could celebrate—that the brother of their own well-loved-but-injured quarterback Payton Manning had defeated the team Colts fans most loved to hate and that their city had successfully hosted one of the world's major sporting events. National news outlets put out stories about "a cold-weather, landlocked, midsize burg surrounded by corn" (that written by a CNN reporter from Indiana). For an entire week before the big game, however, football fans from all over the world enjoyed a giant outdoor party in downtown Indianapolis. A three-block-long "village" along downtown Georgia Street offered a zip-line, concert stages, restaurants and bars; by the time the party ended, more than 300,000 people had been part of the celebration. The day after the game, ESPN commentator Adam Schefter tweeted: "Every NFL official and media person I spoke with agreed Indianapolis should become a regular part of Super Bowl rotation. Super job, Indy."

February 6, 1923

From 1900 to 1937, sixty-four different makes of cars came from Indianapolis manufacturers. In 1900, Arthur Newby and his partners began to produce electric automobiles at the National Automobile & Electric Company. In 1903, the company introduced its first gasoline-powered auto; one year later, it was renamed the National Motor Vehicle Company. In 1906, National introduced one of the first six-cylinder automobiles in the nation, a seven-passenger touring car known as the Model E. After success at the 1909 test races at the Indianapolis Motor Speedway, National advertisements boasted "the fastest, the most powerful, and most capable car" on the market. The company continued to produce large, luxurious six- and twelve-cylinder automobiles, including the models it displayed at the Chicago auto show in February 1923. The next year, National went out of business, unable to compete with Ford and other companies making automobiles at a lower cost. The first Ford Model T produced in 1908 was priced at $825, and in 1912 the price was lowered to $575. The 1910 National Model Forty, in contrast, sold for $2,500.

February 7, 2015

In 2002, the Indiana State Museum moved to its new home in White River State Park. In its core galleries, the museum offers displays on the natural history, culture and history of the state. Visitors can dine in a re-creation of the L.S. Ayres Tea Room and enjoy IMAX movies focusing on natural

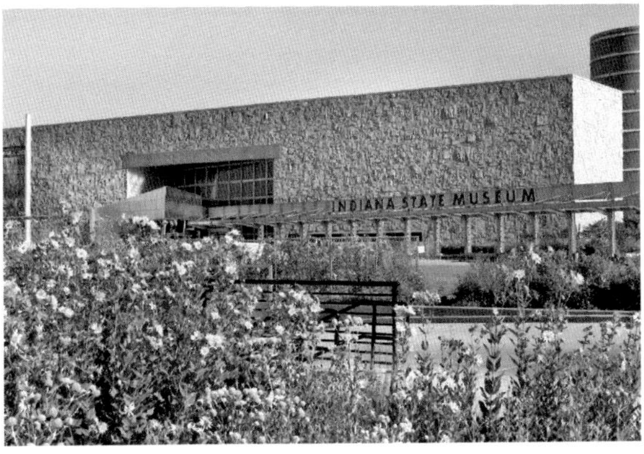

The new Indiana State Museum in White River State Park. *Photo by Dawn Bakken.*

history and history subjects. The museum has become known worldwide for being one of the two partners (the other the Allen County Public Library) holding and digitizing the Lincoln Financial Foundation Collection, one of the most comprehensive Lincoln collections in existence. With over twenty-eight thousand items digitized, online exhibits are added regularly to the collection website (http://lincolncollection.org). On this date, the third on-site exhibit held at the museum highlighting the Lincoln collection—So Costly a Sacrifice: Lincoln and Loss—opened to visitors.

February 8, 1910

A decade before Prohibition, Indianapolis was attempting to enforce its liquor laws, although results were inconsistent. One city hall reporter offered readers of the *Indianapolis Star* a story about one saloon owner who had had enough of a city crackdown: "Throwing on the desk of Mayor Shank the saloon license under which he operated a roadhouse…[Lon] McClure declared dramatically yesterday afternoon that he is through with 'the dirty saloon business' and that he is going to move away from Indianapolis and take up some other line." McClure and an apparent business partner had been arrested when the name on the saloon's liquor license and the business's manager did not match up. McClure declared that he had been arrested nineteen times under the previous city administration and another fifteen times since two police officers were caught drinking in his establishment. Any troubles on his property, he swore, were due to neighbors who would drink elsewhere and arrive at his saloon "fighting drunk…with a bottle of whiskey and a gun."

February 9, 1854

In 1852, Harriet Beecher Stowe's *Uncle Tom's Cabin* was published to acclaim and great success. Many Indianapolis residents speculated that some of the novel's characters were based on people the author had met while visiting her brother Henry Ward Beecher during his years in the town. Stowe's Uncle Tom was believed to be Tom Magruder, a freedman who had lived with his wife in a small cabin on property near the Beecher home. In 1854, a dramatic version of the book, already playing on stage in New York City, arrived for twelve nights of performances at the Indianapolis Masonic Hall. "The new and wonderful version of *Uncle Tom's Cabin*," announced the advertisement in the *Indiana Free Democrat*, "in which the celebrated wonder, little Mary Guerneau Marsh will appear in her original character of Eva!" The producers primed their audiences for the emotional effect of the play's conclusion: "Ladies and gentlemen will please *remain seated until the Curtain descends*, that every effect may be given to the last Grand Tableaux."

February 10, 1992

In the summer of 1991, Indianapolis became the target of unwanted national media attention after boxer Mike Tyson was accused of sexually assaulting a beauty pageant contestant while visiting the city. In July, Tyson had visited a rehearsal for the Miss Black America pageant. Tyson asked one of the contestants for her phone number and later called to ask her for a date. According to Desiree Washington, who came forward after the trial and conviction to tell her story, Tyson sent a limousine to take her to his hotel and then asked her to come up to his room before going out; instead, he assaulted and raped her. Tyson went on trial in the midst of a media circus on January 27, 1992, and on February 10, after nine hours of deliberations, the jury found him guilty of rape and two counts of criminal deviate conduct. Tyson was sentenced to ten years in prison, with four suspended, and began serving his sentence immediately after his March sentencing. He served three years of the six-year sentence and was released from the Indiana Youth Center in March 1995.

February 11, 1861

The *Indianapolis Daily Journal* reported in detail on the day's "Programme for the Reception of Abraham Lincoln, President Elect, at Indianapolis, by the State of Indiana." Lincoln was to leave Springfield in the morning, stopping at towns along the route, and arrive at 5:00 p.m. in Indianapolis, where he would be met by state and city officials, military officers and their units and local citizens. He would be escorted to the Bates House "in grand procession" for the evening's events. The next day, the *Journal* printed the text of the president's speech, given from the hotel balcony. Noting that the large crowd had greeted Lincoln's promise "to maintain the constitution and the laws" with "universal and enthusiastic shouts," the editors concluded that "there can be no two opinions about the course Mr. Lincoln must take if he ever swears to *support* the Constitution of the *United* States. He sees this much more clearly than those whose eyes are not sharpened by a great responsibility…His speech made a good impression, and we are sure it strengthened the feeling which stands by the Union against all assailants."

February 12, 1825

Before Indianapolis could take its place as the official working capital of the state of Indiana, the old capitol building at Corydon had to be emptied out and its contents transferred. In February 1825, the legislature appointed state treasurer Samuel Merrill "to superintend, generally, the removal of the records, documents and public property of every description" and to sell "all the chairs, tables and furniture belonging to the state which, in his opinion, cannot be advantageously removed to Indianapolis." In November, Merrill packed his family and their possessions, as well as all of the state papers and the contents of the state treasury (the latter contained in a single "large and strong" box), into wagons and, accompanied by state printer John Douglass and his family, set off north to Indianapolis, 125 miles away. On their best day, they traveled 11 miles; their worst day saw only 2 miles of progress due to "passages through the woods having to be cut on account of the impassable character of the road." Two weeks later, the families, along with the official papers and the treasury of the state of Indiana, arrived in Indianapolis.

February 13, 1890

Although the practice of sending valentines to sweethearts dated from before the Civil War, printing technology developed later in the century made colorful, fanciful cards affordable, widely available and extremely popular. But according to the *Indianapolis Sun*, not all of the valentines were sentimental or even kind. "Ah, Now for Revenge: Send Your Enemy a Scathing Valentine," read the headline. "Comic and satirical valentines," the article recounted, "were never so numerous or mean as they are this year and dealers have never sold more of them." The article related the story of one buyer, a wagon driver "who wanted a particularly scathing valentine for his landlady" who had refused to install gas lighting in his rental house. The driver was not alone in his anger at his landlady—one of the most popular "mean" valentines was intended for landlords who charged too much rent: "Rasping and grasping and grasping for rent, and never content under fifty percent…May such creatures find neither home nor repose, and never see rent, save a rent in their clothes."

February 14, 1944

How to sell romance and valentine sentiment in the midst of winter and war? Indianapolis department store advertisements evoked both wartime frugality and a woman's desire for a pretty new spring dress. On Valentine's Day 1944, an L.S. Ayres ad ran under the title "All from the Budget Shop and Aren't They Beautiful. Pretty and Positive Proofs That, This Year More Than Ever Before, There Is No Price Penalty for a Lovely Look!" The sketches showed tailored suits in light spring fabrics with a ruffle or two, all priced from $16.95 to $22.95, and complemented with hats from the Budget Hat Shop, priced from $5.95 to $7.95 Another Ayres ad invited women to "get personal about the wearability of your rayon stockings." Rayon had replaced the silk and nylon being used for war manufacturing, but "Realtex Rayon Stockings" offered "More Elasticity! Soft 'Silky' Feel! Higher Snag Resistance!" and "Miss Indianapolis" could buy the bargain irregulars now at $0.85 per pair instead of $1.35.

February 15, 1841

James McCready was mayor of Indianapolis from 1854 to 1856; he was also the bass trombone player of the Indianapolis Band, incorporated in February 1841. Concert bands enjoyed enormous popularity in nineteenth-century America. Groups including the German Military Band, the Sax

Horn Band, the Union Band and Bradshaw's Band played summer concerts at Indianapolis parks and performed at halls and theaters across the city all year long. In 1875, the When Clothing Store began an employees' band. The *Indianapolis News* formed a band composed of its newsboys; a group of local women composed the Indianapolis Ladies' Cornet Band. Even neighborhood celebrations seemed to require a band: a July 1888 "jollification" by residents of Woodruff Place prompted by "the completion of the street railway line to their suburbs" offered the Springdale Brass Band. When Benjamin Harrison conducted his front-porch campaign for the presidency, crowds arriving daily by train were escorted to his home led by local bands, including the African American Hotel Brotherhood Band, which led one thousand Harrison supporters through downtown Indianapolis one day in June, playing "Hail to the Chief."

February 16, 1942

Indianapolis high school students, like their counterparts across the nation, responded to World War II in a variety of ways. One young woman told the *Shortridge Daily Echo* that "just a few months ago we were a perfectly normal American family." Now both her parents worked long hours in manufacturing jobs and her brother had left school to join the armed forces; "the job of running the house," she said, "is now left to me." Many teenagers were still able to pursue their usual school and after-school activities but, as one girl said, you "want to do your part too." The Arsenal Tech 1942 yearbook showed girls who had "invaded the drafting classes to learn to fill vacancies," girls in welding classes and girls learning to remake their families' clothing to adjust to war shortages. More young men at Tech were enrolled in classes in airplane mechanics. High school students at Shortridge, Manual, Arsenal Tech and Crispus Attucks joined the ROTC, purchased war bonds, participated in scrap metal drives and planted victory gardens.

February 17, 1961

In February 1961, the first basketball player to ever appear on the cover of *Time* was Oscar Robertson. At the beginning of his professional career,

Robertson had already been co-captain of the gold medal–winning 1960 U.S. Olympic team and Rookie of the Year in his first season with the NBA. Before all that, however, Robertson had made an indelible name for himself in the annals of Hoosier high school basketball. Robertson grew up in Indianapolis in Lockefield Gardens and attended the segregated Crispus Attucks High School. Attucks basketball coach Ray Crowe, like all the teachers and administrators at the school, encouraged the pursuit of excellence. "I never had a teacher," Robertson later recalled, "who said a single word to me about basketball. That wasn't what they cared about." Nevertheless, in Robertson's sophomore year, the Attucks team reached the state quarterfinals (losing to eventual champion Milan). In his junior year, the Attucks Tigers went 31-1 and won the state championship. In Robertson's senior year, Attucks went undefeated and again took the state title. Robertson was named Indiana's Mr. Basketball for 1956.

February 18, 1827

On February 17, 1827, the citizens of Indianapolis received news that the 1826 treaty with the Potawatomi Indians had been ratified. The treaty granted land from Indianapolis all the way to Lake Michigan that would allow the state to build a road linking the new capital with the northern part of the state. Betsey Goldsberry Martin, living in the town with her first husband, Mr. Goldsberry, described the celebration that ensued: "We had a grand turn-out of all the citizens…After marching through the streets, or the main ones, which were Washington and Meridian, they marched down to old Dunning's tavern on the river, and all got tight and had a dance." Several hours later, in the early morning of February 18, Betsey's husband arrived home "as tight as a brick" and "very jolly." Since the couple were devout Methodists and normally shunned alcohol, Betsey might have condemned her husband, but she recalled that "that was the only time he drank too much and he was excusable when the Governor [James B. Ray] was tight, and all concerned. There were a lot of sick folks the next day."

February 19, 1895

"The Industrial and Manual Training School, occupying nearly an entire block at Meridian Street and Madison Avenue, was opened to the public yesterday morning...The equipment of the school is complete except in the wood-turning and iron-forging departments," wrote the *Indianapolis Journal*. In the 1880s, American educators began to recommend that manual training be offered at the high school level; Indianapolis High School offered some classes starting in 1888, but growing demand for such curriculum as well as the call for a second high school to serve the south side of the city led to the establishment of Manual Training School in 1895. On opening day, 278 boys and 248 girls arrived at the school designed for 500 students. Principal Charles Emmerich and his staff emphasized academic learning as well as technical skills, exemplified by the yearly student publication *Mind and Hand*. The title page of the publication proudly noted that the "literary work herein contained...has been done by the students of our school."

February 20, 1827

"It will be gratifying to many of our readers to learn," the *Indianapolis Gazette* announced, "that a revival of religion has taken place in the different churches in this place. The greatest accession of members has taken place in the Methodist Episcopal Church. Within the past two or three weeks between thirty and forty persons have joined that church." In 1821, Baptist, Methodist and Presbyterian preachers began organizing groups of the faithful under their denominational wings. The Presbyterians erected a simple wooden-frame building the same year; the Methodists bought a log cabin the next year and in September 1822 conducted a six-day camp meeting on the grassy circle at the center of town. The revival that added thirty to forty members in less than one month, as the Methodists experienced in 1827, would indeed have been noticeable in a small town. As the capital grew in the 1830s and 1840s, the religious landscape expanded to include Lutherans, Disciples of Christ, Episcopalians and Roman Catholics. The city's first synagogue was organized in the 1850s, as was the first Quaker meeting.

February 21, 1934

Indianapolis was still trapped in the Great Depression. Government relief programs had begun to put some residents back to work, but factories were closed or running on part-time schedules, some local banks had gone under and many men and women in the workforce were making do with low-paying jobs that could pay the rent and keep food on their tables. Nevertheless, for the still-wealthy members of Indianapolis society, life went on much as before. "Dress Me With Distinction at Any Cost!" exclaimed the beautiful woman depicted in the Block's Department Store advertisement—one of "the smartest matrons facing a second April in the Autumn of life this Spring." The smart matron was wearing a wool coat liberally trimmed with fox fur, "the ne plus ultra of elegance…the thrilling lift of the new spring silhouette that fairly drips DISTINCTION." The cost of distinction, in this instance, was $298.50, in a year when, according to IRS records, the average net family income in the United States was $3,125 (or $260 per month).

February 22, 1958

Late February in Indiana in the 1950s meant only one thing for a sports reporter—"Hoosier Hysteria Due to Hit High Schools," wrote Jan Moran, a student reporter from Manual High School for the *Indianapolis Star*. Moran consulted three other high school–aged fans (all from Indianapolis) for their predictions for the winner of the state's high school boys' basketball tournament: all three picked Indianapolis teams to win the championship, with one favoring Shortridge and the other two picking Crispus Attucks. The young Moran concluded his column with as good a description as has ever been written about Hoosier Hysteria: "When the sectional is in full swing, it means days of getting home late; being too excited to sleep; stuffing [oneself] with hot dogs, cokes, popcorn, peanuts, cotton candy, snowballs and malts…screaming until hoarse; running around Butler Fieldhouse like madmen between halves and games; and sleepless nights at slumber parties." The 1958 state champions were Fort Wayne South.

February 23, 1910

Holidays such as presidents' birthdays, which today bring little notice, were celebrated in the early twentieth century. The day after George Washington's birthday, the society page of the *Indianapolis Star* reported on some of the local parties. The Caroline Harrison chapter of the Daughters of the American Revolution had met in the third-floor ballroom of a member's home for "colonial entertainment," with a gold-framed portrait of Washington on one wall "encircled with red, white and blue electric lights. The ceiling of the room was decorated with a canopy effect of red, white and blue bunting and there were many flags." The afternoon included a vocal concert and "a minuet…danced by members of the chapter," each costumed as "a well-known woman of the colonial period." The group also enjoyed "dainty refreshments," including "ices…served in patriotic form." The Woodruff Place clubhouse hosted a "George Washington card company" with "forty tables of bridge and euchre." With the focus on cards, the room was decorated with flags and smaller flags on each card table.

February 24, 1928

In 1874, New York businessman Lyman Ayres assumed full ownership of the Trade Palace in downtown Indianapolis. In 1875, L.S. Ayres & Company moved across the street. In 1905, a new eight-story building—featuring elevators, modern lighting and an expanse of display windows—opened at the corner of Washington and Meridian Streets. The store offered affordable fashions in its basement shops and higher-priced clothing, jewelry, cosmetics and home furnishings on its other floors. Smaller "shops" within some floors, such as the French Shop, catered to wealthier city residents. The mix was well reflected in Ayres's daily advertisements in local papers, which from 1936 onward featured the phrase "The Ayres Look," meant to evoke the style of a woman who regularly shopped at the store. Ayres also became known for its high level of customer service and its well-trained sales staff. Employee newsletters stressed the characteristics of a good staff member, describing one departing employee's popularity owing to "her unfailing courtesy to everyone with whom she came in contact."

February 25, 1822

An advertisement appeared for the first time in the February 25 issue of the *Indianapolis Gazette*: "Law Notice: Calvin Fletcher proposes practicing LAW in the fifth judicial circuit of the state of Indiana…and all business submitted to his care at Indianapolis, where he resides, or while on the circuit, will be attended to." Fletcher was a young Vermont-born lawyer who moved to Indianapolis shortly after his marriage to Sarah Hill in May 1821. Calvin's circuit, which he traveled twice a year for many years, took in ten central Indiana counties. While Sarah kept their home, remained active in the community and raised the couple's eleven children, Calvin practiced law, served for a time in the state senate, was active in Whig and later Republican politics, helped organize the second State Bank of Indiana, promoted railroads, farmed and supported the state Agricultural Society and generally had his hand in much of what went on in the city. Calvin also found time to keep a diary, which began in 1817 and continued until 1866, providing one man's perspective on much of the history of early Indianapolis.

February 26, 1938

"Mass Moving Day in Indianapolis," announced the *Pittsburgh Courier*. Twenty African American families began to move into the first five completed units of Lockefield Gardens, which the reporter described as "the most beautiful slum clearance project yet to be built." The project was part of the federal Public Works Administration Housing Division's plan to create affordable, good-quality urban housing. The project offered a neighborhood of twenty-four buildings, containing 748 units with spacious rooms and modern electrical appliances. Within the project were playgrounds, a shopping arcade and an elementary school. In a highly segregated housing environment, Lockefield Gardens became an important center of African American life in Indianapolis. By the 1950s, as black families moved into more neighborhoods throughout the city, the Gardens lost tenants and conditions deteriorated. In 1983, despite the efforts of historic preservation groups, seventeen of the original buildings were demolished to allow IUPUI to expand. The remaining seven original buildings were later renovated and eleven new buildings added. Lockefield Gardens apartments now house IUPUI students and others wanting to live in a historic downtown neighborhood.

February 27, 1862

Indiana had raised ten thousand troops for the Union in response to President Lincoln's call in April 1861. Regiments continued to form across the state, and existing regiments were in continual need of new men as they lost soldiers to injury and death. Recruiting notices—and offers of bounty (payable upon discharge) for signing up—became a commonplace sight across the state. One advertisement began, "200 Recruits Wanted for the Battalion of the Eleventh Infantry. One hundred dollars bounty in gold. Pay from $13 to $22 per month, with rations, quarters, medical attendance…The term of enlistment is only THREE YEARS." The Nineteenth Indiana Infantry was also recruiting, offering the same bounty and "an abundance of good food, clothing, quarters, fuel and medical attendance free of charge." The recruiting officers for both regiments offered the chance of promotion and higher pay: "In this Regiment [the Nineteenth], most of the Second Lieutenants and Non-Commissioned Officers are yet to be appointed thus affording rare opportunities for promotion."

February 28, 1942

In 1913, James Allison, one of the founders of Prest-O-Lite and the Indianapolis Motor Speedway, began a machine shop, which was renamed the Allison Engineering Company in 1917. During World War I, the company received government contracts for airplane engines; after the war, Allison engineers worked with the government to retool those engines. After General Motors purchased the company in 1929, Allison engineers spent seven years developing the first one-thousand-horsepower engine for military use, the V-1710. Even before the United States entered the Second World War, Allison GM produced aircraft engines for the British fleet, and in 1942, it began production on a massive scale to meet the needs of U.S. air forces. From its plant on the west side of Indianapolis,

Allison GM produced seventy thousand aircraft engines during the war; peak employment at the plant was twenty-three thousand men and women working three shifts seven days a week. Company employees could follow the success of their products in the *AllisoNews* weekly newsletter. In August 1941, the British minister for aircraft production sent "the thanks of our fighter pilots for these grand machines."

MARCH

March 1, 1916

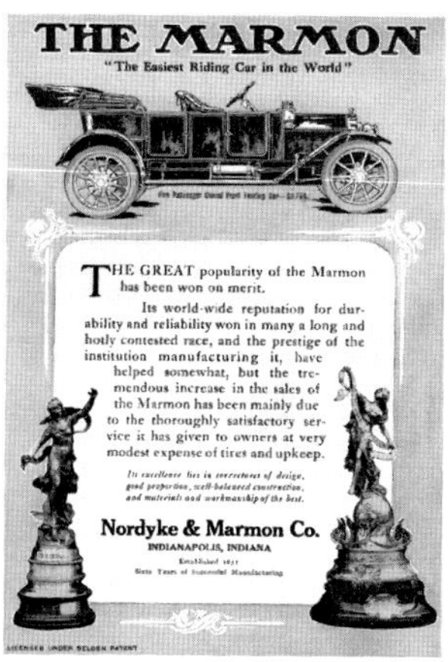

A 1911 Marmon advertisement for the five-passenger touring car. *Author's collection.*

On the first day of March 1916, five Russian engineers toured the Nordyke Marmon & Company's manufacturing plant. The men were driven to the plant in the company's latest model—the four-door, six-cylinder Marmon 34—and then taken on a city tour in the automobile. Marmon autos ("the easiest riding car in the world," according to a company advertisement) were manufactured in Indianapolis from 1903 to 1933. Owner Howard Marmon built his first car in 1902; in 1911, his Marmon Wasp, driven by former company engineer Ray Harroun, won the first Indianapolis 500 race. The company also produced luxury passenger vehicles, including the Marmon 34, distinctive for its use of aluminum to reduce the weight of the vehicle and boasting the "Marmon economy" of fourteen miles to the gallon.

March 2, 1819

Depending on whose family was telling the story, either George Pogue or John McCormick was the first known white man to settle with his wife and children within the geographic area that would become Indianapolis. The Pogue family version was that George and his wife, Cassa Ann, along with the younger five of their eight children, arrived on March 2, 1819, at the White River. The river being too flooded to cross, the family decided to build their cabin on nearby high ground. Almost a year later, in February 1820, the McCormick family arrived, stayed with the Pogues for a brief time while constructing their own cabin and then settled in the vicinity. The story passed down in the McCormick family is that John and his family, accompanied by two brothers and several employees, settled and built a cabin on high ground near the White River in February 1820—the Pogues did not arrive until a month later and settled in a cabin deserted by some earlier pioneer. When Jacob Piatt Dunn Jr. wrote his two-volume history of Indianapolis, he recounted both versions as they had been told to him by descendants of the two families, all of whom swore to the veracity of their particular family claim.

March 3, 1863

By 1863, many Hoosier Unionists believed that they were fighting not only Confederates but also the threat of insurrection by Southern sympathizers in their own state. Few issues evoked stronger feelings among Northern soldiers than the presence of pro-Southern Copperheads in their hometowns. One member of the Forty-third Indiana wrote home to an Indianapolis newspaper on behalf of his entire regiment: "As some of the Copperheads of Indiana have claimed the soldiers as being their constituents in the work of treason, I send you these resolutions, unanimously adopted by this regiment upon the reception of the news that it was currently reported...that we had laid down our arms and refused to fight any longer." The men of the regiment had resolved that "we never will lay down our arms until the present unholy rebellion is put down" and "that we hold it to be the duty of every loyal man to support the administration." "We will ever be found ready," the soldiers concluded, "to put down treason wherever it may exist."

March 4, 1852

When Hungarian freedom fighter Lajos Kossuth arrived in Indianapolis, he was welcomed and fêted as a great hero. Kossuth had been the leader of the Hungarian struggle for independence from the Hapsburg Empire, but after the nationalist forces were put down by Hapsburg and Czarist armies, Kossuth was forced to flee Europe. He embarked on a tour of England and the United States, trying to raise support from Hungarian exiles and sympathetic westerners. Kossuth had already dined at the White House and addressed a joint session of Congress when he arrived in Indiana in March 1852. When his special train arrived, Governor Kossuth, as he was titled, was met by a welcoming committee and driven down Washington Street, to the cheers of an assembled crowd. At the statehouse, both Kossuth and Governor Joseph Wright spoke; after the public ceremonies, the governor hosted Kossuth and his party for dinner. Although Hungary did not achieve independence with its revolution, Lajos Kossuth became a Hungarian national hero, celebrated to this day.

March 5, 1923

"Shank on Record for Race Bill," reported the *Indianapolis News*. From the first year it was held on Memorial Day, the Indianapolis 500 created controversy for offering entertainment on a day traditionally set aside to remember those who had fought for the Union during the Civil War. Unable to convince track owners to change the date of the race, members of the Grand Army of the Republic, the Civil War veterans' organization, supported legislation in the state General Assembly that would prohibit all "commercialized sporting events" on Memorial Day. The Moorhead Memorial Day bill, introduced in 1923, caused considerable controversy. Mayor Lew Shank supported the bill; many Indianapolis residents argued that attendance at the race was a matter of personal choice and that the bill unfairly targeted one event. Members of the American Legion (veterans of World War I) had begun to celebrate Armistice Day on November 11, and many opposed the bill. The Moorhead bill passed the legislature but was vetoed by Governor Warren McCray; the Indianapolis 500 continued to be held on Memorial Day.

March 6, 1900

The meeting of a national political party to choose its nominees for president and vice president of the United States would generally merit a welcome from that city's mayor and other officials. When the fifty delegates from the Social Democratic Party and the one wing of the Socialist Labor Party convened in Indianapolis for their first national convention, they were welcomed by "a member of the local branch." The two socialist groups met to combine their memberships under the banner of the Social Democratic Party and to choose candidates to represent their united group: Terre Haute native and Social Democratic Party leader Eugene V. Debs as presidential candidate and Socialist Labor Party leader J.B. Harriman for vice president. The Social Democrats dissolved their political party in 1901 and became part of the Socialist Party, which nominated Debs for president four more times in 1904, 1908, 1912 and 1920.

March 7, 1823

Many early residents of Indianapolis grew much of their own food and raised livestock. Bartering for goods was widespread in the town, and cash was reserved for a few necessary items. The first issue of the *Western Censor and Emigrant's Guide* carried a single advertisement for a local store: Robert Siddill announced that he had available for cash purchase "dry goods, queensware, hardware, & groceries." Metal goods included "knives, spoons, butts, hinges, screws, nails"; groceries included coffee, tea and "loaf sugar," as well as a few spices and tobacco. Siddill offered to pay cash for one important trade item: "N.B. CASH given for FURS and HIDES of every description." The fur trade continued into the 1830s as an important business in the capital. In 1834, businessman John Jamison advertised in the *Indianapolis Journal* for "HIDES CASH! CASH!" announcing that he would pay "the highest price" for ten to fifteen thousand animal skins: "Otter, Mink, Black Fox or Fisher, Raccoon, Grey Fox, Wild Cat, Deer, Bear and Wolf."

March 8, 1931

Apparently Hoosiers take their fried chicken as seriously as they do their sports and their politics, at least according to a tongue-in-cheek editorial in the *Indianapolis Star*. Under the title "Upholding Hoosier Traditions," the editors related events at a recent dinner held in New York City by the Indiana Club of New York. When dinner was set before the members, club president Mrs. Medea Wager was horrified to realize that the evening's entrée, "the famous Hoosier fowl," had been "encrusted in the batter so sacred to the residents of Maryland." The assembled company "balk[ed] at having the internationally famous dish known as fried chicken, Indiana style, maltreated" in such "a barbarian fashion." "The offending fowl," the editors continued, "was ordered removed to the kitchen, where the batter was scraped off and the chicken properly sprinkled with flour and fried in hot grease." The editors commended Mrs. Wager "for the courage in delaying the meal long enough to uphold the traditions of Indiana fried chicken."

March 9, 1936

At 6:00 a.m. on Monday, March 9—as on so many others days in the 1930s and early 1940s—people across the Midwest were rising, dressing and preparing for the day and listening to Indianapolis evangelist Howard Cadle on the radio. Each weekday morning, Cincinnati's WLW Radio offered *The Nation's Family Prayer Period*, a fifteen-minute show featuring the evangelist and his wife, Ola. Ola opened the show singing "Did You Think to Pray," Howard offered a brief message and then Ola closed with "Sweet Hour of Prayer." On Sunday mornings, a one-hour broadcast came live from the Cadle Tabernacle. From 1932 until Cadle's death in a plane crash in 1942, the enormously popular show brought Howard Cadle into homes. Cadle had begun leading religious revivals in Indianapolis in 1921; later that year, he built the ten-thousand-seat Cadle Tabernacle. Cadle lost control of the building in 1923 and regained it in 1931, but his widest influence came through his radio show. "We got up by it every morning," a former listener from Tennessee reported in an oral history interview done in 1996. "It was a touch of the outside. It was inspirational."

March 10, 1943

In the midst of war, Indianapolis residents enjoyed reading stories of local soldiers who had fought in important battles and returned home to tell their tales. The *Indianapolis News* interviewed First Lieutenant Bernays Thurston, on leave at his parents' home. Thurston, with the 111th Army Air Forces, had co-piloted a B-17 bomber over Guadalcanal during the Battle of the Solomons. While on a search mission, Thurston's plane encountered, engaged and destroyed a Kawanishi 97 enemy bomber. The story of the dogfight between the two bombers had already appeared in a book and in *Reader's Digest*. In the *News* interview, Thurston recounted his early service in Pearl Harbor, including the day of the Japanese attack, and his transfer to the Solomons. Thurston added that he had sung a song to his crew as they returned from their victory—one he "used to sing out at Butler University." On September 4, 1945, Major Bernays Thurston was piloting a B-29 that took off from the Marshall Islands en route to California. It was the last B-29 nighttime takeoff—shortly after takeoff, the plane flew into the ocean, apparently due to blinding runway lights, killing all on board.

March 11, 1897

"We'll Be 200,000," stated an *Indianapolis Sun* front-page headline. The city council was about to consider consolidating several suburbs—Brightwood, Irvington, West Indianapolis, Haughville and Mount Jackson—into the city of Indianapolis. The annexation would add 25,000 new residents and create a city of 200,000; the alternative, according to the paper's editors, was "to remain a second-class city throughout another generation." Mayor Thomas Taggart and a majority of council members favored the proposal. A special council meeting on March 13 was flooded with supporters from the affected suburbs, including 100 Haughville residents wearing white badges that read "Annexation. Haughville." Separate ordinances for each locality were brought up as "numerous voices announced that every person in those suburbs is in favor of 'comin' in.'" On the morning after the council vote, the paper announced "A Blissful Union. Five Municipalities Bow at Hymen's Altar and All Are Soon Made One…Irvington Alone Remains a Solitary Old Maid." Irvington was annexed by the city of Indianapolis on February 17, 1902.

March 12, 1869

An indignant contributor to the *Indianapolis Journal* wrote in defense of a controversial new means of transport—the bicycle. In a column entitled "The Velocipede Question," the writer defended "the elegant, quick moving bicycle." The new contraption, some were arguing, would take up the entire width of a sidewalk, mowing down people in its path. Those who were "afraid of being 'run down' and 'crushed into an unrecognizable mass,'" the author replied, did not realize that "the thing can, even when going at a high rate of speed, be easily and instantly stopped." The writer offered several points in the bicycle's favor: first and foremost that it was "a means of speedy transportation from one point to another, and, perhaps, distant one, making, with quiet, ease and *safety*, a mile in, say, *seven* minutes—in this city of magnificent distances, an important consideration." The new machine also offered "a means of powerful and healthy exercise in the open air" and, unlike a horse, "eats no corn, hay, or oats, requires no stabling, nor runs away." By the 1890s, with improvements in design and manufacture, bicycles were the rage of Gilded Age America, and Indianapolis boasted numerous bicycle clubs.

March 13, 1915

When members of the Indianapolis Medical Society gathered in March 1915 to pay tribute to John Hurty, he had been the secretary of the Indiana State Board of Health since 1896. Hurty served in the position until 1922, and during his long career he brought modern principles of public health to the state. Hurty had come to Indianapolis in the mid-1870s to work in pharmaceutical production for Eli Lilly. As secretary of the Board of Health, he worked to establish standards and practices for clean water, healthy food and pure medicine. He insisted that the state begin to keep vital statistics on births, deaths and disease. Hurty also encouraged public health education; his 1914 *Indiana Mothers' Baby Book* taught women basic principles of nutrition, child care and first aid. Unfortunately, Hurty also subscribed to eugenic theory and supported the practice of Indiana prisons and asylums sterilizing those deemed unworthy to reproduce. Hurty left behind a complex legacy, but many of his principles remain today as foundations of Indiana's public health system.

March 14, 1915

The *Indianapolis Star* offered an editorial in support of the upcoming fundraiser for the city's Flower Mission: "In the years since the Flower Mission came into existence many other organizations for the performance of good works have developed, but none has ever undertaken a service more needful or useful than the one to which the Mission is devoted—that of caring for the sick poor." The mission began in 1876 when a few Indianapolis women visited patients at City Hospital, taking flowers and food. In the 1880s, a group organized as the Flower Mission made home visits to those who were ill but too poor to seek medical treatment. The work of the Mission quickly grew in scope—it sponsored the city's first training school for nurses at City Hospital; it founded the short-lived Eleanor Hospital for Sick Children; and for several decades it operated a Flower Mission Hospital (at three different locations), which offered treatment for patients with tuberculosis. Throughout its history, the Flower Mission remained a private group that relied on donations and fundraising.

March 15, 1950

Newspaper editors, even those who worked at the most respectable city papers, knew that a little bit of sexual impropriety would attract readers' attention. "Strip Tease 'Snake Goddess' Jailed on Bad Check Charge" was the *Indianapolis Star* headline, accompanied by a photo of Norita Lane, posed in a side profile looking back and smiling at the camera, with one foot propped up (not too high) on the bar of her jail cell. "It's easier to get out of my clothes," she remarked to the reporter, "than it is to get out of here." Lane had been arrested for writing a bad check—for gowns that glowed in black light—in Chicago. Lane explained that in her former burlesque act she had earned "$250 a week doing a dance with seven 9-foot snakes" but had changed her act because "the snakes weighed 125 pounds and I was losing weight." The black-light act had been less successful and therefore less profitable—hence the bad check—and Lane vowed: "When I get out of this mess, I'm going back to my snakes."

March 16, 1962

After their March 12 defeat of Bowling Green by a single point, Coach Tony Hinkle and the Butler Bulldogs took to the court in Iowa City, Iowa, to play their second game in the NCAA national basketball tournament. For the first time in his career, Hinkle had led his team to the NCAA tournament, and although Butler lost to Kentucky that day, Hinkle and his team had gained national attention. In 1921, after graduating from the University of Chicago where he made a name for himself playing basketball, Paul "Tony" Hinkle arrived in Indianapolis to coach athletics at Butler University. By the time he retired in 1970, his baseball, basketball and football teams had amassed over one thousand wins. In basketball-crazy Indiana, Hinkle was best known for coaching that sport. Already by 1929, he had led his team to a national championship. Hinkle became a huge influence within the game, introducing his own "Hinkle Offensive Strategy," used by high school and college coaches for generations. Hinkle is also credited with introducing the orange basketball—easier to see than the traditional brown ball.

March 17, 1934

On this Sunday afternoon, a crowd gathered at the Senate Avenue YMCA to hear author, teacher and civil rights advocate W.E.B. DuBois speak on the topic of "Segregation." The address was one of many heard at regular "Monster Meetings" held at the segregated Indianapolis YMCA. The Senate Avenue YMCA was dedicated in 1913; Faburn DeFrantz became its executive secretary in 1916 (a position he held until his retirement in 1952) and began to transform the Y into a leading force in the city's African American community. Among the many programs he initiated, DeFrantz began a series of Sunday afternoon forums for black and white speakers from the city and from all across the country. Audiences heard from professors and university leaders; they listened to ministers, politicians, writers and artists speak about current issues, religion, economics, education and science. In 1928, NAACP assistant secretary Walter White spoke about his investigations into lynchings and race riots. One 1931 debate featured both sides of the question "Prohibition: Shall Indiana Stay Dry?"; a postwar 1944 panel discussed "Industry, Employment, and the Negro." Olympic gold medalist Jesse Owens spoke in 1952 and again in 1953, the same year Eleanor Roosevelt gave a speech on "International Human Rights."

March 18, 1918

Covering the annual exhibition of Indiana artists held at the Herron Art Institute, a reporter for the *Indianapolis Star* noted in particular the grouping of six large paintings "by the senior member of the original 'Hoosier Group,' Theodore C. Steele." Steele had moved to Indianapolis as a young man; his subsequent years of study in Europe were sponsored by local patrons. In the 1880s and 1890s, Steele painted portraits and taught art in the city; in 1891, he was one of the founders of the Indiana School of Art. By the late 1890s, Steele had begun to travel elsewhere during the summer and early fall to paint landscapes, and although he became primarily associated with Brown County during the last decades of his life, he returned to Indianapolis many winters to paint there. The exhibition featured two of his winter cityscapes: *Christ Church, the Deep Snow*, a view of the Episcopal church on the Circle with "the charm and subtlety of a snowy atmosphere," and *The Soldiers' Monument, Midwinter Afternoon*, described as "full of the sparkle of sunlight."

March 19, 1955

"City Hails 1st and Greatest State Champs," announced the *Indianapolis Recorder*. The Fighting Tigers of Crispus Attucks had beaten Gary Roosevelt to become the first high school basketball team from Indianapolis to ever win the Indiana High School Athletic Association (IHSAA) state tournament. Attucks High School opened in the fall of 1927, after the city's school board created a segregated high school for all of the city's black high school students. Principals Matthias Nolcox and Russell Lane, whose tenure combined to last until 1957, set the standard for the school, hiring faculty from across the country, many from black colleges. By the early 1950s, Coach Ray Crowe had built a basketball team with regional presence. The Tigers achieved three state wins in a single decade: 1955, 1956 and, under Coach Bill Garrett, 1959. After their March 1955 victory, Crowe and his team rode on a fire truck from Hinkle Fieldhouse to Monument Circle, escorted by eight policemen on motorcycles, Mayor Alex Clark and busloads of Attucks supporters. After speeches and presentations, the team continued to Northwestern Park, where they were met by twenty-five thousand cheering fans.

March 20, 1916

After the death of Indiana's U.S. senator Benjamin Shively, Governor Samuel Ralston announced on March 20, 1916, that Indianapolis businessman and politician Thomas Taggart would take his place. Taggart had arrived in Indianapolis in 1877. The ambitious, entrepreneurial young man became involved in various business ventures, including part ownership of the city's Denison Hotel, and in politics. In 1886, he ran a successful campaign for Marion County auditor and by 1895 won election as Indianapolis mayor, serving three terms in that office. Taggart became a powerful force in state and national Democratic Party politics. For four years, he served as chair of the Democratic National Committee. In 1912, he helped to secure the vice-presidential nomination for Hoosier Thomas Riley Marshall. Beginning in 1901, Taggart was perhaps best known for his part ownership and management of French Lick Springs Hotel, linked to Indianapolis and Chicago (thanks in part to Taggart's influence) via the Monon Railroad. Taggart's resort attracted wealthy and politically important patrons, offering a spa, golfing and (illegal) gambling. Taggart lost the fall 1916 election to keep his Senate seat, but he continued to manage French Lick until his death in 1929. Two years later, Franklin D. Roosevelt garnered the support of other governors for his presidential run during a stay at French Lick.

March 21, 1948

The war was over and middle-class Americans were moving to the suburbs and enjoying their prosperity with their families, including at least one slightly rebellious but basically obedient teenager—or so the postwar myth went. The *Indianapolis Star Magazine* offered a fictional version of that myth in its weekly "Another Adventure in the Frenzied Life of the Dailey Family." On March 21, 1948, the adventure centered on teenaged daughter Liz's new boyfriend Bix and his love of that new music called be-bop. Bix, Liz and an increasing crowd of their friends began to hang out at the Dailey house, clustered around the record player. George Dailey left wife Abby in charge of dealing with Bix and his be-bop, and "although Abby's taste in music was far from being as longhair as her husband's…Be-Bop thoroughly eluded her." As the story ends, Abby finally rids her home of Bix but is surprised when Liz accepts the change so easily. Bix, Liz explained, had been "a drip" and she was "awful tired of Be-Bop," but she liked riding in his "swell little convertible." In the background, the record player "was crashing away at Wagner."

March 22, 1961

Postwar demand for housing saw the eastside Indianapolis area known as the Meadows develop rapidly. Single-family houses and apartment complexes, including the 1953 Meadowbrook development with its fifty-six apartment buildings, attracted middle-class families to the area. Businesses followed, including those in the Meadows Shopping Center, finished in 1957. As a 1961 advertisement for the center illustrates, Meadows offered a wide variety of shopping choices—including a branch of the downtown Wasson's Department Store, Woolworth's and Murphy's discount stores, Hook's Drug Store, Ludlow's furniture store and a grocery store—and it offered two thousand parking spaces for all those new cars. Unfortunately, by the 1980s, the neighborhood had become a textbook example of urban decline. The shopping center closed, and a brief attempt in the 1990s to reopen it was unsuccessful. City officials and neighborhood groups still struggle with revitalization efforts. In 2015, plans were underway for eight hundred mixed-income residential units and a community wellness center, through the work of the Meadows Community Foundation.

March 23, 1963

Since its inception after World War I, the American Legion promoted what it saw as "American-ness" and condemned political and social movements that its members believed threatened the American way of life. One of its longest-running disputes was with the American Civil Liberties Union and its state branches. For years, disagreements between the Indiana Civil Liberties Union and the Legion centered on the interior of the World War Memorial in downtown Indianapolis. Since the ICLU's founding in 1953, its members had applied to meet inside the building, which was state property. The Legion, believing that the ICLU was "at the very least, sympathetic to Communism," worked successfully to keep the group out. When the ICLU met in 1963 to celebrate its tenth anniversary, it still could not meet inside the War Memorial. But, as the *Indianapolis News* reported, Governor Matthew Welsh, unlike his predecessors, publicly supported ICLU access to the memorial "as a fundamental right of free speech and assembly." In fact, the ICLU did not gain access to the interior of the War Memorial until October 1973, after a ruling by the State Supreme Court.

March 24, 1912

Harry Stutz had always wanted to design and manufacture automobiles. After moving to Indianapolis in 1903, he designed cars for American Motors, worked as chief engineer for Marian Motor Company and then in 1910 founded Stutz Auto Parts. In 1911, Stutz built his first car and entered it, untested, in the first running of the Indianapolis 500. The car finished the race (eleventh out of twenty-two) and was nicknamed "The Car That Made Good in a Day." By August 1911, Stutz automobiles were coming out of the Indianapolis production line. The Stutz Bearcat, with a top speed of 72 miles per hour, debuted in 1912. Stutz advertisements touted the car's machinery: one March 1912 ad touted "The Sturdy Stutz," in this case the two-seat, four-cylinder Stutz Roadster, priced at $2,000 and "equal in mechanical perfection to any car built, no matter what the price." The company also produced larger luxury and high-performance models, such as the 1928 Touring Car, marketed as "The Splendid Stutz," and the Black Hawk, whose new design eight-cylinder engine allowed the car to reach a speed close to 110 miles per hour. The company ceased production in 1935 in the midst of the Depression.

March 25, 1913

The rain began to fall on Easter Sunday, March 23. For five days, rain poured down on the Midwest—twelve inches on Indianapolis. After a wet spring, the water had no chance to soak into the ground. As the White River rose, earthen levees began to give way. On the morning of March 25, the *Indianapolis Star* reported the damages across the state and warned, "City Danger Grows." Later that day, the Morris Street levee failed, and the neighborhood of West Indianapolis (bounded by Washington and Belmont Streets on the north and south, the White River on the east and Raymond Street on the west) was filled with ten to fifteen feet of floodwater. Thousands of homes nearly disappeared beneath the muddy water. The White River finally crested at nineteen and a half feet above flood stage. Railroad bridges were washed away; the city lost its water supply for four days.

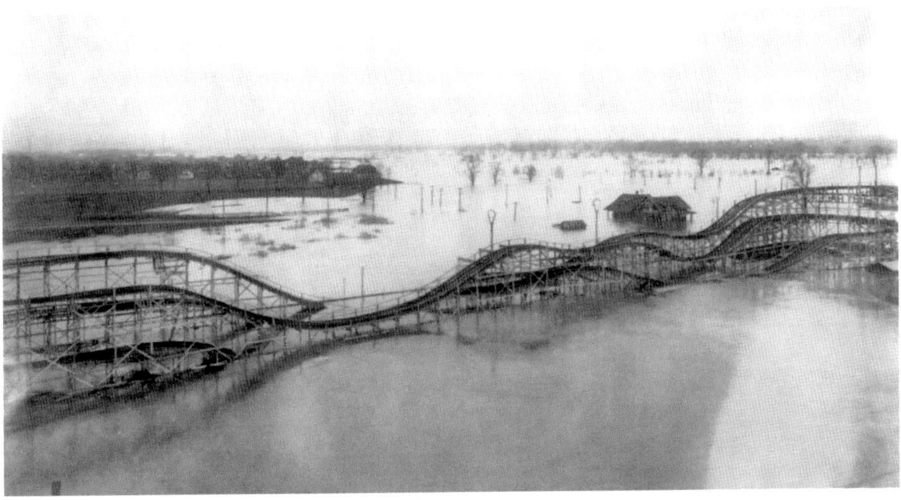

Riverside Park submerged in the flood of 1913. *Courtesy of Library of Congress, Prints and Photographs Division.*

March 26, 1883

In 1870, the Indianapolis Society of Friends opened the Indianapolis Asylum for Colored Children. At a time when few social services were available to black adults, even fewer resources existed for children who were orphaned or displaced from their homes due to poverty or abuse. The Friends put up a large brick structure meant to house several dozen children and their adult caretakers. Boys and girls occupied separate dormitories; infants and very young children had their own space. The asylum also included a school. The IACC was the only such facility for African American children in the state of Indiana. In its first year, 18 children lived on site; by 1890, an average of 170 children per year lived in the facility. Regular reports, such as the one for March 1883, reveal that diseases regularly swept through the crowded institution, especially affecting children under five. The children lived under a rigid schedule, but they also received a decent education in a safe environment. Children who were old enough to be apprenticed were placed out or adopted. The IACC was turned over to the county in 1922.

March 27, 1863

The first military execution of the Civil War to take place in Indianapolis (and in Indiana) occurred on this date. Robert Gary was a schoolteacher who had enlisted in the Seventy-first Indiana Volunteer Regiment. Just a few days after becoming a Union soldier, he was captured in Richmond, Kentucky, and while a captive swore an oath of loyalty to the Confederacy. Upon his release, he was charged with treason, tried and sentenced to death. The execution took place at the Burnside Barracks, located between Eighteenth and Nineteenth Streets. Gary said that he had "never intended to desert" but instead "intended only to get home, that I might stay, for I did not feel able for service." Gary admitted his guilt and the justice of his punishment; he was bound, blindfolded and seated on his coffin. Ten soldiers fired, and Gary was dead. A reporter for the *Indianapolis Journal* concluded: "The coffin was put into undertaker Weaver's wagon, the troops were dismissed, and the most impressive and dreadful scene ever witnessed in Indianapolis, and the first military execution in the West, was over."

March 28, 1958

By 1958, Indianapolis had four television stations. Daytime programming was mostly local: cooking shows, variety shows, children's shows, game and contest shows, sports (including Indians baseball games) and news. Evening network programs included variety shows, such as the *Ed Sullivan Show* and the *Milton Berle Show*; dramas and westerns, including *Dragnet* and *Gunsmoke*; family comedies, such as *Leave It to Beaver* and *I Love Lucy*; and game shows and soap operas. In 1950, TV ownership was uncommon in Indianapolis; by 1960, not owning a television was unusual. Stores began promoting bigger and bigger console sets and the newer portable sets as well. In March 1958, the Major Appliance department of L.S. Ayres offered a sale price for two sets—an RCA Victor Whitman Console (with "3-speaker panoramic sound") and a "personal portable set" for the combined price of $349.95, because "if junior insists on a Western, but you'd rather hear the news…a portable extra set puts an end to family squabbles!"

March 29, 1984

As most Indianapolis residents slept, fourteen Mayflower moving vans began to depart from the headquarters of the National Football League's Baltimore Colts, bound for the capital city of Indiana. Colts owner Robert Irsay had made it clear that he wanted his team to leave Baltimore, with its small, aging stadium and what he perceived as a lack of fan and city support. The city of Indianapolis, led by Mayor William H. Hudnut III, had been aggressively pursuing Irsay and the team. A new domed stadium already stood in downtown Indianapolis; tax incentives guaranteed ticket sales for the first seven years of an NFL team in the city. The state of Maryland, in response to Irsay's open courting of other cities, was preparing to finalize legislation that would allow the city of Baltimore to seize the team by eminent domain. Irsay and Indianapolis officials responded with a midnight raid: late on the night of March 28, moving vans emptied most of the contents of the team's headquarters and, before daylight, taking various routes out of the metro area, headed west. Each van was met at the Indiana border and escorted to Indianapolis by the state police. The *Indianapolis Star* headline declared: "It's Confirmed: Colts on Way" and in a front-page story advised fans to "hold their horses" on trying to buy tickets. The media dubbed the night's events the "midnight ride" of the Colts.

March 30, 1908

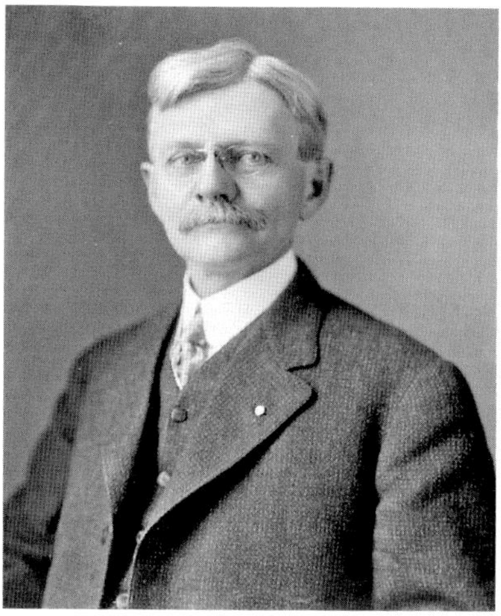

Thomas Riley Marshall, 1912. *Courtesy of Library of Congress, Prints and Photographs Division.*

"I am in the limelight now," conceded Thomas R. Marshall "in cheerful resignation" to a reporter from the *Indianapolis Sun*. Since 1875, Marshall had enjoyed a successful legal career and, although active in Democratic Party politics, had never held any public office. When the 1908 state party convention erupted into controversy with one candidate backed by political powerhouse Thomas Taggart and another backed by an anti-Taggart faction, Marshall emerged as a compromise candidate and took the nomination. Marshall served one term as governor. During his time in Indianapolis, he successfully promoted weekly wage laws and child labor laws, although his attempts to add progressive reforms to the state constitution failed. Marshall was a popular governor, and in 1912, when the Democratic Party was looking for a strong candidate from a swing state to run with presidential nominee Woodrow Wilson, it chose Thomas Marshall.

March 31, 2015

One of the most unusual and visually striking front pages of the *Indianapolis Star* appeared on the last day of March 2015. The top half of the page was black; the words "Fix This Now" were printed in giant white letters. Underneath the headline ran an editorial, addressed to Governor Mike Pence and Republicans in both houses of the state General Assembly: "We are at a critical moment in Indiana's history," it began. The state's just-signed Religious Freedom Restoration Act had created a national firestorm of controversy; the city of Indianapolis, in particular, was already feeling the effects. Within a few days, the city would again host the Final Four NCAA men's basketball tournament, and NCAA president Mark Emmert had publicly condemned the law, saying that it allowed discrimination against LGBT citizens and went against the organization's "core values." Local corporate giant Eli Lilly & Company spoke out against the act; Indianapolis-based Angie's List cancelled a planned expansion of its facilities. On April 2, flanked by business and community leaders, House Speaker Brian Bosma and Senate President Pro Tem David Long announced that both houses had approved changes to the law that prevented it from superseding local ordinances against discrimination; later that day, Governor Pence signed the legislation.

APRIL

April 1, 1893

James Naismith introduced the game of basketball at the Springfield, Massachusetts YMCA training school in the winter of 1891. The game spread quickly through YMCA directors who had attended the school and via Y publications. "Foot Ball Made Over! Basket Ball, a New and Popular Game," read a page of the September 1892 issue of *Physical Education*. "Instead of Kicking the ball, Toss it. Instead of Kicking a goal, Throw it. Instead of 'Downs' keep the ball Up." By 1893, the game had reached YMCAs in Indiana. An April 1 *Indianapolis News* article indicates that local Y physical director William McCulloch had already formed a league of four nine-man teams that had played three games. The reporter was intrigued: "The game, if played right, is full of snap, life and vigor, and is without any element of brutality or roughness." The game quickly spread to high schools and colleges, and through the 1890s, teams from all three types of institutions played one another on a regular basis. By 1898, girls, including a team from Shortridge, had joined in the game.

April 2, 1925

When the Marion County prosecutor issued a warrant for the arrest of D.C. Stephenson on charges of kidnapping and assault, he began the process that would end the career of Indiana's most notorious member of the Ku Klux Klan. Stephenson had arrived in Evansville, Indiana, in 1921 as a Klan organizer. On July 4, 1923, he became the grand dragon for a state that claimed one-third of its white men as Klan members. From his Indianapolis office, Stephenson wielded political power in the city and throughout the state. Stephenson also amassed considerable personal wealth; he made front-page news in the *Star* in December 1924 when he offered a reward for the person who had attempted to destroy his yacht in a Toledo, Ohio marina. But in March 1925, Stephenson viciously assaulted and raped a young woman he had met at an Indianapolis party two months earlier. He was arrested for assault; when she died a few days later, he was arrested again for murder. After a trial that caused a media sensation, Stephenson was convicted of second-degree murder. He was sentenced to life in prison but pardoned in 1956.

April 3, 2000

The city of Indianapolis was looking forward to hosting the Final Four of the NCAA men's basketball tournament, for the fourth time, in 2000; city leaders were also hoping that by the time fans arrived in downtown Indianapolis for the games, they would be able to visit the new headquarters of the NCAA. The association had been headquartered in Kansas City since 1952; in 1997, it asked for bids for a new location. Indianapolis community leaders from government, business and sports saw an opportunity to expand the city's identity as a sports destination and enhance the new White River State Park. Their pursuit paid off, and in 1999 the NCAA headquarters

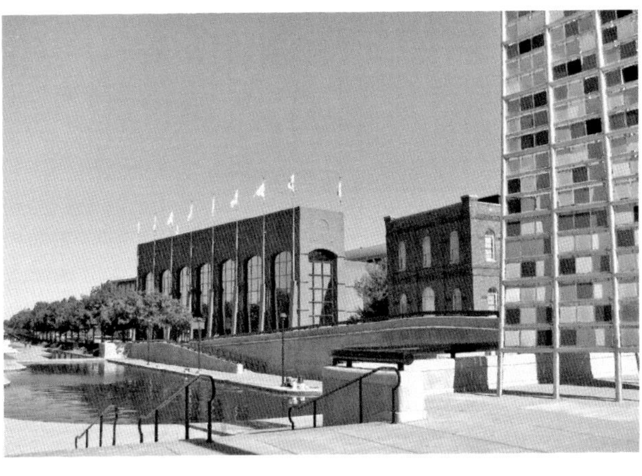

NCAA headquarters in White River State Park. *Photo by Dawn Bakken.*

moved to downtown Indianapolis, along with the NCAA Hall of Fame. Both buildings took their place along the canal, next to the Indiana State Museum, in time for the Final Four.

April 4, 1968

Throughout the afternoon of April 4, news spread through the country of the assassination of Dr. Martin Luther King Jr. Robert Kennedy, campaigning for the Democratic nomination for president, had just arrived in Indianapolis to give a speech when he and his aides heard the news. Fearful of unrest, Kennedy's aides urged him to cancel. Instead, Kennedy scrapped his planned address and hastily scribbled a new one. Told by the city's police chief that the force could not provide protection in the largely black neighborhood where he had been scheduled to speak, Kennedy asked a group of black community leaders to accompany him. Standing with them on a small platform, he announced Dr. King's death to the gathered crowd of black and white supporters. He spoke about King's work "to replace that violence, that stain of bloodshed that has spread across our land, with an effort to understand, compassion and love." He spoke about his own brother's murder and asked the audience to pray for the King family and for the nation. The city of Indianapolis remained peaceful that night and through subsequent days. On June 6, 1968, Robert Kennedy was assassinated. His Indianapolis speech did not garner widespread attention for decades.

April 5, 2010

The city of Indianapolis was again hosting the Final Four in NCAA men's basketball. The championship game between the Butler Bulldogs from Indianapolis and the Duke Blue Devils was scheduled for that evening at Lucas Oil Stadium. Butler had enjoyed success in the national tournament for many years, but this was its first trip to the final game. How were team members preparing on game day? When reporters inquired, they were shocked to find out that the players who had classes scheduled for that day were in their classrooms. Media stories the next day featured that news as well as the details of a hard-fought but heartbreaking game for the Bulldogs. In front of a loudly partisan hometown crowd, Butler kept pace with Duke throughout the game. With almost no time on the clock and the score standing at 61–59 in favor of Duke, Butler forward Gordon Hayward had the ball. His last-second shot hit the rim but then bounced out rather than in. The Butler basketball team gained recognition as a national contender; Butler University gained national notice as a school that valued academics as much as sports. In 2011, the number of applications to attend the school went up by 41 percent.

April 6, 1944

Rationing was a fact of life by 1944. Newspapers ran regular notices of what foods and other restricted goods were available and which ration stamps could be used to obtain them. Grocery stores, automotive supply stores and many other businesses ran ads to help shoppers keep track of what they could buy and when. The April 6, 1944 issue of the *Indianapolis News* was typical, with its front page "Rationing Calendar" that reported that the standard meat and processed food stamps were all valid and that the regular five-pound sugar stamp and the five-pound sugar-for-canning stamps were also valid. Stamps and coupons for gasoline, tires and fuel oil were explained in detail. An advertisement for the local A&P grocery stores attempted to make things easier with "value in low point and no point fine food." Eggs were a featured item: "You don't need ration points for these!" Canned tomatoes were five points per can, but canned green peas and wax beans were point-free.

April 7, 1915

By the early twentieth century, home economics was a practical science taught in schools and through home extension services. Everyday household tasks, including cooking and cleaning, could be done according to modern, scientific standards to the benefit of a homemaker and her family. In 1915, the *Indianapolis Star* co-sponsored a multi-day exhibit that filled Tomlinson Hall with cooking demonstrations, booths displaying "pure" foods and offering recipes and a final baking competition. The Cooking School and Pure Food Show opened with a lecture and cooking demonstration by Sherwood P. Snyder, "noted food expert," who spoke on "Foods and Their Relation to Health." "Many persons regard cooking as insignificant and, at best, woman's work," Snyder told his female audience. "There is no other agency that affects physical health more than proper food, proper cooking and proper eating. There is nothing that will add more to the happiness of womankind than to be able to keep her family well and happy by understanding the chemistry and science of cooking. More than 75 per cent [*sic*] of all illness is the result of wrong eating."

April 8, 1990

When eighteen-year-old Ryan White died on April 8 in Riley Children's Hospital in Indianapolis, the news spread around the world. His *New York Times* obituary noted that he "put the face of a child on AIDS." Ryan was a thirteen-year-old Kokomo schoolboy who had been receiving blood transfusions for his hemophilia when, in December 1984, he was diagnosed with AIDS, a disease that was just gaining national attention. The local school board, fearful of the disease being transmitted, banned Ryan from attending classes. Ryan and his mother, Jeanne, attracted local and national attention that ranged from acceptance and support to vicious hate speech. The family moved to Cicero, Indiana, where, welcomed by the community, Ryan continued to attend school and enjoyed normal teenage pursuits. But Ryan also became a national advocate for understanding the disease free of fear and misinformation. A few months after his death, Congress passed the first comprehensive legislation dealing with HIV/AIDS, which carried his name; Jeanne White Ginder continues to work as an advocate for those who carry the disease.

April 9, 1918

As the German immigrant population in Indianapolis grew, so did the demand for German-language instruction in the public schools. Until 1900, despite regular petitions from the public, there were few classes available even at the high school level. After the school board appointed a supervisor for German instruction, the number of students studying the language nearly doubled in two years. Classes were offered on a regular basis at both of the city high schools and in thirty-four district schools; enrollment grew apace with the student population. High schools offered clubs for advanced students. Then the outbreak of World War I began a progression of increasingly intense protests against German-language instruction. In January 1918, German instruction in grade schools was discontinued. In April 1918, the board banned the use of any textbook that did not "awaken and nourish…love of country." In March 1919, by act of the state General Assembly, all German-language classes in Indiana were banned.

April 10, 1931

Few Hoosiers today would believe that at any point in the state's history, anyone would have opposed holding an annual state boys' high school basketball tournament, and yet in April 1931, the editors of the *Indianapolis Star* felt it necessary to address critics. The first objection concerned "improper conduct on the part of the thousands of pupils who flock to the contests." Easily answered, replied the editors: "The residents of Indianapolis are in position to judge of the deportment of the tournament visitors and they will vouch for [their] good behavior." Second objection? "The battle for the championship imposes a severe physical strain on the players, particularly those of the winning and runnerup teams." Improving the schedule will solve the problem, the editors insisted, without "doing away with the contests." Critics also objected to "the effect of the basketball rivalries on scholarship." "Overestimated," replied the editors. Young people would benefit from "relaxation and a chance to give vent to enthusiasms. Basketball offers a fine opportunity and it engenders school spirit that is valuable."

April 11, 1831

When Indianapolis was chosen as the site for the state capital, planners hoped that the White River would be navigable for travel and trade. In reality, the river lacked sufficient depth, width and flow to allow regular steamboat traffic from the south. Hence the excitement when the *Indianapolis Journal* announced "the safe arrival" of the steamboat *General Hanna*, towing a keelboat (both vessels loaded with stone for bridge building). "No event is recollected," the editors claimed, "since the first settlement of this town, which produced a higher excitement." "Delighted spectators" crowded the riverbank; the day after the steamboat arrived, it was welcomed by members of the local artillery company, who "marched to the river with their cannon, and fired a salute." The boat, having unloaded its cargo, made two trips farther up the river and back, both times filled with Indianapolis residents. "We hope," the article continued, "our Legislature will be induced to take some efficient steps to remove the artificial obstructions in this river, and render it susceptible of being successfully navigated every spring." Railroads, and later automobiles, would make Indianapolis a transportation hub of the Midwest, but the city never became a river port.

April 12, 1861

In the months leading up to the Civil War, many Hoosiers (like other Northerners) supported making the necessary concessions to keep Southern states within the Union. As state after state seceded into the Confederacy, Hoosiers accepted the possibility of war while hoping for a peaceful solution. Then news reached Indianapolis and other Northern cities of the Confederate attack on Fort Sumter. "WAR BEGUN!" announced the front page of the *Indianapolis Indiana Daily Journal* on the morning of April 12: "Civil war has been commenced. The forces of the seceding States have attacked Fort Sumter. Without waiting even for an attempt to supply the Fort with provisions, they have begun a conflict which may last for years." The editors echoed the sentiments of the vast majority of their readers—support for the Union now required complete and forceful repudiation of the South and its cause. "We heard more than one or two or three men last night rejoicing in the prospect of the massacre of Major Anderson and his band." Such people, the editors declared, were "traitors and the meanest of traitors."

April 13, 1841

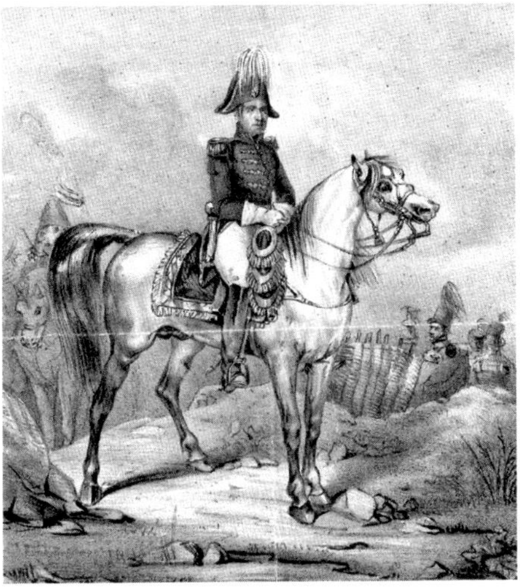

Detail from an 1840 campaign banner for William Henry Harrison. *Courtesy of Library of Congress, Prints and Photographs Division.*

In November 1840, Indianapolis newspapers closely followed the vote in the presidential election. William Henry Harrison's campaign for the presidency, built on images from his early military exploits while Indiana's territorial governor, had been closely followed in the Indianapolis press. In March 1841, the *Indiana State Sentinel* reported in detail on "the glorious Fourth of March" and Harrison's inauguration. The story noted that the sixty-eight-year-old president displayed "manifestly perfect" health and delivered his inaugural speech in a "full and commanding tone." Barely one month later, the *Sentinel* reported on the president's death, which "cast a deep gloom over our citizens." After a "solemn procession" from the courthouse, Indianapolis residents gathered to listen to memorials by Governor Samuel Bigger—who extolled at length Harrison's "virtues, as a patriot, a soldier and statesman"—and Reverend Henry Ward Beecher.

April 14, 1869

Already an archaeologist of some repute (although his first excavations seeking the site of ancient Troy lay two years in the future), Heinrich Schliemann arrived in Indianapolis on the first day of April 1869 for reasons unrelated to his scholarship. In 1852, he had married Catherine Lishin, who subsequently refused to leave her native Russia. Schliemann left his wife and sought a divorce, which she also steadfastly refused. Finally in March 1869, Schliemann sailed to New York and shortly after his arrival became an American citizen. Because Indiana had some of the most lenient divorce laws in the country, he took up residence in

Indianapolis until his petition for divorce could be granted. On April 14, he wrote to a friend: "I have rented a small house here…Three railroads are located 100 metres from my house…Just imagine—Indianapolis, a city of only 40,000 inhabitants, has 12 railroads." Schliemann was far less impressed with the city's culture: "Believe me…there is nothing here for the intellect." His divorce granted in early July, Schliemann at once made plans to sail from New York.

April 15, 1861

President Lincoln had just issued a call for the governors of the Northern states to raise 75,000 men to fight for the Union. On this day in 1861, Indiana governor Oliver P. Morton began the first of what would become a series of dispatch books, recording his telegrams related to the war. His first telegram went to the Ordnance Department, inquiring whether "the arms intended for Indiana" were on their way. "The arsenal," Morton informed them, "is prepared to receive." The second telegram went to Lincoln: "On behalf of the State of Indiana, I tender to you for the defense of the Nation and to uphold the authority of the Government, Ten thousand men." By the end of the war, 197,000 Indiana men had fought for the Union, making Indiana the state with the second-highest proportion of soldiers to its population.

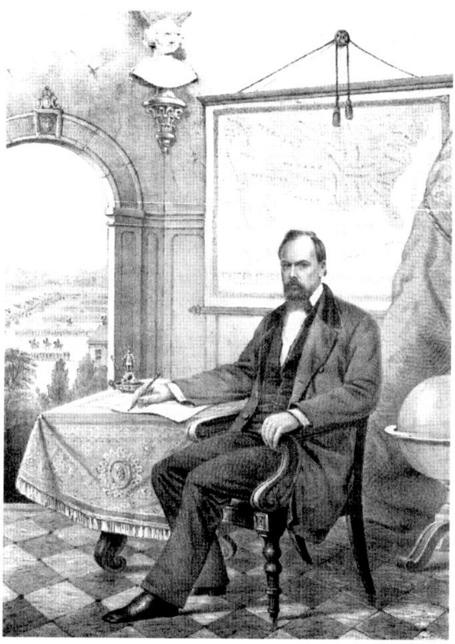

An 1862 lithograph of Oliver Morton as governor of Indiana. *Courtesy of Library of Congress, Prints and Photographs Division.*

April 16, 1920

In the spring of 1920, with women's suffrage assured, the Indianapolis Branch of the Women's Franchise League of Indiana re-formed itself as a local chapter of the League of Women Voters. The league, begun just two months earlier in Chicago, promised to promote "education in citizenship" and support "needed legislation." In 1924, chapter members began staffing booths at downtown department stores promoting voter registration. Later in the decade, the group began to offer citizenship classes. The league conducted get-out-the-vote drives, produced candidate questionnaires and sponsored candidate forums. For decades, the group offered demonstrations of the most recent voting machines. League members also became involved in a variety of issues related to government accountability and efficiency. In the 1940s and 1950s, members advocated for streamlined city government and against wasteful duplication of services. Many of their desired reforms were embodied when Unigov became law in 1970.

April 17, 1867

The process of freezing milk, cream, sugar and flavorings into the smooth, cold treat called ice cream was perfected well before the Civil War, but until the late 1860s, residents of Indianapolis had to make their own at home. By 1867, more than one establishment was offering downtown residents and shoppers the chance to enjoy ice cream on a warm day. The April 17 *Indianapolis Daily Journal* carried an advertisement placed by Mrs. Cunningham, who had "added to her immense establishment several new improvements for the manufacture of Ice Cream" and was now not only serving from her place of business but could also provide the treat for "parties and festivals at the shortest notice." The same day's edition announced that Mr. Moesch "at No. 33 North Pennsylvania street, first door south of the Post Office, will open his Ice Cream department today and will at all times keep a supply of the best creams and other confectionaries."

April 18, 1910

In the 1850s, Indianapolis became a state railroad hub. After the Civil War, larger railway companies began to connect the Hoosier capital with Michigan, Ohio, Illinois, Missouri and the West, as well as with Pennsylvania and New York. By the early 1890s, twenty-five thousand passengers were passing through the city's new Union Station every day, with 120 daily passenger trains. An April 1910 advertisement for the New York Central Railroad suggests the type of train service available: "Four trains daily to the heart of New York. Departures from Union Station, Indianapolis, 7:30 a.m., 2:20 p.m., 3:05 p.m., 6:55 p.m. All these trains arrive at Grand Central Station…Subway, surface and elevated trains from its doors to all parts of the city." Passengers would arrive in New York City, the company assured them, "ready for business or pleasure." In 1913, the Pennsylvania Railroad and the New York Central joined together to pay for improvements at Union Station, providing a new train shed and elevated crossings so that passengers would no longer have to cross tracks to reach their trains.

April 19, 1998

The morning after the NFL draft, months of speculation ended for Colts fans. The team, by virtue of possessing the worst record in the previous season, had the first pick in the first round of the draft. The team was going to pick a quarterback, but which one? The two top draft picks of the season were Ryan Leaf, quarterback for Washington State University, and Peyton Manning, quarterback for the University of Tennessee. Both players were expected to have distinguished pro careers. According to later reports, Colts manager Bill Polian and coach Jim Mora debated for hours, almost up until the time of their draft pick. The Colts chose Peyton Manning, and Ryan Leaf went to the San Diego Chargers. "The heady youngster is heading to Indianapolis," wrote the *New York Times*, "a franchise in need of a savior." Leaf's four-year NFL career was short and famously undistinguished. Peyton Manning led the Colts to two Super Bowls, including a championship in 2006.

April 20, 1914

The day's news was all about the new Federal League baseball team in Indianapolis and the upcoming opening of its new park. In thirty-two days, local construction and steel contractors had raised a stadium on a vacant lot in an industrial area along Kentucky Avenue. The construction company took out an ad bragging that "the pictures of the new Federal League Ball Park will show you the vast amount of work that can be accomplished in the short time of thirty-two days if handled by C.R. Pease Construction Company." Team managers and coaches would not guarantee an outright championship but predicted a winning season and perhaps more; sports writers were more sanguine, having seen the team barely win the previous day at St. Louis. The Federal League comprised eight teams, all playing in new ballparks. At the end of the season, the Indianapolis Hoosiers were on top, but the team went out of business after the season ended, and the league did the same in 1915.

April 21, 1861

Days after President Lincoln called on Northern governors to recruit volunteers to fight for the Union, Oliver P. Morton began to assemble Indiana regiments and provide for their training at a site just north of Indianapolis. Camp Morton filled up with five thousand troops, most civilian volunteers who had to be drilled and instructed before they could fight. The camp took on something of a festive atmosphere: on April 18, a large group of German recruits from Indianapolis arrived accompanied by the local German Turners band. The camp was also overrun with spectators. The citizens of Indianapolis journeyed up in their carriages or in rented hacks (the fare from the Circle was ten cents). On Sunday, April 21, ten thousand visitors descended on Camp Morton. Families and friends also sent supplies to the soldiers—on April 27, the *Indianapolis Journal* reported that two captains had received "divers boxes and baskets" filled with "all the delicacies of high life." On Sunday, April 28, to restore the necessary order, the camp was ordered to be closed to all outsiders "as a matter of justice to the men."

April 22, 1911

In October 1910, a dynamite-fueled explosion and subsequent fire destroyed the *Los Angeles Times* building, killing twenty-one people and injuring at least one hundred more. The bombing was soon linked to labor unrest, in particular the increasingly violent relationship between the National Erectors' Association and the International Association of Bridge and Structural Iron Workers. On April 14, private detective William J. Burns, assisted by local police, arrested union activists James McNamara and Ortie McManigal in Detroit. On April 22, Burns and two Indianapolis detectives forced their way into a meeting at the Iron Workers' headquarters on Monument Circle and arrested James's brother, John McNamara, the union's secretary-treasurer. With a warrant signed by Governor Thomas Marshall, Burns whisked McNamara (without legal representation) before a local judge who approved extradition; less than an hour after his arrest, McNamara was on his way out of the state for trial. The trial was a national sensation. Hoosier Socialist Party leader Eugene Debs was among many who decried the arrests and the trial and helped raise money to hire Clarence Darrow to defend the accused. McManigal turned states' evidence; the McNamara brothers eventually agreed to plead guilty. James died in prison in March 1941; John served his sentence and died in May1941.

April 23, 1861

In 1853, the Bates House, a luxurious four-story brick hotel, opened at the corner of Washington and Illinois Streets in downtown Indianapolis. When presidents and congressmen, foreign dignitaries and wealthy businessmen came to town, they stayed at the Bates House. So when city residents heard that Illinois senator Stephen Douglas was visiting Indianapolis, they went looking for him at the Bates House. Hearing that a large crowd had gathered outside in the rain, Douglas came out onto the hotel's main balcony and gave a brief speech. "The time has arrived," he told his audience, "for true and loyal citizens to rally in support of the Constitution and the laws. This is no time for crimination and recrimination as to the causes that have produced the present disaster; it is enough that the Government is assailed, and our liberties imperiled, and that every American citizen should rally in their defense." At the end of the speech, "three rousing cheers were given for Douglas and the Union." Douglas had undertaken a speaking tour through the Midwest at Lincoln's request. By the end of May, worn by his travels, he contracted typhoid fever; he died in Chicago on June 3.

April 24, 1847

Indianapolis began its existence with no local government other than that of Marion County. In 1832, voters elected five town trustees; a local sheriff and a volunteer fire department soon followed. As the population grew, new problems arose. A cholera epidemic in 1832 and 1833 highlighted the need for a board of health; the financial panic of 1837 left trustees wondering how to care for indigent citizens. In 1838, a new town charter added some governance, but Indianapolis did not officially incorporate until 1847. The "new" city needed a mayor and a city council. In 1832, Samuel Henderson had been the first president of the town trustees; he had also worked as the first postmaster of Indianapolis. Henderson was a landowner and businessman, as well as a director of the first bank in Indianapolis. On April 24, 1847, he won the mayoral election and served in the office for two years. Henderson did not remain in Indianapolis: he sold his land and businesses and headed west in the California gold rush.

April 25, 1853

In 1851, there were eleven schools in Indianapolis: four were available to residents of particular districts, four were available by subscription only, one was run by the county and two were private "female seminaries." The editor of the *Common School Advocate* presented his readers with the hard facts: "There are in this city 1,928 children between the ages of 5 and 21 years. In all the schools of our city there are less than 550 names upon the registers, and the average daily attendance is only 462…Here at the Capital, a place so renowned for its intelligence…we have 1,466 [children] receiving no instruction." In the same year, city voters approved a mandatory school tax. Each city ward became a school district overseen by trustees. Local leaders and education advocates rented buildings and hired staff, and in April

1853 the first free city schools opened with two men and twelve women as teachers. By fall, the schools had arrived at a common course of instruction and textbooks, as well as a grading system. The city's first free high school opened on September 1.

April 26, 1986

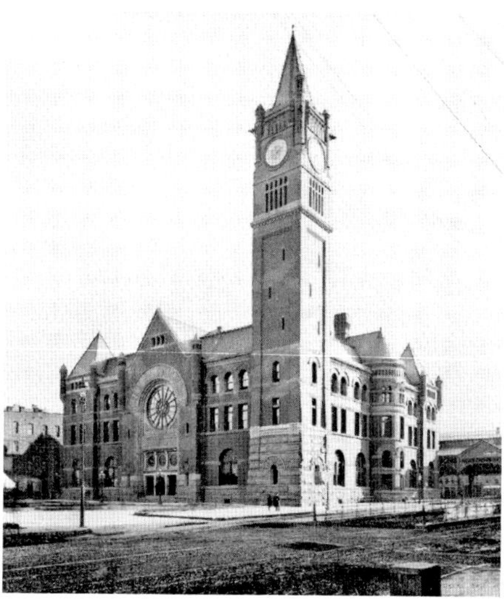

Indianapolis's 1888 Union Station. *Author's collection.*

On this day, Indianapolis's Union Station reopened as a festival marketplace filled with restaurants and shops, part of the larger downtown renewal. Indianapolis's first railway station had been built in 1853—the nation's first Union Station, built by a consortium of railroads. In 1888, a much larger and grander Romanesque station replaced the first. The brick and granite building, with its beautiful central hall and its distinctive 185-foot-high clock tower, began to decline after World War II, as the popularity of automobiles affected passenger rail service. By the 1970s, the decaying building was in danger of demolition, but it survived to be placed on the National Register in 1982. The festival marketplace began the rebirth of the station, which now houses a hotel (including "rooms" in twenty-six Pullman cars still on their tracks) and a banquet and conference center in the Great Hall.

April 27, 1950

Most Americans went through World War II driving the same car. New car production stopped in February 1942 and did not resume until October 1945. Rubber rationing made it difficult to obtain new tires, and gasoline rationing frequently restricted driving. Immediately after the war, car companies retooled their factories and waited for their supplies of raw materials to regain prewar levels. By 1950, American consumers were exuberantly moving away from austerity. The cars of the decade were out-sized, often weighted down with shining chrome. Engines were powerful, and gas mileage was unapologetically low. An advertisement in the *Indianapolis News* for the new Chevrolets was typical of the era in automobiles: "Enjoy all these finer things of motoring...new style-star bodies...new two-tone interiors...[and] Chevrolet's exclusive new power-glide automatic transmission." As the illustration made clear, the most distinctive feature of the car was its size: "Biggest of all low-price cars. Biggest in every way, for Chevrolet is the longest, heaviest car in its field, and has the widest tread."

April 28, 1962

By the early 1960s, the Indianapolis 500 had reached new heights of popularity. On opening day in 1962, seventy-two cars were entered for qualification into a field of thirty-three, with fifty drivers already committed to vehicles. Car number one and car number two were to be driven, respectively, by relative newcomers A.J. Foyt and Eddie Sachs, both of whom had first raced at Indy in 1957. Car number three would be driven by veteran Rodger Ward, who had competed at Indy since 1951. Fifteen of the drivers were rookies, including the only two foreign drivers. Track officials were hoping, as an *Indianapolis News* reporter noted, that "a firm groove of rubber [would] be laid on the track" in time for qualifications, since the track was now "almost fully asphalt paved." On the first day of qualifications, Parnelli Jones took the pole and became the first driver to break 150 miles per hour on the track. Rodger Ward, 1959 champion, took his second victory in the 1962 race.

April 29, 1952

Hoosiers have often been wary of federal and state government programs, and many residents of Indianapolis have exemplified the sentiment. "Suburbanite Wants Super Duper Four Lane Highway to Bypass the

City," read the title of a letter to the editor in the *Indianapolis Star*. The State Highway Commission was planning to extend Highway 37 into and through Indianapolis, and Mr. Joseph Waite, living on North Allisonville Road, objected strongly to the planned route. He understood, he wrote, that the commission and the city of Noblesville had already come to an agreement that the highway would bypass their town. So why, he wanted to know, did it have to come right through his part of the city? "I believe we non-political, tax-paying, home-owning, reliable citizens should be the ones to decide and agree upon whether we want to have this speedway built right through our front yards or not."

April 30, 1865

On the last day of April, Abraham Lincoln's funeral cortege passed through the state of Indiana. The train carrying the president's body arrived at Union Station in Indianapolis at 7:00 a.m. Lincoln's casket was placed into an ornate black carriage, which processed to the statehouse. A military honor guard lined the streets on either side of the route, and as the *Indianapolis Daily Journal* described the scene, "in the falling rain, and amid the sound of the tolling bells, all along the entire line of march, the citizens thronged the sidewalks, balconies, and housetops." At the statehouse, the coffin was placed on a catafalque and the lid opened for viewing. From early morning until 11:00 p.m., crowds—estimated to be close to 100,000—filed past to view "the features of a great and good man" who had "carried the nation through perils only now beginning to be comprehended."

MAY

May 1, 1961

The 1960s saw Indianapolis transform into a modern regional transportation hub. In 1961, that change was just beginning to take place. On May 1, the *Indianapolis Star* announced: "Indianapolis Jet Service Opens in Grand Style." The first jet-engine commercial aircraft, a Trans World Airlines SuperJet, "streaked off the runway" at Weir Cook Airport in Indianapolis bound for Idlewild International Airport and New York City. In the terminal, an official from TWA presented a plaque to Indianapolis mayor Charles Boswell, who pronounced that it was "a great day for Indianapolis." TWA flight 158 would now offer once-daily service from Indianapolis to New York, with a flying time of one hour and forty minutes. According to the *Star*, "The airport observation deck was packed with onlookers as the huge airliner knifed through the morning sky…Cars lined streets near the field after motorists halted to watch."

May 2, 1977

"Stay tuned for the greatest spectacle in racing"—to generations of radio listeners, the words evoke the excitement of listening to the Indianapolis 500 on the radio. And from 1953 to 1976, there was one voice that listeners associated with the race: Sid Collins, dubbed "the voice of the 500" by track owner Tony Hulman. Collins was an Indianapolis native and a graduate of Shortridge High School. He went to work at local radio station WIBC in 1947 and in 1948 became one of the track announcers for the 500. At the time, radio offered thirty minutes each of beginning and ending coverage of the race and updates broadcast each hour. Collins persuaded station executives to broadcast the entire race live, and in 1953, he went on the air as the lead announcer. Collins broadcast thousands of sporting events at WIBC, but he was best known in Indianapolis and all over the world for his work one day a year at the Indy 500. Just a few weeks shy of the 1977 race, Collins, who had been diagnosed with Lou Gehrig's disease, took his own life.

May 3, 1913

At a meeting of the city's Board of Parks Commissioners, landscape architect George E. Kessler presented a series of plans for Riverside Park, including an "extensive system of driveways and a system of lagoons. Every spot of natural beauty will be enhanced." Kessler was a German immigrant who began his work in the United States in Kansas City, Missouri, where in 1892 he designed a system of parks and boulevards. He also designed the grounds for St. Louis's 1904 Louisiana Purchase Exposition. From 1908 to 1915, he worked in Indianapolis, designing a system of boulevards as well as a "chain of parks" across the city. Among his accomplishments was the

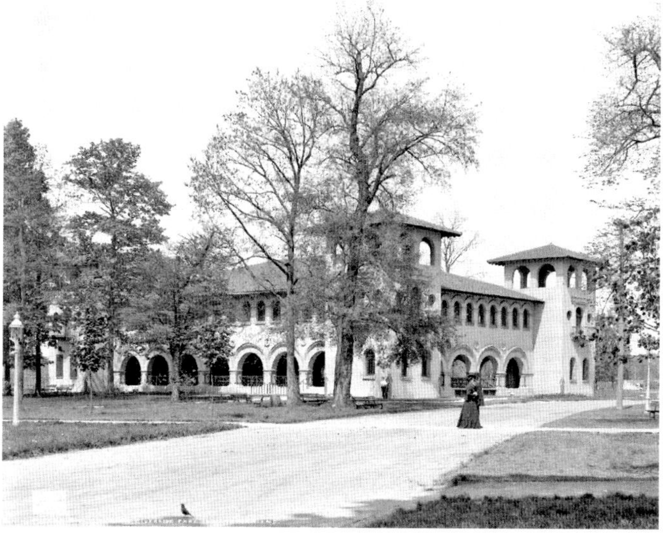

Shelter House in Riverside Park, 1907. *Courtesy of Library of Congress, Prints and Photographs Division.*

redesign of Garfield Park, the city's oldest public park, where he added its featured Sunken Gardens. Kessler Boulevard—another of his designs—was named in his honor at its completion in 1929.

May 4, 1893

Indianapolis has seldom been studied as a center of labor unions and union activity, but during the late nineteenth and early twentieth centuries, the city was home to the headquarters of at least twelve labor unions. In 1893, the International Association of Machinists held its annual convention in the city. Among the questions before the delegates on May 4 was a proposed revision in the union constitution that would strike the word "white" from the membership requirements and allow African Americans to join the union. The proposal was "voted down…in a unanimous manner." The next day, Samuel Gompers addressed the delegates on behalf of the American Federation of Labor, hoping "to remove the somewhat strained feeling" between the two labor groups. Over subsequent days, the delegates approved the federation of several smaller groups (including molders, blacksmiths and pattern makers) into the union, worshipped at Second Presbyterian Church to hear a sermon "for their special benefit" and elected officers. Not until 1947 was the race clause finally eliminated from the union's constitution.

May 5, 2005

On this day, the "new" Indianapolis Museum of Art (IMA) reopened to the public. The museum had its beginnings in 1883, as the Art Association of Indianapolis, and acquired its first permanent home at the turn of the century, on the grounds of the Herron School of Art. By the 1960s, the museum's collections had vastly outgrown its location, and in 1970, the IMA opened on the grounds of the Josiah Lilly Jr. estate, donated by the Lilly family. The Krannert Pavilion was joined by the Clowes and Showalter Pavilions, all showcasing the museum's collections of Asian, European and American art. In 1990, the museum acquired the African and South Pacific art collection of the Eiteljorg family. In 2005, the newly expanded museum featured the Wood Pavilion, a new Family Entrance Pavilion and a special events pavilion. The museum has also restored Oldfields, the Lilly home, as a showcase for the decorative arts. The recently added one-hundred-acre Fairbanks Art and Nature Park makes further use of the museum's beautiful grounds and features outdoor art installations.

May 6, 1950

Political infighting can produce odd results. In the 1950 primary elections for Indianapolis city government, the reigning faction of the Democratic Party lost several offices to its inter-party challengers. The city administration had been turning a blind eye to large-scale gambling in the city for years, but the other Democratic faction had received large amounts of funding for its primary campaigns from the gambling interests. Thus the city police were sent out in early May to put "a glove-tight crackdown" on all organized gambling within the city limits. The results, reported by the *Indianapolis Star*, were temporarily impressive: "Orders were given to operators of the some two dozen horse race bookie parlors in the city to remove all telephones and other equipment...It was as hard to find a slot machine within the city limits last night as it is to hit a jackpot. Big time gamblers were making speedy preparations to move their illicit businesses into outlying areas of Marion County to escape the shutdown...A well-known casino at 4444 West Washington Street—outside the city limits—was reported expanding to handle the increased trade."

May 7, 1919

"Thousands Pay Tribute to Hoosier Heroes" read the main headline of the *Indianapolis Star* the day after the grand parade held on May 7 to welcome back Hoosier soldiers from the war. Crowds gathered downtown all morning, serenaded by bands and choirs and entertained by airplanes flying overhead. The parade began through a Victory Arch as a mounted police escort led thousands of returning soldiers past cheering, flag-waving crowds. "To look up Meridian Street" from an Ohio Street viewing stand, as one reporter described the scene, "was to see what appeared to be a solid line of flags." At one point, soldiers passed through the Court of the Allies, with flags of the Allied nations flying from every building and "schoolgirls [who] strewed flowers in the path of the soldiers." At the foot of the Soldiers and Sailors Monument, one section of the steps was filled with women dressed in red and in white, forming a "Living Red Cross." Another front-page headline described the celebration as "One of Most Joyous and Colorful Events in City's History."

May 8, 1833

On May 11, Indianapolis citizens learned the results of a coroner's inquest into the death of William McPherson. On May 8, McPherson and Michael Van Blaricum had been crossing the White River in a canoe, when Van Blaricum overturned the canoe in about ten feet of water and McPherson drowned. The jurors found that Van Blaricum had acted "intentionally and with malice aforethought," causing the death of McPherson "against the peace and dignity of the state of Indiana." Van Blaricum was taken to jail to await a county trial; McPherson was given a funeral at the Presbyterian meetinghouse and was laid to rest in the town's "new burying ground." Stories of the murder, one of the first recorded in Indianapolis, continued to circulate throughout the area, and when Maine lawyer Ebenezer Chamberlain visited the town in October, he was told a much-embroidered version of the story. The canoe became a ferry, and Van Blaricum became a "brutal" ferryman who told passenger McPherson that "he would be damned if he would not drown him before he got over." In this version, McPherson was able to swim to shore, but Van Blaricum "seized him by the throat [and] pulled him under the water."

May 9, 1922

The Indianapolis Home Show, a popular fixture at the state fairgrounds for decades, began in 1922 as the Home Complete Exposition. To attract visitors, the city's real estate board donated a five-room model house to go on display at the exposition and to be given away to the person who submitted the best answer to "Why One Should Own His Own Home in Indianapolis." The exposition, promoters promised, "will show you the latest developments, the newest and best methods...It will give you new inspiration." Most exhibitors were local and state manufacturers and businesses. Indiana furniture makers displayed rooms of their newest designs. Many companies promoted the latest in home technology, such as the Cataract Electric Washer, "the Machine that Completes the Home." The Indiana Bell Telephone company promised that four times daily "a group of our young lady operators will present...the 'Telephone Tangle,'" described as an "educational playlet."

May 10, 1876

By the time Colonel Eli Lilly opened a drugstore just off Washington Street in Indianapolis in 1876, he had led a life of some distinction as well as hardship. A pharmacist by training, Lilly had just opened his first drugstore in Greencastle, Indiana, when the Civil War began. He enlisted at once and served first in Wilder's Lightning Brigade and later with the Ninth Indiana Cavalry. After the war, Lilly tried and failed at cotton farming in Mississippi and headed north, first to Illinois and then to Indianapolis, again taking up the drugstore business. Within a few years, the medicines he sold from his Pearl Street store made him a successful businessman, with a staff of one hundred and annual sales of $200,000. After a move to larger headquarters on McCarty Street south of downtown, the colonel retired in 1890 to the life of a wealthy philanthropist, leaving the business to his son Josiah. Lilly was a founder and major supporter of the city's Commercial Club, which promoted paved streets, city sewers, a new county jail and a pipeline to supply the city with natural gas. When the *Indianapolis Sun* announced his death in June 1898, its editors remembered him as "among the best friends Indianapolis ever had."

May 11, 2013

In 1999, the City of Indianapolis designated six distinct cultural districts, all part of or close to the city center: Massachusetts Avenue, Fountain Square, the Canal and White River State Park, Indiana Avenue, the Wholesale District and Broad Ripple. Worried that many residents failed to explore their own city and that most tourists rarely ventured beyond

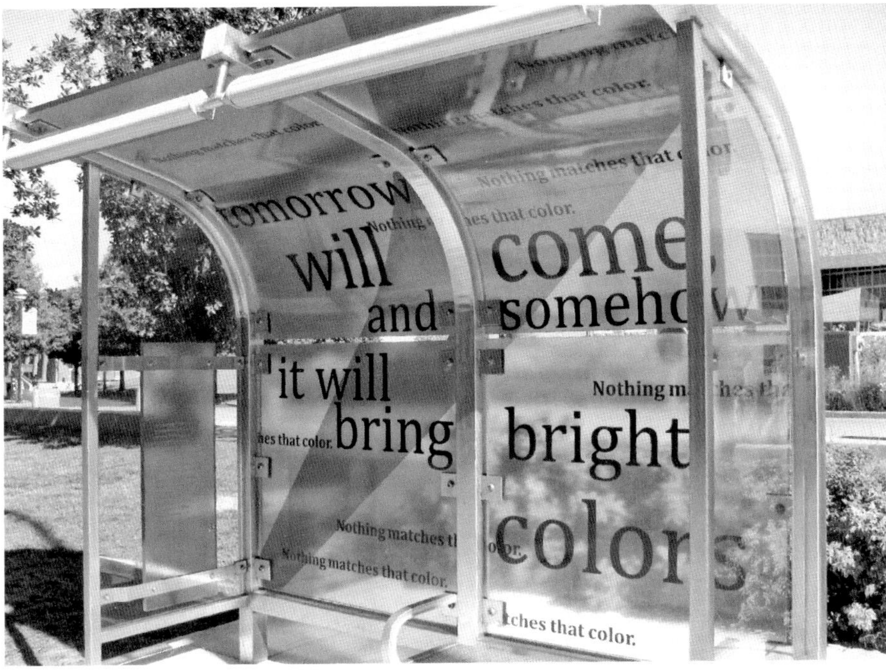

One of seven transit shelters that make up *Moving Forward* by Donna Sink, part of the Indianapolis Cultural Trail. *Photo by Dawn Bakken.*

the same downtown spots, the Central Indiana Community Foundation, working with the city, developed the idea of an Indianapolis Cultural Trail that would wind through each of the cultural districts. On May 11, 2013, a two-day celebration marked the completion of the eight-mile trail, laid out to encourage walking, running and biking. Several pieces of public art, many integrated into the urban landscape, have been installed at various locations; major donors Eugene and Marilyn Glick were commemorated with the Glick Peace Walk, featuring luminary sculptures honoring twelve world peacemakers.

May 12, 1948

In 1948, thirteen-year-old "Little David" Walker, "Miracle Boy Preacher," was just beginning to travel around the country with his manager, Reverend Raymond Hoekstra, and preach at religious revivals. Walker claimed that at the age of nine he had been taken up into heaven, where he experienced a vision and received a call to preach. In May 1948, Walker was traveling and preaching in the South when he and Reverend Hoekstra, along with Indianapolis lawyer James Dawson, his guardian, were called before the Marion County Juvenile Court in Indianapolis. David's parents had charged Hoekstra and Dawson with endangering David's "health and education" and had sued for custody of their son. The hearing took place on June 17. David testified that he opposed his parents' custody suit and that his father, Jack, "had beaten him with a belt and forced him to preach day after day without rest." The court ruled against the parents, and David Walker continued his worldwide preaching career. In 1979, David and his wife, Kathy, founded Bible Missions, Inc., a nondenominational evangelism organization.

May 13, 1923

An advertisement in the *Indianapolis Star* announced the summer grand opening of the Riverside Amusement Park, which offered guests "fireworks each evening of opening week" and "many new rides." Weekly ads through the summer of 1923 reveal a variety of special events to lure in crowds, including "Capt. Skivers' Balloon Ascension and Five-Parachute Drop" in mid-August. The park had first opened at the turn of the century, offering rides such as a "double-eight toboggan railway" and a "Shoot the Chutes" waterslide, as well as a roller-skating rink. In the 1920s, the park added two roller coasters. Riverside Amusement Park continued to add attractions and to draw Indianapolis residents for decades—in 1952, more than one million people visited the park. By the 1960s, the park had begun to deteriorate and lose money; owners also drew criticism for the park's decades of discrimination against African Americans, with occasional "Colored Frolic Days" in an overall setting of whites-only segregation. The park closed at the end of the 1970 season.

May 14, 1961

In 1961, Indianapolis was on the verge of a massive interstate construction program that would last through two decades. Interstate 465 was proposed as a beltway around the city, Interstate 70 would run east and west through the middle of the beltway circle, and Interstate 65 would connect the city to Chicago and Cincinnati and would cut through the center of downtown. On May 14, the *Indianapolis Star* printed a map of the state, with lines indicating the proposed interstates, under the headline "$850,000,000 Highway Program Changing State Road Map's Face." "The enormous public works program," the reporter noted, "has been called everything from the biggest boondoggle since Hadrian's Tomb to a magnificent impetus for economic growth." The interstate highways transformed Indianapolis in many ways. They were indeed an impetus for the continued physical growth of the city as well as its economic expansion. They connected a relatively unconnected midwestern capital to the region in ways that had not been imagined, and they destroyed or literally cut apart many historic city neighborhoods.

May 15, 1902

If asked to pick an iconic landmark in downtown Indianapolis, most locals and visitors would choose the Soldiers and Sailors Monument on the Circle. In 1887, the state legislature approved the design and construction of a memorial, to be located in the state capital, to Hoosier veterans of the Civil War. From the seventy submitted designs, commission members chose the proposal of German architect Bruno Schmitz. At the center of the structure was an obelisk of Indiana limestone, ornately finished with statuary on all sides and a bronze Victory at the top. Construction was not complete until 1901, and the monument was dedicated on May 15, 1902, in a lengthy ceremony that began with a parade honoring veterans from the Mexican War, the Civil War and the Spanish-American War. Union veteran and author Lew Wallace served as master of ceremonies, and poet James Whitcomb Riley recited "The Soldier," a poem he had written for the occasion. Bands played during much of the day; "Messiah of the Nations," a new march composed for the occasion by John Philip Sousa, was a feature of the morning ceremonies.

May 16, 1899

It is hard to imagine today how intensely popular bicycles were during the 1890s. In that decade before the automobile, the bicycle was exciting, fast, romantic, sometimes dangerous and sometimes even morally questionable. In May 1899, the *Indianapolis Sun* reported on a local minister's concerns regarding female bicyclists. Reverend Warren Reynolds, pastor of the Brightwood Methodist Episcopal Church, had written to the chief of detectives for the Chicago police department "inquiring if the use of the bicycle among women has affected their morality in any perceptible manner." Captain Luke Colleran replied: "Women of refinement and exquisite moral training addicted to the use of the bicycle are not infrequently thrown among the uncultivated and degenerate element of both sexes. Many doubtless escape the contamination. A large number of our female bicyclists wear shorter dresses than the laws of morality and decency permit, thereby inviting the improper remarks of the Depraved and Immoral. I most certainly consider the adoption of the bicycle by women as detrimental to the advancement of morality."

May 17, 1952

As the popularity of the Indy 500 grew, fans who could not hope to obtain or afford great tickets for race day flocked by the tens of thousands to the first day of qualifying, when the pole position was awarded and most of the top drivers secured their places in the field. In May 1952, fifty thousand people crowded the Speedway on a Saturday morning for the first day of qualifications, paying one dollar each for unreserved seats. The track record—138.122 miles per hour for a single lap and 136.872 for four laps—had been set the previous year by Walt Faulkner, who had returned to race this year. The car that had set the record, owned by J.C. Agajanian, would be driven by Troy Ruttman. Both drivers were expected to be competitive in qualifying and on race day. Faulkner failed to qualify. Ruttman, a twenty-two-year-old who had been "a terror on the sprint circuit," won both the pole and the race and became the youngest Indy 500 champion.

May 18, 1918

"Help the Red Cross: It Helps Our Men in France—Fill the War Chest" read the banner of the *Indianapolis News*. A front-page story detailed the "Great War Chest," which had been dedicated the day before in ceremonies on Monument Circle. Indianapolis mayor Charles Jewett called on every city resident to contribute to the fund, intended to meet "all war and charitable demands in the coming year." The chest, with a glass window showing the money and war bonds piling up inside, was guarded by soldiers and stood on the monument steps as a sign of the city's commitment to support soldiers through such groups as the Red Cross as well as charitable groups at home. The city also promoted a war savings program with a giant cash register sitting on a downtown street, with a sales counter where the cash drawer would have been found.

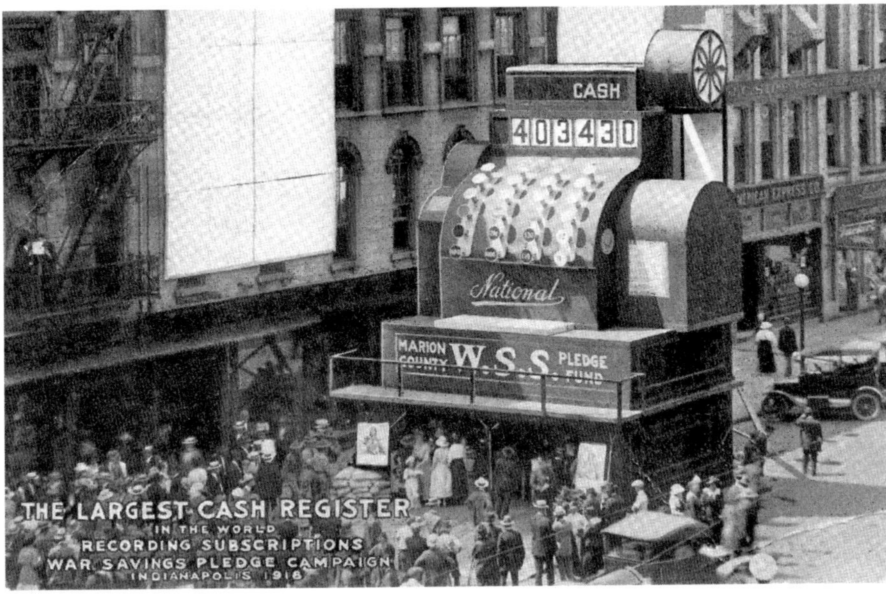

"The World's Largest Cash Register," downtown Indianapolis, 1918. *Author's collection.*

May 19, 1840

In 1840, Indianapolis society was provincial by the standards of Boston or New York, but its wealthy families were enjoying a high standard of living.

In June 1840, Catherine Noble, the daughter of former governor Noah Noble, wrote to a friend who had not been invited to Catherine's wedding on May 19. After profuse apologies and assurances of her continuing regard, Catherine settled down to a description of the day. For the ceremony, which took place in front of two hundred guests, she had worn a white satin gown with white kid gloves and shoes and silk orange blossoms in her hair. Catherine went on to describe her friends' gowns, the groom's formal attire, the elegant evening supper that followed the ceremony and the dessert table with a "splendid" cake and many confections. The letter continued with news of the parties the young couple had attended in the days after their marriage. "I feel as if I had indeed," Catherine wrote, "entered into a new state of being…I wish you were near me to begin the world with me… marry some person and come and live in Indianapolis."

May 20, 2015

Indianapolis mayor Greg Ballard declared May 20, 2015, as "David Letterman Day" to celebrate the last broadcast of *Late Night with David Letterman*. The future comedian and television star was born in Indianapolis and grew up and went to high school in the Broad Ripple area. After graduating from Ball State, Letterman returned to Indianapolis, where his 1970–74 tenure as a television host and weather announcer at local ABC affiliate WLWI yielded odd moments. A satellite film of cloud cover over the United States was missing some of the state lines, prompting Letterman to announce: "The higher-ups have removed the border between Indiana and Ohio, making it one giant state. Personally, I'm against it." He congratulated a tropical storm that had been upgraded to a hurricane and described an approaching thunderstorm as carrying hailstones "the size of canned hams." Letterman left Indianapolis for California in 1975. With his success in national television, in 1996 he realized every Indy 500 fan's dream: becoming a partner in an Indy Car team. Rahal-Letterman Racing brought Letterman back to Indianapolis almost every May, as it did in 2015 just a few days after his retirement from network television.

May 21, 1964

A three-day auction of a northeast-side Indianapolis house and its outbuildings began on this day, attended by an estimated fifty thousand people. City residents had turned out for their last glimpse of the infamous House of Blue Lights, a subject of urban folklore for two decades. The property had belonged to local realtor Skiles Test, who, with his first wife, built a home and established a farm just off Fall Creek Avenue. The house boasted a large outdoor pool, lit at night with blue lights (the owner's favorite color). At Christmastime, the couple lighted up their home and property with blue lights, and the house gained its popular name. Around the name also grew legends: Skiles was an unhappy recluse who lived with the body of his dead wife in a coffin surrounded by blue lights. The story was untrue, but by the early 1950s, local residents regularly went over, under or through the fences around the property, hoping to catch a glimpse of the coffin and the lights. When Skiles died in March 1964, the curious flocked to the auction. The buildings were razed in the 1970s; the property became Skiles Test Nature Park, part of the Indianapolis park system.

May 22, 1942

With little fanfare and minimal publicity, Navy Rear Admiral William H.P. Blandy commissioned the navy's newest ordnance plant in Indianapolis. When the United States entered World War II, the best available technology gave bomber pilots a relatively low chance of hitting small and exact targets, often forcing pilots to execute dangerous low dives. Existing bombsights also required that planes be leveled out before dropping their bombs, making accuracy difficult during combat situations. The Indianapolis facility, operated during the war by the Lukas-Harold Corporation, went to work manufacturing the new, top-secret Norden Bombsight. The Norden featured an analog computer that used actual flight conditions to calculate the bomb's trajectory; it also linked to the plane's autopilot system for quick corrections based on wind and other factors. The device required extensive training, and its complicated internal machinery sometimes broke down, but the Norden allowed U.S. bombers to accurately hit targets from high altitudes and was used in Europe as well as in the Pacific throughout the war.

May 23, 1904

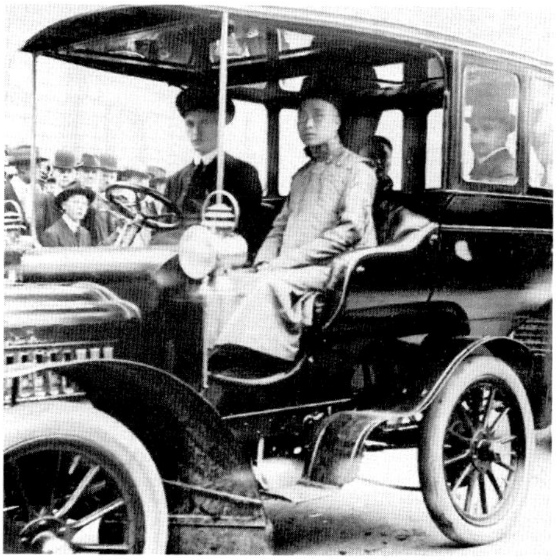

Courtesy of Library of Congress, Prints and Photographs Division.

Local newspapers followed the visit of Chinese crown prince Pu Lun to Indianapolis. The prince and his party visited several local schools and factories; they toured city sights, including Crown Hill Cemetery, where the prince alighted from his car at the tomb of Benjamin Harrison. The prince also enjoyed a high school baseball game featuring Indianapolis Manual versus Louisville and was taken to Fairview Park, at his request, to see its famous diving horses. One day was given over to an excursion sponsored by the Automobile Club of Indiana. A line of cars left downtown Indianapolis at 10:30 a.m. and arrived in Lafayette, where the prince was scheduled to visit Purdue University, more than four hours later.

May 24, 1946

Few Indianapolis residents knew that during the 1940s and 1950s, the city was home to a major research and design center for commercial and military aviation. The Indianapolis Experimental Station, operating under the Civil Aeronautics Authority, opened in May 1939. Early experiments resulted in improvements in radio navigation, precision guidance systems for landings and stronger cockpit windshields that could withstand in-flight collisions with birds. The tests for the last involved firing chicken carcasses at glass panels at a speed of two hundred miles per hour. After World War II, the engineers at the Indianapolis Station were able to begin testing military technology for civilian use. Some of the earliest postwar tests involved radar, a revolutionary technology that allowed airport controllers to "see" every aircraft within a set radius, allowing better spacing of aircraft in flight, as well as safer (and faster) takeoffs and landings. By the early 1950s, radar was being used at several major U.S. airports, thanks to experiments carried out in Indianapolis.

May 25, 1919

On this date, former Indianapolis resident Sarah Breedlove died in New York City. Better known as Madame C.J. Walker, she was the nation's first self-made female millionaire, all the more remarkable in a time when there were restricted economic opportunities for African Americans. Walker had already developed a system of hair and skin care for black women when she moved to Indianapolis in 1910. She built a home, laboratory and manufacturing facility. In September 1911, when the Madame C.J. Walker Manufacturing Company was incorporated, she was its president and sole shareholder. The company marketed through newspaper ads and sold through a nationwide network (numbered at fifteen thousand) of Madame Walker agents, trained in product application and sales techniques. During her years in Indianapolis, Walker was active on behalf of the city's African American community, particularly as a major founding donor and board member of the Senate Avenue YMCA. In 1927, the company built a larger headquarters along Indiana Avenue. Today, the Madame Walker Theater Center, in the words of its mission statement, "exists to advance the legacy of our namesake through art, entertainment, cultural education, youth empowerment, entrepreneurship and civil engagement."

May 26, 1833

After Hugh McCulloch left his native Maine to practice law in Indiana, his first decision was "whether I should settle in Indianapolis or seek a home somewhere else." McCulloch discovered that Indianapolis did not meet his expectations: "The parks, in which were the State House, just then completed, and the court-house, had been enclosed with post and rail fences, but nothing had been done to the streets except to remove the stumps from two or three of those most used…There were no sidewalks, and the streets most in use, after every rain, and for a good part of the year, were knee-deep with mud…I have seen many of the incipient towns of the West, but none so utterly forlorn as Indianapolis appeared to me in the spring of 1833." McCulloch settled in Fort Wayne—"about as uninviting in every respect except its site as any of the towns through which I had passed"—where he became a banker and played an important role in the second State Bank of Indiana. In the 1860s and again in the 1880s, he served as U.S. secretary of the treasury under Presidents Lincoln and Arthur.

May 27, 1982

William H. Hudnut III had been a minister at Indianapolis's First Presbyterian Church and had also served in the U.S. Congress as representative from Indiana's Eleventh District when he was elected as the mayor of Indianapolis in 1976. For sixteen years, he headed up an administration that worked to transform the city, in particular its still-mordant downtown, through a series of private-public partnerships. One such partnership formed under the aegis of the Indiana Sports Corporation, which sought to re-create Indianapolis as a sports destination. One of Hudnut's most controversial, and ultimately successful, projects was the Hoosier Dome, an $80 million building financed in part by the Lilly Endowment and the Krannert Charitable Trust and in part by the sale of revenue bonds and a 1-percent tax on city restaurant and hotel sales. The dome was intended to house an NFL team, although at the time Indianapolis had no team and no guarantee of getting one. On May 27, 1982, at a celebration of the official start of construction, Hudnut cut a cake in the shape of the Dome. Construction was complete in May 1984, just a few weeks after the Baltimore Colts became the Indianapolis Colts.

May 28, 1994

In 1957, the city of Indianapolis first hosted the 500 Festival, a series of events designed to complement the race. The first festivals were three-day weekends, with a ball, an evening parade downtown and a square dance on the War Memorial Plaza. In 1960, the 500 Festival Associates added a golf tournament at the Speedway Golf Course. Over the years, the festival grew to encompass the entire month, with a pageant to crown a festival queen and princesses, a mayor's breakfast, a mini-marathon and an art festival. By the 1990s, the 500 Festival Parade—the only event that has been part of the festival every year since its inception—was the nation's second-largest parade, with tens of thousands of spectators on the streets of downtown Indianapolis and hundreds of thousands more people watching on national television. The parade features the thirty-three drivers and their families, as well as celebrities who are also race fans. Grand marshals have included Peyton Manning, Reggie Miller, Jane Pauley and Jim Davis (with Garfield).

May 29, 1822

When Alexander Ralston laid out the town of Indianapolis, he predicted that four months out of the year rains would swell the White River, making it navigable for transportation and commerce. Early government officials shared Ralston's hope, so when two keelboats arrived in Indianapolis at the end of May 1822, the newly elected county commissioners paused their very first organizational meeting to walk down to the river, greet the captains and view their cargo. One of the keelboats brought a variety of supplies, including salt, tobacco and dried fruit. The second boat carried Hugh Walpole and his family, along with their furniture and possessions, and merchandise for the new store that Walpole planned to open in Indianapolis. Unfortunately, the *Eagle* and the *Boxer* did not prove to be harbingers of things to come along the banks of the White River. When the steamboat *General Hanna* arrived in town in April 1831, it was a major event in local newspapers.

May 30, 1949

Television was introduced widely in 1939 at the New York World's Fair, but it would be ten years before Indianapolis residents could watch a TV show broadcast locally. Ironically, by the late 1940s, Indianapolis had become one of the major manufacturing locations for RCA television sets—the plant employed 3,300 people in 1947 and expanded rapidly in the following years. But a 1948 newspaper survey suggested that only 150 homes in the city owned a television set, since owners had to attempt to capture signals from another city on their antennas. In May 1949, the owners of local radio station WFBM launched the city's first commercial television station. The station was a CBS affiliate, and on its first day of operation, it broadcast a live feed of the Indianapolis 500. Local business owners saw an opportunity—stores selling television sets invited customers to come in and watch the race. During the first months of operation, with limited programming available, the station broadcast for a few hours each evening.

May 31, 1937

The first Indianapolis 500 Mile Race was held in May 1911. Suspended only for two years during World War I and four years during World War II, it continues as the most defining event in the city. Generations who grew up in Indianapolis could name their favorite drivers and dreamed of coming to their feet with hundreds of thousands of other fans as the pace car pulled into the pits and the field swept down the front straightaway to start the race. For much of the mid-twentieth century, one of the most popular drivers associated with the race was Hoosier native Wilbur Shaw, who on this day in 1937 took the first of his three victories at the track. In a self-designed, self-built car, Shaw came in first by two seconds; he went on to win in 1939 and again in 1940. After the war, Shaw persuaded Terre Haute businessman Tony Hulman to purchase the aging racetrack and all its facilities. Wilbur Shaw became the president of the Indianapolis Motor Speedway, and until his death in an airplane accident in 1954, he and Hulman worked together to make the Indy 500 the "World's Greatest Spectacle in Racing."

JUNE

June 1, 1864

In October 1863, 236 acres of farmland was purchased for a cemetery for the city of Indianapolis. Crown Hill was dedicated on June 1, 1864, one day before the first burial took place onsite. After the end of the Civil War, a section of Crown Hill was dedicated as a National Cemetery. Over the decades, Crown Hill continued to add acreage and became the burial site for many famous Indianapolis residents. In 1878, Oliver Morton was the first Indiana governor to be buried there. Benjamin and Caroline Harrison, Eli Lilly, Meredith Nicholson and Booth Tarkington are just a few of the famous Hoosiers buried at Crown Hill. At the Crown, James Whitcomb Riley lies in a classical temple-style tomb that is still one of the most popular sites for visitors to Crown Hill. The cemetery's other favorite visitor site is the tomb of Indianapolis native and Public Enemy Number One John Dillinger.

June 2, 1919

When the Pulitzer Prizes for 1919 were announced, the fiction prize went to Booth Tarkington for his novel *The Magnificent Ambersons*. Tarkington won the prize a second time in 1922 for *Alice Adams*. Tarkington was born in 1869 in Indianapolis. His first novel, *The Gentleman from Indiana*, was published in 1899, and from that time until his death, Tarkington was a best-selling author of stories, essays and books. His three Penrod books, featuring the adventures of a young boy growing up in the Midwest, were especially popular. *The Magnificent Ambersons* was set in a fictionalized version of the Woodruff Place neighborhood of Indianapolis and followed three generations of the Amberson family from the years after the Civil War into the early twentieth century. In the Ambersons—and their neighbors and rivals the Morgans, whose fortune was based on automobile manufacturing—Tarkington embodied the decline of a traditional, nineteenth-century way of life and the rise of the new industrial class. The book was made into a movie in 1942 by director Orson Welles and revived again for television in 2002.

June 3, 2005

In 1902, a gift from John Herron began the Herron Art Institute, which would train many of the state's most important artists and serve as the city's art museum and site of innumerable art exhibitions for decades. The Herron's first home was an elegant building designed by local architectural firm Vonnegut & Bohn. Several of its early teachers were members of the Hoosier Group of artists, including T.C. Steele, J. Ottis Adams, William Forsyth, Otto Stark and Richard Gruelle. In 1970, the newly built Indianapolis Art Museum took over the Herron's collections; in 1996, the art school became part of IUPUI. In 2000, the university unveiled a new sculpture and ceramics facility; five years later, the renamed Herron School of Art and Design moved into the new Eskenazi Hall on the downtown IUPUI campus.

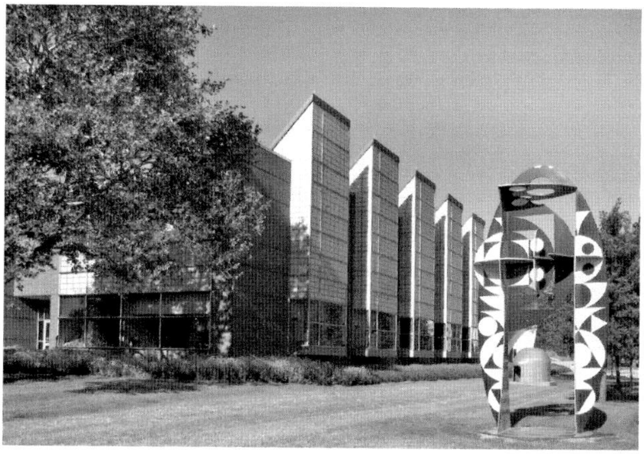

Eskenazi Hall, home of the Herron School of Art and Design, IUPUI. *Photo by Dawn Bakken.*

June 4, 1959

In 1861, Gilbert Van Camp started a canning business in Indianapolis and won a contract to provide provisions to the Union army. By the 1880s, millions of cans of Van Camp's Boston Baked Pork and Beans (a "triumph in cookery," according to the label) were distributed all over the country. In 1933, the Van Camp & Son Packing Company merged with a Tennessee vegetable packing company owned by the Stokely family. Stokely–Van Camp produced a wide variety of canned foods as well as a line of frozen foods. During World War II, Army C Rations were developed in Indianapolis by Stokely–Van Camp. A June 1959 ad from the A&P Supermarket in Anderson, Indiana, advertised a "Stokely–Van Camp Pantry Sale" including the favorite Pork and Beans (four cans for sixty-nine cents) as well as canned applesauce, peaches, cherries, fruit cocktail, peas, green beans, lima beans, corn, creamed corn and a pineapple-grapefruit drink called Ping. The company operated in Indianapolis until the early 1980s, when it was broken up and sold.

June 5, 1909

On this day in 1909, the Indianapolis Motor Speedway was inaugurated with a balloon race, watched by an estimated fifty thousand spectators. One of the participants was Carl Fisher, co-owner of the new racetrack. Fisher had gained a name in Indianapolis as an automobile racer and salesman. In 1904, he co-founded the Prest-O-Lite Storage Battery Company, which made batteries for car headlights and went on to become a major manufacturer of automotive batteries. The company made Fisher and his partner James Allison wealthy men. Fisher and Allison, joined by Arthur Newby and Frank Wheeler, built the IMS test track across from their factory. Fisher continued his fascination with automobiles for the rest of his life. He was one of the founders of the Lincoln Highway Association in 1910. Having helped establish an east–west transcontinental highway, during the next decade, Fisher promoted the Dixie Highway, which ran from Michigan to Florida. He also promoted tourism along the highway and became one of the founders of the resort town of Miami Beach.

June 6, 1881

The 1881 summer term at Butler University was managed by four professors, including Catherine Merrill, "teacher of English literature and history." Merrill was the Demia Butler Professor of English, and when she took the position in 1867, she became the first professor at a U.S. university to hold a chair endowed for a woman. Merrill was also only the second female university professor in the nation, after Maria Mitchell at Vassar. Before her teaching career, Merrill had worked as a nurse during the Civil War. Her experiences gave her the perspective for a job she was asked to do by former governor Oliver Morton. Merrill wrote a two-volume chronicle titled *The Soldier of Indiana in the War for the Union*, published in 1866 and 1869. The book appeared with an anonymous author; only much later was Merrill given credit for her work. Her second book, *The Man Shakespeare and Other Essays*, was published under her name but two years after her death in 1900. The book included an appreciation from naturalist John Muir, who had been befriended by Merrill in 1866. He described her as "one of the kindest, wisest and most helpful [friends] of my life."

June 7, 1820

John Tipton left Corydon, Indiana, on May 17, bound northward "to select & locate a site for the perminant [*sic*] Seat of Government of the State of Ind." On May 22, Tipton and his associates arrived at the trading post of William Conner, one of the few white settlers in the area. The men spent several days surveying the countryside, and on June 7, meeting at the log cabin of the McCormick family, they "came to a resolution" and drew up papers specifying the boundaries of the new capital. Emerging from the cabin after signing the final report, Tipton noted in his journal: "The first Boat landed that ever was Seen at the seat of Government. It was a small Ferry Flat with a cannoe Tied along side boath loaded with the household goods of 2 Families moving to the mouth of fall creek. They came in a keel Boat as farr as they could get it up the river then unloaded the Boat and B[rough]t up their good in the F[erry] & cannoe." In January 1821, the state legislature formally approved the site choice and named the future city Indianapolis.

June 8, 1905

The twenty-first century may see the demise of the print newspaper, but for two centuries, most Americans relied on a local newspaper for news of their city and the world. A large number of newspapers appeared and disappeared in nineteenth-century Indianapolis. Two of the longest lived (under variant titles and a host of owners) were the *Sentinel* and the *Journal*; the *Sun* and the *Times* also appeared in the 1870s and 1880s, the latter remaining in print until 1965. Several newspapers served specific readerships, including African Americans, German Americans, temperance advocates and farmers. In December 1869, the *Indianapolis News*, the only evening newspaper in the city, began a run that would last until 1999. The twentieth century saw the rise of the *Indianapolis Star*, which began in June 1903, acquired the *Journal* on this date in 1905 and then acquired the *Sentinel* one year later.

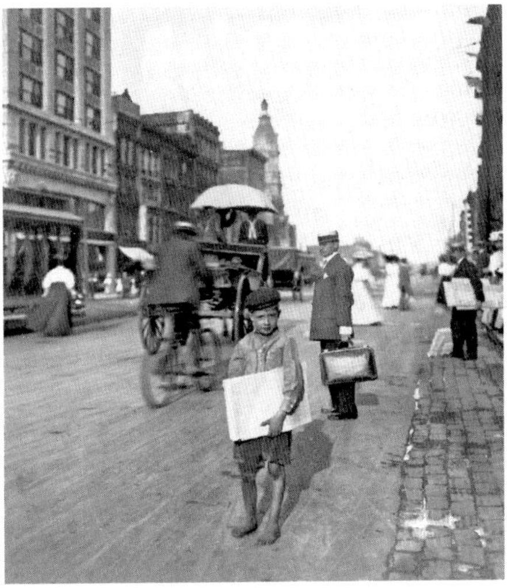

A newsboy in downtown Indianapolis, 1908. *Courtesy of National Child Labor Committee Collection, Library of Congress, Prints and Photographs Division.*

June 9, 1920

The city of Indianapolis threw itself a five-day centennial celebration. On the evening of June 9, some residents sat along either side of the White River watching a water pageant and fireworks. Others were in the Coliseum at the state fairgrounds, watching a two-thousand-person, eight-episode historical pageant of the city's history, offered for two nights due to popular demand. Two female narrators, portraying Indiana and Indianapolis, provided the pageant's structure. White settlers appeared in the first episode after Indiana declared: "Pioneers who long have waited, eager for this vast New Purchase, come and make your homes upon it, come and people it with heroes!" Other episodes included selecting the site and platting the town, the first railroad and the Civil War. The pageant concluded with a "massed chorus," joined by the audience, singing (to the tune of "Battle Hymn of the Republic") "We have builded us a city which foundations hath in God/Out of wilderness upspringing at consecrating nod/Blessed every towering battlement, blest every foot of sod/In-di-an-ap-o-lis!"

June 10, 1930

The keynote address at the 1930 state Democratic convention in Indianapolis was given by Hoosier Paul V. McNutt. McNutt grew up in Martinsville and graduated from Indiana University and then from Harvard Law School. After stateside duty during World War I, McNutt became a law professor (and then dean of the law school) at Indiana University; he also became involved locally and then statewide with the new American Legion. In 1928, McNutt was elected national commander of the legion; his national prominence also made him a rising star within his political party. McNutt ran for and was elected governor in 1932. He served from January 1933 to January 1937 and was an effective ally of the Roosevelt New Deal, utilizing the Works Progress Administration to bring seventy-five thousand jobs to Indiana during the Depression. Although his ambitions for the presidency were never realized, he remained in public service after he left the statehouse, serving as high commissioner to the Philippines, administrator of the Federal Security Administration, chair of the War Manpower Commission and first U.S. ambassador to the Philippine Republic.

June 11, 1988

The new Indianapolis Zoo, one of the first developments of White River State Park, opened on this day. The city's first zoo had opened in April 1964. The popular attraction offered twenty-four acres of grounds and five hundred animals, most displayed in fairly restrictive, traditional enclosures. The new zoo was designed around four biomes—waters, deserts, forests and plains—where visitors encountered animals in re-creations of their natural habitats. The zoo continued to add new habitat areas to its collections, building the Marine Mammals Pavilion in 1989 and opening the International Orangutan Center in 2014. The zoo has also become an important international center for research and conservation, now housing more than 320 species and, through its own Hix Institute for Research and Conservation, participating in conservation efforts worldwide for endangered animals including Amur tigers, African mountain gorillas and Madagascar's lemurs. The zoo grounds also encompass the three-acre White River Gardens.

June 12, 1909

It was a typical hot summer day in Indianapolis. The *Sun* offered news of the new bathing beach at Riverside Park: "Fresh water swimming…A new retreat from warm weather." Park officials created a fifteen-acre lake by diverting water from the Central Canal into an artificial lakebed; water flowed back into the White River, keeping the small lake fresh. The lake offered beaches at the deep end and at the shallow end, as well as thousands of electric lights on buildings and the lake's boardwalk, enabling nighttime swimming. "Five thousand bathing suits, with a drying machine which will cleanse them all two or three times a day if the demand makes it necessary," would be available at the locker building. Weber's Band from Cincinnati, along with a quartet of singers, was hired to entertain the crowd during the first week of the beach's opening.

June 13, 1923

The *Indianapolis Star* reported a closed-door meeting between Mayor Lew Shank and City Controller Joseph Hogue. Shank had been mayor of Indianapolis for the first time from 1910 to 1913; he proved to be an outspoken opponent of Sunday saloon sales and illegal gambling and a supporter of women's suffrage and the local police. During the Indianapolis streetcar strike of 1913, many policemen refused to attack the strikers or staff the streetcars as they had been ordered to do. Shank, rather than enforce the governor's order, resigned his office. He became mayor again in 1922 and this time took on Prohibition-era bootleggers and the Klan.

The Klan held the allegiance of Hogue and many other city employees. Shank was being attacked in the pages of the Klan newspaper, the *Fiery Cross*; he responded by pressuring Hogue to help stop the stories. Shank paid a political price for his stand. In 1924, he lost the Republican nomination for governor to Ed Jackson, a Klan supporter (and probable Klan member) who went on to become governor of Indiana.

June 14, 1893

In 1893, the bicycle was the fastest conveyance between two points not directly linked by a railroad, so why not make use of its speed and convenience as a method of emergency communication? So was the reasoning of the Zig-Zag Bicycle Club of Indianapolis and other bicycle clubs in Illinois and Kentucky. On June 14, the clubs conducted an experimental relay race to deliver a message from the governor of Illinois to the governor of Indiana and from there to the governor of Kentucky, all via bicycles; cyclists would then repeat the trip in reverse order. The relay race was intended "to furnish a practical demonstration of the utility and value of the bicycle in cases of emergency." Each cyclist was assigned a segment of about eight miles, with "an average of a mile in four minutes." A brief report on the results a few days later deemed the experiment "quite a success," but there is no record of the bicycle ever being used by state officials for such a purpose.

June 15, 1826

Indianapolis was a small frontier town when John Scott included an entry on the site in his 1826 *Indiana Gazetteer or Topographical Dictionary*. Scott, one of the earliest newspaper publishers in Indiana, had established a newspaper in Centerville and had also begun to print other materials. The gazetteer, like others of its sort, was intended to educate and entice potential emigrants. Scott's entry on Indianapolis described a town laid out across one square mile, with wide streets, and one of its squares containing "a large elegant brick house, which is used as a court house and state house; several of the public offices are also kept in it." The square intended for a new statehouse was "not yet improved." "It is supposed," Scott wrote, "this place now contains about 800 inhabitants, 7 stores, 4 taverns…2 printing offices, a post office, a library, a sundy [*sic*] school, a bible society, and a masonic lodge—3 clergymen, 3 physicians, and several lawyers." Scott also noted other town businesses, including "1 clock and watch-maker, several cabinet-makers, carpenters, saddlers, hatters, shoe-makers, tailors, brick and stone masons, plasterers, chair-makers, wheel-wrights, &c."

June 16, 1936

In the months leading up to the election of 1936, Indiana voters were split almost evenly between President Franklin Roosevelt and Republican challenger Governor Alf Landon. Roosevelt visited the state three times during the summer; his June visit also included First Lady Eleanor Roosevelt. The couple parted in Vincennes, with the president continuing into Kentucky and the first lady traveling to Indianapolis. On the afternoon of June 16, Mrs. Roosevelt arrived at the Governor's Mansion and was welcomed by Governor and Mrs. McNutt and a delegation of local Girl Scouts. That same evening, she spoke at a town hall meeting at the Murat Theater on housing issues and then attended a performance by the local troupe of the Federal Theater Project. The next morning, she traveled to West Lafayette to tour a housing research project at Purdue and then returned to Indianapolis to visit a WPA sewing project that employed nine hundred women. The brief visit left a lasting impression on many who met the first lady, including Roberta West Nicholson, the supervisor of the WPA project, who described "what a natural, lovely and simple person she was, as I guess all real people are."

June 17, 1922

In June 1922, Eli Lilly wrote to reassure James Macleod: "Our chemists here have been working very intently." Eli Lilly & Company was being run by the founder's son, Josiah Kirby Lilly, and his sons Eli and Josiah Kirby Jr. In 1920, two researchers at the University of Toronto had developed a possible treatment for the deadly disease of diabetes, but Frederick Banting and James Macleod were unable to perfect a process that would produce the drug in stable, pure form and in large quantity. In 1921, Lilly was granted the right to produce the drug commercially should they be able to develop it for the market; two years of research and controlled experiments conducted with patients at Indianapolis City Hospital produced Iletin, an animal-derived insulin that Lilly manufactured on its modern production line. The drug revolutionized the hitherto primitive treatment of diabetes. Lilly began to sell the drug in January 1923, and by October, 7,500 doctors across the country were prescribing it to 25,000 patients. In the early 1980s, marking the first use of recombinant DNA to produce pharmaceuticals, the company introduced the first human insulin product.

June 18, 1927

When the Indiana Theater opened in June 1927, it was the epitome of the movie palace—an elegant building with an ornate interior, spacious public areas and a huge theater where audiences could view the newest motion pictures. The Indiana offered patrons a romantic glimpse of an imagined Spain; its Baroque Spanish style included beautiful ironwork and ornate painted plasterwork. Above the theater was the equally elegant Indiana Roof ballroom, where couples could dance to an orchestra or a big band in a setting that suggested the plaza of a Spanish village at night, complete with

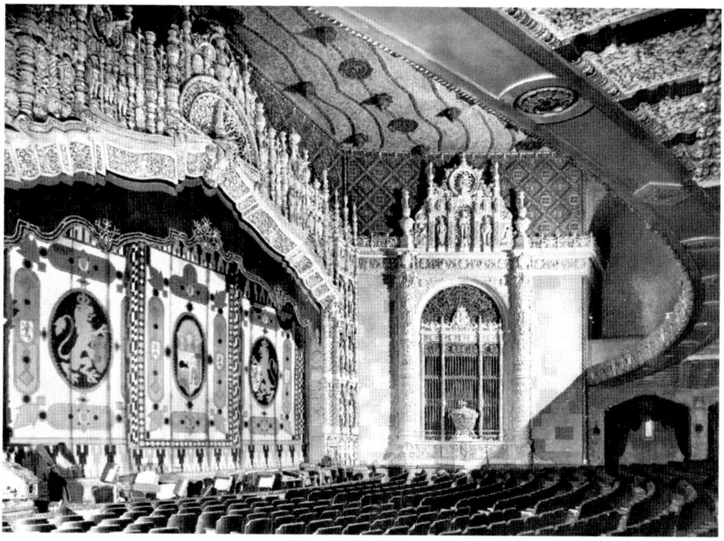

Interior of the Indiana Theater, 1927. *Courtesy of Historic American Buildings Survey, Library of Congress.*

a star-studded sky. Like other grand movie theaters, the Indiana began to deteriorate by mid-century but was rescued when it was restored to become the new home for the Indiana Repertory Theater in 1980.

June 19, 1971

On this day in 1971, as part of the sesquicentennial celebration for the city of Indianapolis, Indiana Black Expo premiered at the State Fairgrounds. The two-day event, designed to "showcase the achievements of African-Americans in the areas of culture, art, history and economics," attracted 50,000 visitors. Exhibitors offered seventy-five booths, ABA and NBA players squared off against one another in a game and the Dells performed a concert. The next year, the event moved downtown to the convention center. In 1973, attendance hit 100,000 and doubled again by 1988. As the expo grew, it hosted, among other events, an employment fair and business seminars, concerts, a Miss Black America pageant, family and children's events and a health fair. IBE organized as a nonprofit community service organization and added events apart from the summer expo, including the Circle City Classic, begun in 1984 and held yearly, featuring a football game between two historically black colleges and drawing alumni from all over the country.

June 20, 1826

In January 1825, Thomas Carter's log tavern caught on fire. Neighbors helped save the furniture, but the town of Indianapolis had no fire brigade and the building was destroyed. More than a year later, in June 1826, the town finally formed the Indianapolis Fire Company. Unfortunately, lack of funds meant that the company consisted of a group of volunteers with leather buckets and ladders. The fire alarm was a church bell. Only in 1835, when the statehouse was finally completed, did local leaders admit that their buckets were insufficient to protect many buildings in the growing town and that not one of their ladders was tall enough to protect the statehouse. The town purchased a used fire engine and a set of hoses, as well as four taller ladders and many more buckets. An engine house was built on the north side of the circle. In 1840, the town purchased its second engine, and the fire company grew from there. In 1851, the original engine house, constructed of wood, had to be replaced after it was destroyed by fire. A new brick engine house was built several blocks to the north.

June 21, 1821

Speaking to the Indiana Centennial Association on July 4, 1900, Amos Hanway recalled his life as a young boy in Indianapolis. In early June 1821, five-year-old Amos and his family left their home in Vincennes and boarded a flatboat down the Wabash River. Arriving at the mouth of the White River, Amos's father and another male passenger "poled along up the stream the entire way." According to family stories, the trip took nearly three weeks. The tiny settlement they found upon their arrival on June 21 consisted of "eighteen houses…all cabins…built along the bank of the White River." Hanway also related his memories of the first bridge across the White River, begun in 1832. The "fine poplar timbers" used to build the bridge were located "up the river eight miles." Amos was one of the men who rafted the roughly hewn lumber "down to the place where it was whip-sawed into proper shapes." Amos also recounted the excitement when widely scattered settlers joined together for activities, including the first Methodist camp meetings with "a great crowd" in attendance.

June 22, 1947

As postwar prosperity swelled the ranks of the middle class, more families were able to buy their own homes. New suburban developments appeared in every city, including Indianapolis, and in those developments a new housing style also appeared. The mid-century modern home was markedly different from earlier Victorians, bungalows and cottages. Magazines and newspapers began to feature plans for these new houses. One Sunday *Indianapolis Star Magazine* offered "The Changing House" designed by architect Richard Neutra—a single-story house with an interlocking layout that allowed for variations in size and adaptation to the landscape. Many of the rooms were large and open, with options to subdivide them for various purposes. The dining room and living area were "merged" together but could be separated "by a colored plastic or spun glass curtain." The living room featured glass doors that opened onto a terrace for "an outdoor feeling." The house offered "easy, simplified home management and maintenance," as well as "spaciousness within a limited floor area."

June 23, 1910

Many middle- and upper-class white Protestant Christians were part of the temperance movement through local clubs and national movements such as the Woman's Christian Temperance Union (WCTU). But the idea of reforming alcoholics within homelike group settings—a practice begun in the late nineteenth century by many groups such as the Gatlin Institute, the Empire Institute and the Neal Institute—often caused the same reformers to reply, as the modern phrase puts it, "Not in my backyard." The residents of Woodruff Place in Indianapolis reacted in just that way when they realized that one of the houses in their neighborhood had become a home to rehabilitate alcoholics. A group of fifty property owners brought a suit for a permanent injunction against the Neal Institute conducting its business in their neighborhood. "Woodruff Place is on fire about this thing," said one of the residents. "Mothers are afraid to permit their children to play on the esplanades and everyone regards the institute [as] a possible source of danger. We don't want these drunkards brought out here."

June 24, 1943

As the war continued and industries needed more workers, federal, state and local governments conducted recruitment campaigns, urging able-bodied men and women who were not in the armed forces or already working to join the war effort. "Indianapolis got off to a fairly good start in its campaign…to recruit 25,000 workers for its war industries," the editors of the *Indianapolis Star* noted in a June 1943 editorial, but only 1,400 prospective workers had registered in the ten days since the campaign began and "too many people with time on their hands that the war factories desperately need are holding off." The Bridgeport Brass Company advertised open positions "to persons not now engaged in essential war industries...but who ought to be." Another advertisement sought women needed as volunteers "to help mail out war ration book[s]." "Here's your war job," the ad announced, "and your help is badly needed NOW! The work is easy, pleasant—and there are three daily shifts...choose the one convenient for you."

June 25, 1888

The delegates to the Democratic National Convention in Chicago had voted the third ballot of the day, the eighth of the convention, to decide their nominees for president and vice president. The consensus finally rested on Indianapolis lawyer Benjamin Harrison for president and New Yorker Levi Morton for vice president. "Harrison Is the Man" ran the headline of the next day's *Indianapolis Journal*. Harrison ran a front-porch campaign, receiving visitors at his home on North Delaware Street and sometimes speaking in University Park when crowds grew too large for his lawn. Indianapolis became one of the political centers of the nation for the summer of 1888. Every day, hundreds of Harrison supporters arrived at the downtown train station and were met by escorts and bands provided by the campaign. They marched through downtown streets carrying banners and gifts for Harrison; they listened to the candidate speak and then shook hands with Harrison and his wife, Caroline. Harrison estimated to one reporter that he could greet more than sixty people per minute, shaking with both hands. The strategy and Harrison's message were successful; he was elected as the twenty-third president of the United States and was sworn into office on March 4, 1889.

June 26, 1977

The eighteen thousand fans who filled Indianapolis's Market Square Arena had no way of knowing that they were witnessing history—Elvis Presley's last live concert before his death on August 16 at age forty-two. By the time he reached Indianapolis, Presley had been touring since mid-February, with a few short breaks. Rita Rose, reviewing the concert for the *Indianapolis Star*, described his entrance "in a gold and white jumpsuit and white boots, bounding on stage with energy that was a relief to everyone." Presley performed many of his favorite songs from his long career, including "Jailhouse Rock," "It's Now or Never" and "Can't Help Falling in Love." Rose described the overall performance as "true Presley style" and noted of his fans that "just about everything he did created mass hysteria." The full arena, she concluded, offered "indication enough that Elvis was still as popular as ever." After the concert, Presley returned to his home in Memphis. He was scheduled to travel the night of August 16 for a concert the next day but died that morning. Market Square Arena was demolished in 2001; a memorial plaque stands in a parking lot on the site, commemorating Presley and the concert.

June 27, 1839

By the mid-1830s, Indiana was in the grip of canal fever. To the east, the Erie Canal had transformed the economy of a region in the 1820s; Indiana, in contrast, still lacked decent roads and was without a large-scale transportation system. The state's Mammoth Internal Improvement Act of 1836 set off the construction of a system of canals, including the Wabash and Erie to connect much of the state to Ohio and New York and the Central Canal, planned to reach from southern Indiana through Indianapolis and connect with the Wabash and Erie at Peru. The Panic of 1837, the huge costs of the undertaking and the crippling interest on borrowed funds soon stalled or greatly slowed most of the plans. Not until June 1839 did a significant section of the Central Canal through Indianapolis open. The 9-mile segment through downtown north to Broad Ripple encouraged many manufacturing businesses to open along the canal, but only 24 of the planned 296 miles were ever completed. In the late nineteenth century, the canal assumed an important role in city life when it became part of the city water system laid out by the Indianapolis Water Company.

June 28, 1904

After the Spanish-American War, the United States had a large standing army and not enough sites to house and train soldiers. In 1902, the army

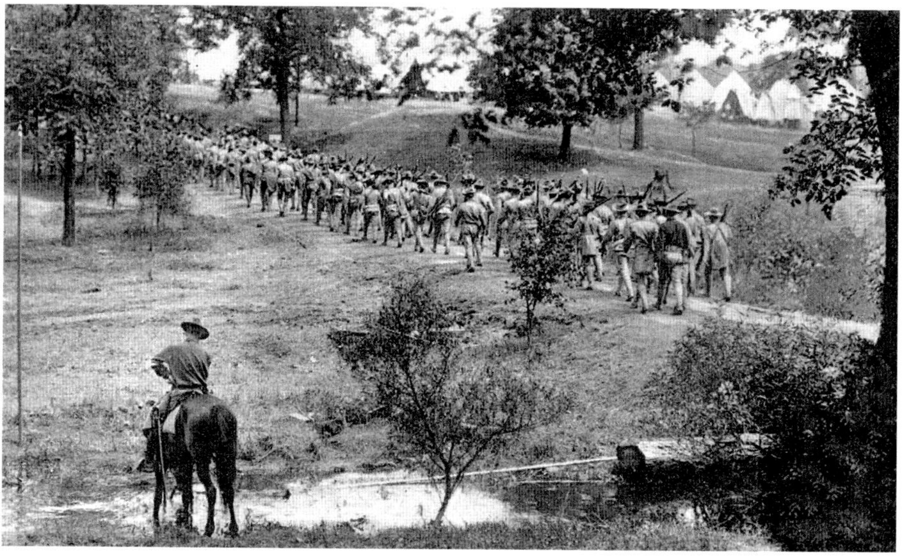

Infantrymen on a hike through Fort Benjamin Harrison, circa 1910. *Author's collection.*

purchased land northeast of Indianapolis for what became Fort Benjamin Harrison. Barracks were constructed for enlisted men; brick houses were built for officers and their families; and service buildings, parade grounds and training facilities completed the de facto small town adjacent to the city. As needs changed, the fort was used as a military hospital, as a training center for Civilian Conservation Corps workers during the 1930s and as an induction center during World War II. In 1951, the army moved its Finance Center to Fort Ben, and the complex continued to serve that role until the cutbacks of the mid-1990s finally closed the facility. Today, the land and some of the buildings have been repurposed for a variety of private uses.

June 29, 1913

By 1893, James Whitcomb Riley's poems had appeared in newspapers and magazines; the poet regularly performed his work to appreciative audiences. Unable to find a publisher, Riley printed his own paperbound book, which attracted the attention of Indianapolis publishing company Bowen-Merrill. For more than two decades, Riley's work would be published in small collected volumes by the Indianapolis firm—later known as Bobbs-Merrill—

to the considerable mutual benefit of poet and publisher. Bobbs-Merrill also published many other best-selling authors, in particular Meredith Nicholson, but few were as successful as Riley. In June 1913, the *Indianapolis Star* reported on the newest special edition of Riley's *An Old Sweetheart of Mine*. A vice-president of the publisher wired from its New York office that on the first day of printing, 100,000 copies of the book had already been ordered. Riley, reading the telegram in the Indianapolis office, gave his reply in verse: "You ain't no sinner and you ain't no saint, but when it comes to selling books, there's nothing that you ain't."

June 30, 1950

Tucked in on page nine of the *Indianapolis Star*, among ads for fall coats and junior sportswear, was a map showing routes from Indianapolis southward to Greenwood, Franklin and then Camp Atterbury. The news was that Johnson County was the first in central Indiana to be "ready for defense" and that the county was prepared "to provide 100,000 with aid in case of emergency." The impetus behind the preparations was evident on page one of the newspaper: "Red Tanks Break Through. South Korea Reels After Earlier Rally, Allies to Join U.S." The civil defense programs that would become so commonplace in the Cold War America of the 1950s and 1960s had begun. Johnson County had already formed its own "department of civil defense," and "plans were ready to provide food, shelter, medical treatment and clothing to 'refugees' on a moment's notice and begin evacuation of southern Marion County in a matter of minutes."

JULY

July 1, 1924

One of the most unusual parties of 1924 did not make the Society page of the *Indianapolis Star*, although it did merit considerable column space on page three. "Five Women Wish to Act as Hostess for Gigantic Snake," announced the headline. The Murat Shrine Circus was coming to Indianapolis in two days, bringing, among other attractions, "King, the gigantic boa constrictor." As a publicity stunt, the circus had announced a Snake Hostess Contest. The local shrine was "besieged with inquiries." The winner, to be chosen that evening, would be "required to enter the den of monster reptiles and see to it that the big crawlers do not fight or otherwise misbehave at King's party. The hostess will be expected to serve luncheon for the snakes…live mice, toads and kindred delicacies." "We are advised," continued the chair of the local organizing committee, "that the snakes are not poisonous, but they kill their prey by squeezing." He guaranteed that circus employees would ensure that the hostess did not become "a victim of too much squeezing."

July 2, 2014

Officials of the new Indianapolis International Airport announced plans for a larger-than-life bronze statue of aviation pioneer and war hero Harvey Weir Cook to stand in the ticketing area. Weir Cook was a World War I flying "ace" who was twice awarded the Distinguished Service Cross; in August 1918, the young pilot attacked six German planes, destroying one and driving the others away, and in October of the same year, he repeated the feat with three more enemy planes. In the early 1920s, Weir Cook helped form the army's U.S. Air Mail Service; in 1928, now a civilian, he served as vice-president and general manager of Curtis Flying Service, located at Stout Army Air Field in Indianapolis. In 1931, he played a key role in establishing the first Indianapolis Municipal Airport on the same site. Weir Cook reenlisted during World War II and was training pilots when he was killed in an air crash in 1943 in New Caledonia. Indianapolis renamed its airport in his honor; the name remained for many years until it was changed, to considerable public opposition, to Indianapolis International. The statue, unveiled in April 2015, greets all who arrive to check in for their flights.

July 3, 1909

The *Indianapolis Sun* announced a garden concert featuring the Indianapolis Military Band to be held at Das Deutsche Haus in downtown Indianapolis. Designed by local architects Vonnegut & Bohn in the German Renaissance Revival style and built in two phases from 1893 through 1898, Das Deutsche Haus was an embodiment of German immigration to Indiana and to Indianapolis in particular. The first generation of immigrants to the city had founded a German-heritage Turnverein society in 1851. Das Deutsche Haus became an important center of German American life, offering meeting rooms, a concert hall, an open beer garden, a restaurant

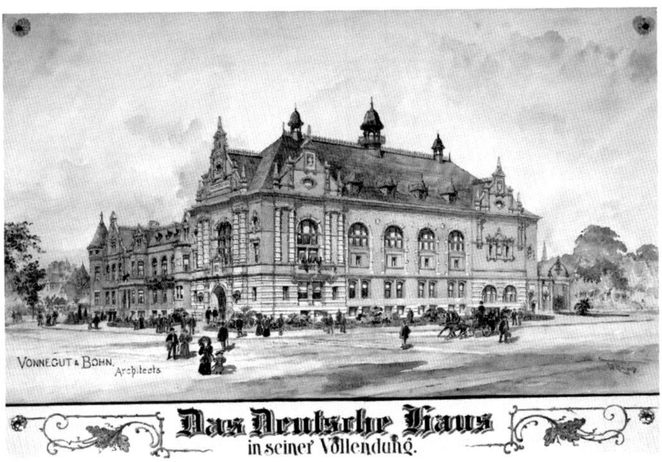

Courtesy of Historic American Buildings Survey, Library of Congress.

and extensive athletic facilities with teams that included one of the earliest basketball teams in Indianapolis. Society members enjoyed lectures, concerts and special celebrations. During World War I, the building was renamed the Athanaeum; by the 1990s, extensive renovations ensured that the building would continue into its second century.

July 4, 1822

Settlers were still putting up log cabins when the citizens of Indianapolis, few in number, gathered to celebrate their first Fourth of July. A committee of residents had established a formal program for the day, which began with singing, prayers and a sermon. The Declaration of Independence was read to those assembled and then Washington's Inaugural Address and his Farewell Address. More singing and prayers concluded the program. The men of the town then sat down to enjoy a barbecue set up in the middle of Washington Street—a deer that had been shot near one end of that same street—after which they repaired to Jacob Crumbaugh's tavern for the evening. Sarah Fletcher's diary entry for the day records the events: "This day there apered to be a great stir & livelaness among the people. The men had a barbacu & dined under the green sugar trees at the West end of Washington St. The Evening of the same day Mr. Crumbaugh had a large party held at his dwelling."

July 5, 1911

"Taft Honor Is Genuine. Marked Enthusiasm and Hoosier Cordiality Characterize Reception of President," read the headline of the *Indianapolis Star*. Taft, at the invitation of former vice president and Indianapolis resident Charles Fairbanks, toured the city for an entire day, making ten speeches. He was fêted at the Columbia Club and cheered by "the people of Indianapolis [who] turned out en masse" despite a record heat wave and a high temperature that particular afternoon of 103 degrees. In his impromptu speech after lunch, Taft praised both Indiana and its capital. And as he rode down Meridian Street to a reviewing stand on the Circle, Taft appeared to be impressed by the "inspiring sight" of people "banked in a solid mass of humanity" despite the day's heat, which "danced and pirouetted and turned somersaults on the brick walls and asphalt pavements."

July 6, 1924

As a young woman, Mary Rigg trained first as a teacher, taking her bachelor's degree at Indiana University, and then as a professional social worker, studying in New York City. In 1919, Rigg moved to Indianapolis, where she became the director of the American Settlement House in 1924. In July, she was interviewed by a reporter from the *Indianapolis Star*. Rigg summed up her primary goal as "Americanization…the great, the leading thought in everything we do." In an area filled with immigrants (Rigg mentioned families from Romania, Serbia, Bulgaria, Greece, Poland, Turkey and Italy) all "employed near by in the packing houses, abbatoir, railroad yards and factories," Rigg and her employees offered a medical clinic and dispensary; the services of a visiting nurse and doctor; classes for mothers on childcare, cooking, family health and home sanitation; and classes in English and citizenship. For children, the settlement offered a playground, a day nursery, Boy Scouts and cooking and sewing clubs for girls. In every instance, introducing the immigrants to modern American ways was an integral part of the service offered.

July 7, 1945

When Hoosier journalist Ernie Pyle died on the island of Ie Shima, a nation of readers mourned his death. Pyle had brought the war, as seen and lived by the ordinary soldier, to those on the homefront. Pyle died on April 18, 1945; on July 6, a Hollywood movie titled *The Story of G.I. Joe*, starring Burgess Meredith as Pyle, had its world premiere at the Loews Theater in Indianapolis. The premiere became a tribute to Pyle. As the *Indianapolis News* reported the next day, an afternoon parade through downtown was followed by a reception at the Press Club and a dinner at the Claypool Hotel for family members, celebrities, military officials and local dignitaries. Outside the theater, "the 200th Army ground forces band played for crowds which lined the sidewalks near the theater." A program inside the theater included speeches and an auction of an original film script—the proceeds of which went to buy war bonds—before the movie showing.

July 8, 1863

On July 3, Vicksburg finally surrendered to General Ulysses S. Grant, and Grant and his troops marched into the city on July 4. News of the great Union victory took time to reach Northern newspapers—a boat carrying Union dispatches arrived at Cairo, Illinois, on July 7, and on July 8 the *Indianapolis Daily Journal* announced the "Surrender of Vicksburg." The newspaper tried to summarize all of the news that was coming in from the South as well as from the eastern theater of the war, where details were still emerging regarding a Union victory in Pennsylvania at a place called Gettysburg: "Pennsylvania News. Four thousand more rebels taken. Our forces pursuing closely. Lee thought to be cut off." Indiana regiments had fought at both Gettysburg and Vicksburg, and the news was welcome in a year that had seen too many Union defeats and too many men added to the rolls of the dead. Indianapolis residents would be able to rejoice for a day, until news reached them the next morning that Confederate troops had crossed over into southern Indiana.

July 9, 1863

On the morning of July 9, telegrams began to arrive at Governor Oliver Morton's office in Indianapolis—reports that on the previous evening Confederate captain John Hunt Morgan and a large force of men (variously estimated at four to six thousand) had crossed the Ohio River into Indiana. Morgan's Raiders, as they became known, rode into Corydon, where they defeated a small force of the Indiana Legion and looted the town. Morton issued a call to defend the state: "Satisfactory evidence having been received that the Rebels have invaded Indiana in considerable force, it is hereby ordered and required that all able-bodied white male citizens in the several counties South of the National road forthwith form themselves into companies of at least sixty persons, elect officers and arm themselves with such arms as they may be able to procure." The companies were ordered to drill and then stand ready for further orders. Some of the volunteers were able to skirmish with Morgan's troops and change their course, but the raiders, pursued by Union troops, continued through southern Indiana until they entered Ohio. By the end of July, Morgan and his men had been captured. Morgan's Raid was the only significant Confederate incursion into Indiana during the war.

July 10, 1907

Charles Warren Fairbanks moved to Indianapolis in 1874 to work as a lawyer for the Indianapolis, Bloomington and Western Railroad. The young attorney became a wealthy, influential man, known for his moral probity and in particular for his strong stance on temperance. Active in Republican politics, Fairbanks became chair of the state convention in 1892; in 1897, he became a U.S. senator; and in 1904, he was chosen as vice president on Theodore Roosevelt's ticket and spent four years in Washington, D.C. But in 1907, Fairbanks's political career was ruined by scandal. The vice president and his wife had entertained President Roosevelt and forty other guests in their Indianapolis home on Memorial Day. Fairbanks, known as "Buttermilk Charlie," by all accounts did not drink one of the Manhattans that were passed among the guests by waiters. But the details of the luncheon soon became public. Temperance groups nationwide condemned the vice president for even serving liquor, and Fairbanks gained a new nickname—"Cocktail Charlie"—which, try as he might, he could not shake. On July 10, the Prohibition Party of Indiana, led by Fairbanks's fellow Methodists, condemned his actions; the *New York Times* printed the story the next day, as it (and other national newspapers) had printed the sordid tale from its beginnings. "Cocktail Charlie" had entered the popular imagination, and Charles Fairbanks was never again elected to public office.

July 11, 1996

By the middle of the twentieth century, much of the land along the stretch of the White River running through downtown Indianapolis was home to a variety of mills and manufacturers and a huge meatpacking firm.

By the early 1970s, many of the buildings had closed or burned down and urban decay was setting in. In 1979, as local government officials and business leaders worked to revitalize downtown Indianapolis, the city established a White River Park Development Commission to re-imagine 250 acres of land. The result was a state park that encompasses the restored 1870 Indianapolis Water Company Pumphouse; the new Indianapolis Zoo (1988); the Eiteljorg Museum of American Indians and Western Art (1989); Victory Field, the new home for the Indianapolis Indians (1996); the Congressional Medal of Honor Memorial (1999); the NCAA headquarters and Hall of Fame (2000); the new Indiana State Museum (2002); and the Lawn, an outdoor concert space (2003). New green spaces, gardens, pedestrian paths and bridges and art installations (that tie the park into the city's Cultural Trail) connect the buildings.

July 12, 1893

The Democratic *Indianapolis Sun* reported approvingly that Mayor Thomas Sullivan had again been nominated by his party, this time for a third term. Sullivan was the city's first mayor born in Indianapolis. A successful attorney, he was elected to his first term in 1889, and his administration emphasized modernizing and improving the city. A new city charter, adopted in March 1891, gave Sullivan the power to appoint bipartisan municipal boards, and he used the newly created Board of Public Works and the Board of Public Safety to further his ideas, including better streets with electric streetlights, a modern sewer system and electric trolleys. However, the expansion of city government, including a larger police force and an expanded administrative staff, prompted criticism of tax hikes and claims of fiscal waste. Republicans charged Sullivan with corruption and with making political appointments for kickbacks; by the summer of 1893, faced with his possible reelection, opponents branded his administration "weak, insincere, detrimental to good morals, and dangerous." With the city's economy weakened by the Panic of 1893, Sullivan lost his bid for a third term.

July 13, 1849

From 1832 until the mid-1850s, a number of cholera outbreaks occurred in the United States. Doctors could offer no cure; people followed the progress of the disease and hoped it would not reach their city. On June 14, 1849, the *Indianapolis State Sentinel* reported on the front page: "The cholera is increasing, we regret to state, at…Cincinnati, Louisville, New York, New Orleans, and on the plantations of Mississippi and Louisiana. A few cases have occurred again at New Albany and Mauckport, Ind. Our people should be careful of exposure, and keep cool: fright is about the worst feature in cholera." Calvin Fletcher's diary reveals a city on edge: on February 1, local churches held a day of prayer "to avert the scurge [*sic*] now upon us the Asiatic cholera." On July 5, Fletcher wrote: "cholera rages at Cincinnati & on the river…The scourge has not reached this place." Three days later: "We have apprehension of cholera. It is expected. May God avert it." On July 13, Fletcher joined an effort to prevent a group of Dutch migrants traveling from New Orleans from entering the city for fear of "Cholera & other diseases." Indianapolis was spared in 1849—in 1850, cholera struck the city.

July 14, 1963

The Soap Box Derby was an American institution almost from its beginning in 1933 in Dayton, Ohio. The first race, inspired by a local newspaper photographer who saw three boys racing down a hill in homemade "cars" powered only by gravity, attracted 362 Dayton boys and 40,000 spectators. The first derby cars were made from scrap wood and borrowed wheels; later cars might be constructed from fiberglass, but they were always homemade and built by their drivers. In 1959, *Boys' Life* magazine recorded 160 local races in addition to the national competition. July 1963 saw the twenty-sixth annual Soap Box Derby in Indianapolis. The event was won by three-time entrant and Indianapolis local fourteen-year-old James Clarence Handy, who barely beat out closest competitor James Crookston, aged twelve, from Muncie. Handy won a $500 U.S. Savings Bond, a trophy, a plaque to go on the wall of his school (IPS 101) and a trip to Akron for the national race. He also made the front page of the next day's *Indianapolis Star*, with a photo of the entire family celebrating his win.

July 15, 1848

In 1848, the weekly Indianapolis newspaper *Locomotive* began a series of articles describing sections of the city, apparently in an effort to promote further development. Part nine of the tour began at the city's center, the intersection of Washington and Meridian Streets, and moved northward. Washington Street, designed as the main boulevard of Indianapolis, was filled with ordinary two- and three-story buildings: "On the north side of Washington street, from Meridian to Drake's Hotel, is a row of two story frames, used for store rooms, & c., some of which look as if they would bear removing to a back street very well, to give place to better and more commodious business houses." Moving north from the Circle on Meridian Street was the "block of Churches," including Presbyterian, Episcopal and Lutheran houses of worship. Continuing northward "from New York to north streets, including three blocks, the only building erected within the last year is a one-story frame…We consider this section of the city more desirable than any other for handsome dwellings, and yet a great portion of it is an unfenced common, overrun with dog fennel."

July 16, 2009

The Indiana Fever joined the Women's National Basketball Association as a newly created team at the beginning of the 2000 season. From its inception, the team played at Bankers Life Fieldhouse, also the home of the Indiana Pacers. In the 2002 season, star player Tamika Catchings won Rookie of the Year and the Fever went to its first playoff series. Although the team continued to make the playoffs from 2005 through 2008, attendance began to dip, and there was speculation in local sports media that Indianapolis might lose the team if the 2009 season did not re-ignite players and fans alike. In mid-July 2009, early in the season, the Fever had caught fire: "Double-Digit Run," exclaimed the *Indianapolis Star* headline. The team had just won its tenth straight game the night before, and "if winning 10 consecutive games is no big deal," *Star* sports columnist David Woods asked rhetorically, "why have so few pro basketball teams done it? The Indiana Pacers never have in the NBA." The Fever made its first trip to the WNBA finals in 2009 but ultimately lost to the Phoenix Mercury.

July 17, 1860

Most Americans know that Abraham Lincoln defeated Stephen Douglas to become the president of the United States; fewer know that the 1860 election involved two Democratic nominees, with John Breckinridge standing for the Southern Democratic Party. The Democratic nominating convention in Baltimore had split over the issue of extending slavery into the territories, and both factions laid claim to having the legitimate candidate. In Indianapolis, Southern Democrats promoted their political philosophy and their candidates via the *Old Line Guard*, whose banner announced, "The Constitution, the Union, and the Equality of the States!" The first issue of the newspaper appeared on July 17, 1860, and the editors clearly stated their purpose: "We have no doubt that when the facts are properly understood by the people—when they learn the truth in regard to the prospects of the several candidates—that John C. Breckinrid[g]e will carry nearly every Southern State and that there is no probability of Mr. Douglas receiving a solitary electoral vote in the United States…thousands of Douglas men in Indiana…will rally around the standard of Breckinridge and Lane."

July 18, 1953

Roscoe Turner learned to fly during World War I. During the 1920s, he performed with aerial thrill shows, worked as a charter and promotional pilot and, in 1929, formed Nevada Air Lines. The Depression quickly ended the airline, but in the same year, Turner began to compete in air races. Throughout the 1930s, Turner won short-distance dash races as well as long-distance races, including the MacRobertson Trophy Race from London to Melbourne, Australia. In 1939, Turner began an air school in Indianapolis that trained pilots, mechanics and control tower operators for civilian and military work. In 1947, Turner started a local airline but sold his interest in 1950. In July 1953, Turner was asked to fly a special airplane—one he had raced in 1934—from Indianapolis to Washington, D.C. "Adaptable Annie" was a 1934 Boeing 247-D transport plane used since 1940 by the Indianapolis Experimental Station of the Civil Aeronautics Administration. Most of Annie's controls had been changed, and her wings had been altered to test for icing. The station's engineers, as one reporter put it, "did just about everything short of setting her afire." Annie was retired with honors—she was placed in the Smithsonian's National Air Museum.

July 19, 1883

"Will the girl who reads Homer, who pores over Euclid…be attractive to men who are wife-seeking?" asked May Wright Sewall in her column "Woman's Work" for the *Indianapolis Times*. Her answer was an emphatic "yes": through her writing, teaching and tireless leadership, Sewall spent her life advocating for women's education. Sewall moved to Indianapolis in 1872 when she and her first husband took up teaching jobs at Shortridge High School. In 1880, widowed, she married Theodore Sewall, the principal of the Indianapolis Classical School, and taught at that institution; in 1882, with Theodore, she founded the Girls' Classical School. From 1882 to 1907, the school taught young women the same curriculum as their male counterparts, preparing pupils for the most prestigious women's colleges in the nation. Sewall advocated for women's education and women's rights at the national level as one of the founders of the National Council of Women, which she saw as a vehicle to bring together women at work in women's clubs across the country. She was instrumental in organizing the World's Congress of Representative Women, held during the 1893 Chicago World's Exposition with representatives from 126 nations. In 1900, Sewall was elected president of the five-million-member International Council of Women.

July 20, 1973

In 1968, the federal Justice Department filed suit against the Indianapolis Public Schools for failure to desegregate their school system. The case came to trial in 1971; the school board's attempts at changing the racial balance of schools were deemed inadequate, and IPS was found guilty of *de jure* segregation. The court gave jurisdiction of the case to the U.S. District Court for the Southern District of Indiana; the case fell under the purview of Judge S. Hugh Dillin. Convinced that Unigov had encouraged white residents to move to surrounding townships within Marion County, Dillin ordered in July 1973 that IPS begin an aggressive program of busing black students out from the city of Indianapolis to the six predominantly white township school systems. The controversial decision affected IPS enrollment and funding, and public opinion was highly mixed and generally negative. Legal appeals delayed implementation of the busing plan until 1981; Dillin's order stood until a June 1998 agreement between IPS and the federal government to phase out busing by 2017 and promote other forms of desegregation. When S. Hugh Dillin died at age ninety-one in 2006, newspapers across the country carried obituaries that featured his role in the IPS desegregation case.

July 21, 1893

Newspaper readers who were looking for human interest stories written with adjectival flair could always turn to the pages of the *Indianapolis Sun*. One front-page July 1893 headline read: "Martin's Tragic Death: Crushed Beneath the Wheels of an Irvington Motor." Forty-eight-year-old George H. Martin had stumbled into, or perhaps stood in, the path of an oncoming interurban car and had been killed. Headed westbound on Washington Street at 9:20 p.m., the motorman and passengers of Irvington Car 156 had felt "an unusual jar"; when the car stopped, "the mangled and dead body of a man was found entangled in the machinery beneath the car, while blood poured upon the cobblestones from a dozen wounds. The mass of mutilated flesh was taken out after much trouble and exertion, and removed to Whitsett's morgue." The reporter interviewed witnesses as well as Martin's landlady and employer. Was it suicide? Was he drunk? Martin's landlady "gave out the impression" that she and Martin were to be married soon, yet police located a woman in Michigan claiming to be Martin's wife. The next day's story cleared up the questions—the death was probably an accident, but Martin had been leading a "double life," married to one woman and courting another.

July 22, 1948

American society was still emerging from World War II when a new crisis developed in Germany. With control of the country divided between the

United States, the European Allies and the Soviet Union, the city of Berlin had been split in half. In June 1948, the Soviets tried to gain control of the entire city through a blockade, intended to starve residents into submission. President Truman and U.S. military forces responded immediately: June 26 was the first day of the Berlin Airlift, which lasted until May 11, 1949. The vast majority of Hoosiers, like all Americans, supported the airlift. "The Watch on the Rhine," a July editorial cartoon in the *Indianapolis Star*, summed up public opinion, showing a sky filled with airplanes with the word "food" on the leading plane. Below, on one side of the river stood two smiling German people, the woman carrying a food basket. On the opposite shore stood Joseph Stalin, looking up at the sky in shock, as his hat and a piece of paper with the words "communist prestige" began to blow away in the wind created by the planes.

July 23, 2010

Few men have had as long and distinguished a career in politics and public service as Indianapolis native Richard Lugar. By 2010, however, Senator Lugar was attracting criticism from within his party for his stances on a variety of international and national issues. During the summer of 2010, Lugar voted to confirm Obama administration nominee Elena Kagan to the U.S. Supreme Court. "Lugar stands out for not stooping to partisan strife," wrote *Indianapolis Star* political columnist Matthew Tully. Lugar had just become the second Republican senator to endorse Kagan, explaining that he had looked into her background and qualifications, studied her testimony and concluded that she was "clearly qualified to serve on the Supreme Court." The executive director of the American Family Association responded that Lugar "should retire, or not run again in 2012. Kagan is a pure political activist with views far outside the mainstream of Hoosier voters." Lugar did run in 2012 but was defeated in the Republican primary by Tea Party favorite Richard Mourdock. Mourdock, in turn, lost in the general election to Democratic candidate Joseph Donnelly.

July 24, 1878

On this day, leaders of the Greenback Party of Indiana unanimously chose Indianapolis resident Gilbert De La Matyr as their candidate for Indiana's Seventh Congressional District. The decision attracted controversy because their candidate was also a Methodist minister. De La Matyr had been assigned to the pulpit of Indianapolis's Roberts Park Methodist Church in 1874; having successfully led that congregation through a major building project, he was assigned to Grace Methodist Church, where he began preaching sermons that were regularly reported in local newspapers. De La Matyr had become concerned about corruption in government and big business; he denounced the "moneyed classes" as "oppressors," spoke of the "tyranny of capital" over the impoverished majority and supported the currency and financial reforms of the new Greenback Party. Reverend Thomas Goodwin, another Indianapolis Methodist, spoke for the opposition in labeling him a "communist of the most dangerous type." In September, his Methodist Conference demanded that De La Matyr choose between the church and politics; choosing the latter, the ex-minister was elected to a single term in the House of Representatives, where he continued (with little success) to promote financial reforms. A few years after leaving Congress, he returned to the Methodist pulpit in Denver, Colorado.

July 25, 1934

John Dillinger was born in Indianapolis in June 1903. The first twenty years of his life were marked by a variety of petty crimes, but in 1924 Dillinger was sent to prison after an armed robbery of a grocery store. After his release in 1933, Dillinger quickly began the criminal career that would make him the FBI's Public Enemy Number One. The bank robber became a local and a national sensation; a popular Indianapolis lottery had citizens betting on when Dillinger would be captured. After Dillinger's death, crowds lined up at the morgue where his body lay. And despite efforts by Dillinger's father and local authorities, they lined up again on July 25, 1934, when his body was buried in the family plot at Crown Hill Cemetery. The grave was unmarked for many years; the current headstone is the fourth, the previous stones having been chipped away as souvenirs.

July 26, 1865

The charter for the second State Bank of Indiana expired in 1857. As business and government leaders were preparing to charter a third state bank, the federal government passed the National Banking Act in 1863, allowing for nationally chartered banks. A group of Indianapolis investors responded to the opportunity, founding the Indiana National Bank of Indianapolis in July 1865. The bank settled in a large Neoclassical building in 1897. Through much of the twentieth century, Indiana National acquired smaller banks until it became the city's largest, symbolized by its thirty-seven-story INB Tower built in 1970. In 1992, Indiana National was acquired by a regional banking company.

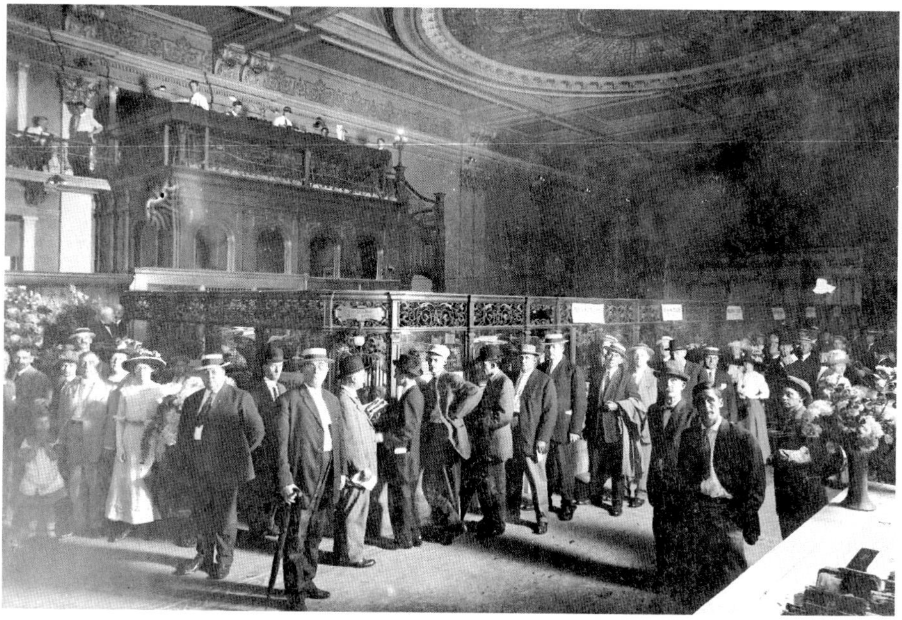

Main banking room of the Indiana National Bank, 1912. *Courtesy of Historic American Buildings Survey, Library of Congress.*

July 27, 1886

A prominent ad in the *Indianapolis Journal* announced: "An Unexampled Opportunity to Get a Valuable Home at a Bargain, in the Finest and Healthiest Part of the City…The Chance of a Lifetime Offered to 24

Persons." James Woodruff and J.R. Cleveland were offering for sale the last available lots in Woodruff Place, one of the first suburbs of Indianapolis. The developers promised "broad substantially paved streets…original forest trees…[a] high and commanding situation" and "esplanades adorned with numerous fountains and fine statuary." "A home almost in the country," the advertisement continued, "while the advantages of the city are at hand." Woodruff Place grew rapidly in the 1890s, as its wide, tree-lined boulevards and architecturally distinguished homes made it one of the most desirable residential areas of the city. By the 1920s, Woodruff Place had been physically absorbed by the larger city, and wealthier homeowners had moved elsewhere. The area gradually declined, but many of the homes were saved when an upswing in historical preservation and renovation began in the 1970s.

July 28, 1821

An advertisement in the weekly Vincennes *Indiana Centinel* announced land for sale: "On the 2nd Monday in October next, the Lots in the Town of Indianapolis will be offered for Sale by Public Auction…This town has been laid out…on the site located for its permanent seat of government… on the East bank of the West Fork of White River, in the centre of the state. It is situated on a high, dry, uninterrupted plane of several miles extant, perfectly free from inundations, marshes and ponds…The plan of the town is calculated to insure the health, comfort, and convenience of its inhabitants, and occupies a space of one mile square…It is confidently expected that the Great National Turnpike Road from Washington City to Missouri, will pass through Indianapolis." Indianapolis, like so many other properties described in glowing real estate ads, had plenty of marshes and ponds, and malaria would be endemic during the first years of settlement. The National Road was not finished through the town for more than a decade.

July 29, 2002

In 1902, Joe Stahr opened a tavern and restaurant three blocks south of the Circle on Illinois Street. One hundred years later, St. Elmo Steakhouse celebrated its centennial for an entire year, including a Centennial Brick fundraiser that not only replaced the old sidewalk in front of the restaurant with new paving bricks inscribed with the names of patrons but also raised $60,000 for two local charities. The traditional steakhouse, known for its huge steaks, its extensive wine and liquor selections and its shrimp cocktail with an incendiary house cocktail sauce, has drawn many, or perhaps most, of the famous people who have visited Indianapolis in the last century. The restaurant's testimonial page on its website lists Hollywood celebrities from Clark Gable to David Letterman; politicians; musicians, including the Rolling Stones, Billy Joel and Elton John; and an especially large number of athletes, including stars of the NBA, NFL, NHL, Indy Car Racing and the Olympics.

July 30, 1945

In November 1932, the city of Indianapolis was honored when the navy cruiser USS *Indianapolis* was commissioned for service. The ship was designed as a fleet flagship, able to carry an admiral and his staff. The *Indianapolis* and its crew joined the war in the Pacific immediately after Pearl Harbor. On July 30, 1945, the ship was en route from Guam to the Philippines when it was hit by two torpedoes from a Japanese submarine. In just twelve minutes, the critically damaged ship rolled over and quickly began to sink. The ship's distress signal was received at three different stations, but not one responded to the call. Of the 1,196 crew members aboard, more than 300 men went down with the ship. For four days, until they were discovered by a PBY seaplane, the survivors began to die off from exposure, thirst and shark attacks—of the almost 900 initial survivors, only 317 were rescued alive. In 1995, after decades of work by an association of survivors and their families, the USS *Indianapolis* National Memorial was dedicated in downtown Indianapolis along the city's Canal Walk.

July 31, 1913

Indianapolis was broiling in a heat wave. The temperature on July 31 was forecast to reach 102 degrees with no immediate relief. Perhaps the heat affected the editors of the *Indianapolis Star*—"Well, If a Split Skirt, Why Not This, Too?" read the front-page headline. "It's the new split trousers for men. Yep, they're coming…A tailor announces them. He predicts that in a short time men will be wearing regular split trousers, prototype in their own way, of the feminine slashed skirt." Men "will have to take to wearing long stockings," the unnamed tailor predicted, "for the slits will likely go to the knee. Too long have women enjoyed the privileges of summery things. Too long have men sweltered in dark woolens when the mercury was flirting with the top of the thermometer." The unknown (perhaps fictional?) tailor's fashion-forward prediction failed to come true.

AUGUST

August 1, 1908

In August 1908, photographer Lewis Hine traveled around Indianapolis photographing children and teenagers laboring in mills, factories and markets and working as newsboys and messenger boys on downtown streets. Hine had been sent by the National Child Labor Committee to document what progressive reformers considered a national disgrace: one in six children ages five to ten (according to the 1900 federal census) were working in some form of "gainful employment." From 1908 to 1924, Hine traveled the country putting faces to the issue of child labor. In Indianapolis, one of his photographs portrayed the noon break at a local cotton mill, where most of the employees were children. Despite the work of the NCLC, it

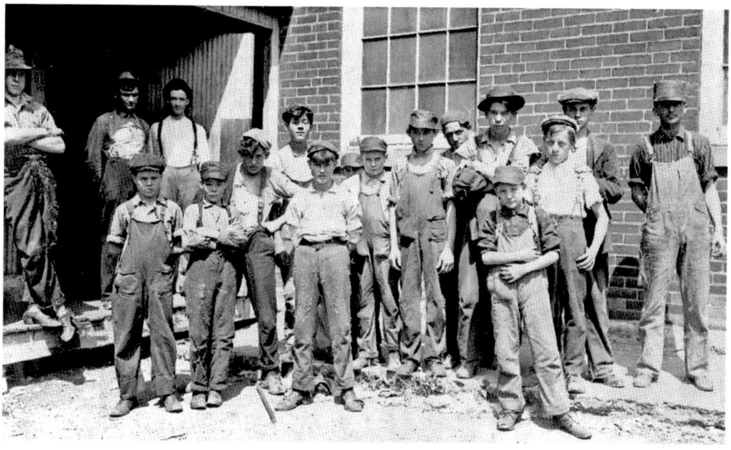

Indianapolis cotton mill workers on their noon break, 1908. *Courtesy of National Child Labor Committee Collection, Library of Congress, Prints and Photographs Division.*

was not until 1938 that President Roosevelt signed into law the Fair Labor Standards Act that, among other provisions, strictly regulated employment for children under the age of sixteen.

August 2, 1943

Ernie Pyle was the best-known journalist who reported from the front lines of World War II, but many newspapers and press services had reporters who were embedded with military units. Readers of the *Indianapolis News* could follow the war thanks to men like Harold Boyle, an Associated Press reporter who, on August 2, 1943, described the battle for "Bloody Ridge," a hill near San Stefano in Sicily. "This natural rock studded fortress held by Germans entrenched with machine guns…was stormed and taken in blinding heat… The third time" up the hill, U.S. troops captured and held the hill "through a fierce counter-attack during which four American machine gunners, one whose arm was blown off, died at their flaming guns." Boyle sat with some of the soldiers after the battle and watched them eating their rations and "reading mail as fast as it was sorted." He described the surroundings as "a peaceful olive grove so quiet it looked like a picnic ground" except for "six freshly dug American graves with dogtags hanging from temporary crosses made from ration boxes."

August 3, 1839

The *Indianapolis Journal* announced that "the Rev. Henry W. Beecher will hold Divine Service on Sabbath next in the Second Presbyterian Church." Henry Ward, the second youngest of the famous family, graduated from Lane Seminary in 1837. After serving his first parish in Lawrenceburg, Indiana, Beecher moved with his wife, Eunice, and their first child to Indianapolis. During his years at Second Presbyterian, Beecher honed his speaking skills, becoming a celebrated preacher and leader of revivals and introducing notes of abolitionism into his sermons, a foretaste of the messages that later made him famous at Brooklyn's Plymouth Church. Beecher became known in Indianapolis for his many interests, in particular his love of gardening and his work in the Indiana Horticultural Society. Life in Indianapolis was difficult for Eunice, who bore eight children (only four of whom survived to adulthood) in a household too poor to pay servants. The Beechers remained in Indianapolis until 1847, when Henry was offered a more generous salary and a far more influential pulpit from which to preach his message.

August 4, 1908

An upcoming concert by the city's Mannaerchor and the Baiser Orchestra included an orchestral performance of "Dusty Rag" by May Aufderheide. In an era when few female composers could claim success with their compositions, Aufderheide's music was published, performed and popular. May was born in Indianapolis in 1890 and received music lessons from her aunt, a classical pianist. At nineteen, she began to write music—not classical sonatas, but "rags." Ragtime music, with its syncopated rhythms, became widely popular at the turn of the century. May's father, John, formed a music publishing company whose clients included his daughter and a small group of other men and women in Indianapolis who were composing in the same style. May's first published work was the 1908 "Dusty Rag." From 1908 to 1912, she wrote several more pieces, including "The Richmond Rag," "Buzzer Rag," "Blue Ribbon Rag" and "The Novelty Rag." As ragtime waned in popularity, May's composing career ended with a song version of "Dusty Rag" in 1912.

August 5, 1876

On this day in 1876, Mary Ritter Beard was born in Indianapolis. At sixteen years old, she enrolled in DePauw University, where she met Charles Beard. After their marriage and the couple's move to England, Mary became active in the women's suffrage movement. In 1902, Mary and Charles moved to New York City, and for more than a decade, Mary was active in workers' rights groups as well as suffrage groups. By the 1920s, Mary had turned to the study of history and to writing. She collaborated with her husband on several books on American history; her individual written work focused on the history of women, anticipating the field of women's studies by decades. Mary wrote about women as "a sex lost to history," as she told a graduating class of the New Jersey College for Women in June 1936. "What is called equal education," she told her audience, actually taught "men's politics, men's wars, men's business adventures, men's books, men's theories and practices. The assumption is that women have no history of their own worth much recognition, if any…that they have no interpretations of history to offer."

August 6, 1994

Although its history began with a motorcycle race and a balloon race, for decades the Indianapolis Motor Speedway was associated with one yearly automobile race. When the Indianapolis 500 ended, the speedway went silent for eleven months. In August 1994, for the first time in the history of the IMS, a race ended with victory laps driven in a NASCAR vehicle, as Jeff Gordon celebrated becoming the winner of the first Brickyard 400. The twenty-three-year-old driver (the youngest in that year's race) started third and led 93 of the race's 160 laps. More than 300,000 NASCAR fans packed the stands, and a new tradition was born. The economic recession of 2008—the same year the race was marred by a succession of tire blowouts that caused 52 laps to be completed under the yellow light—began to reduce attendance, which by 2014 numbered less than one-third that of the first year. Nevertheless, the Brickyard 400 remains one of the most prestigious races on the NASCAR schedule.

August 7, 1987

Long before hosting the Super Bowl, Indianapolis hosted the tenth annual Pan American Games, welcoming more than 4,300 athletes from thirty-eight countries for sixteen days. The dramatic opening ceremonies took place on August 7 at the Indianapolis Motor Speedway. National media attention focused on the presence of a large Cuban team. At a time when relations between the United States and Cuba were tense and travel between the two countries was difficult, considerable negotiation was required to allow the Cuban athletes and coaches to fly directly to Indianapolis. Cuba and the United States were expected to, and did, meet for the baseball gold medal, and the Cuban team took the victory. U.S. fans were shocked when Brazil beat the United States in basketball, although they were able to cheer Greg Louganis to victory in diving and witness gold-medal performances by track and field stars Carl Lewis, Evelyn Ashford and Jackie Joyner-Kersee. After a festive closing ceremony featuring Cuban American singer Gloria Estefan, city leaders described the games as Indianapolis's "coming-out" party in the realm of world-class athletic events.

August 8, 2004

"It's a Dinosaur World in Indianapolis," announced the *New York Times*, profiling the new *Dinosphere: Now You're in Their World* exhibit at the Indianapolis Children's Museum. One of the treasures of the exhibit was Bucky, a juvenile T-Rex skeleton (one of the most complete ever recovered) found by a young South Dakota rancher, after whom the dinosaur was named. The Dinosphere was just one example of the museum's innovative exhibits and programming. Opened in 1925 thanks to the patronage of local business owner Mary Stewart Carey, in its first years the museum was dependent on locally donated objects. In the 1940s, the museum began to collect artifacts ranging from an Egyptian mummy to the Reuben Wells steam locomotive. With a new building in 1976, the museum pursued an aggressive program of redefinition and growth. The facility is now the world's largest children's museum. From every level of the main atrium, visitors can gaze at the forty-three-foot-high tower of blown glass by artist Dale Chihuly. The *Treasures of the Earth* exhibit, developed with *National Geographic*, takes visitors through the tomb of an Egyptian pharaoh, to China to view the terra-cotta warriors and to Captain Kidd's shipwreck.

August 9, 1902

The *Indianapolis Sun* announced "Cruelty of Gardeners to Be Stopped by City Ordinance." A city humane officer was patrolling the City Market to look into "the charge that market gardeners allow their horses to stand on the street all day without feeding them." Officer Frank Wilson told the reporter that most market sellers were "very careful" with their animals, but he was there to ensure compliance with the new law. The City Market building had gone up in 1886 just east of the Circle, allowing

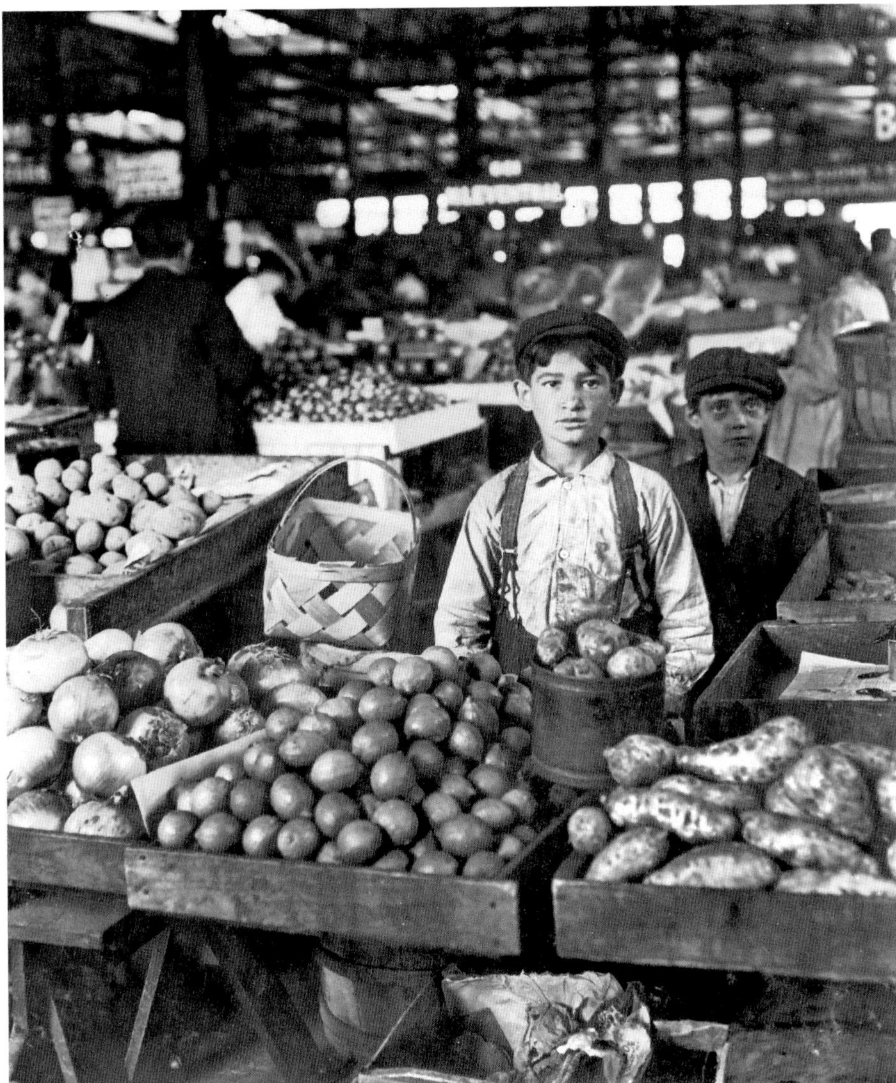

Fruit vendors at the City Market, 1908. *Courtesy of National Child Labor Committee Collection, Library of Congress, Prints and Photographs Division.*

city residents to purchase fresh foods in season. The "City Market" column in the day's newspaper listed crab apples, cooking apples and pears, as well as "Hoosier canteloupes" (two for five cents). "Corn's up, selling 7 to 10 cents a dozen," and heads of cabbage "bigger than a wooden bucket" were selling for one nickel each.

August 10, 1898

By 1898, Indianapolis native Marshall "Major" Taylor was a world-champion cyclist who held seven world records at distances from one-quarter mile to two miles. Taylor was also only the second African American athlete to hold a world record. Taylor began bicycle racing at age thirteen and won many amateur competitions, including, at age sixteen, a seventy-five-mile race held near Indianapolis. In 1896, he turned professional. In August 1898, the *Indianapolis Sun* reported that Taylor had issued a challenge to the winner of the upcoming match race between cyclists Eddie Bald and Tom Cooper. Taylor would race the winner at the distance—from the shortest sprint to the longest road race—of the winner's choice. Bald replied: "I would not ride with Major Taylor or any other man of his color. I have to ride in the open races against him because the others do." In 1900, Taylor finally met and defeated Tom Cooper in a match race held in New York City. Taylor also raced in Europe and Australia. He was banned from competing in many southern states; in many races in northern states, he was verbally or physically attacked or sabotaged. In 1910, Taylor retired from racing. He is remembered today in his home city by the Major Taylor Velodrome Park, the site of many cycling events.

August 11, 1862

Camp Morton opened in 1861 as a training camp for Union recruits; thousands of Hoosier volunteers were drilled and provisioned there before going off to war. In February 1862, Union general Henry Halleck captured Fort Donelson, Kentucky, and needed a place to house thousands of Confederate prisoners of war. Governor Oliver Morton agreed to take many of the men in Indianapolis; by the end of February, 3,700 Confederate soldiers were headquartered at Camp Morton. Prisoner exchanges, such as the one initiated by the governor of Tennessee in August 1862, reduced camp crowding, but Union victories swelled the numbers. The fortunes of the prisoners of war rose and fell with each camp commander. Colonel Richard Owen organized a humane and secure camp, while subsequent commanders exercised less diligence concerning the welfare of their prisoners. More than 1,700 Confederate prisoners died at Camp Morton—one of the lowest figures among Union camps.

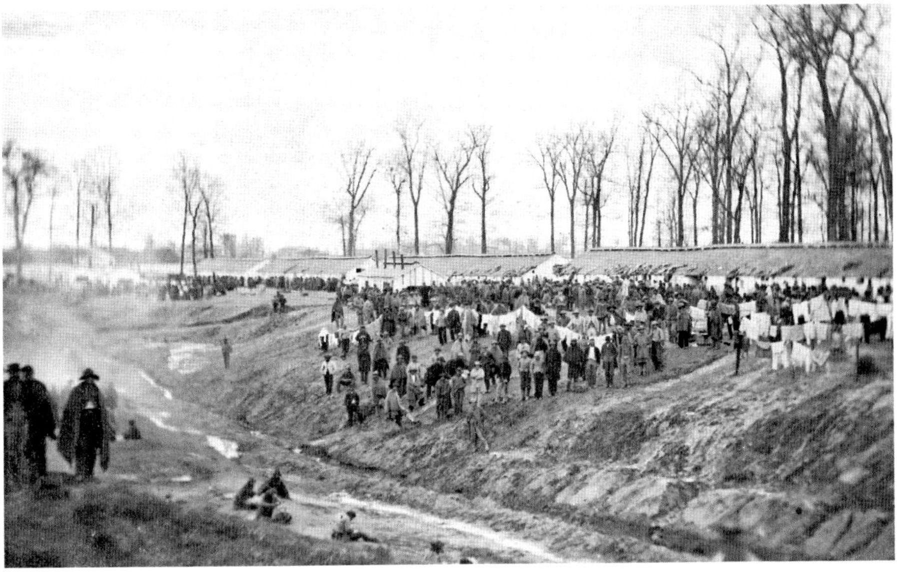

Confederate prisoners at Camp Morton, 1862. *Courtesy of Library of Congress, Prints and Photographs Division.*

August 12, 1899

Beginning in the late nineteenth century, meat markets and grocery stores across the country sold products produced at Kingan & Co. meatpackers in Indianapolis. The business, built by two Irish immigrant brothers, began in 1862. In 1868, after employee George Stockman developed a process for ice curing pork, the company began to operate year-round. By 1899, the Kingan complex of buildings occupied twenty-seven acres on either side of the White River downtown, processing beef and pork as well as animal byproducts, including "Kingan's Reliable Pure Lard." The company was among the largest meatpackers in the nation and throughout the world. An August 1899 ad in a Virginia newspaper for the J.W. Mesic Grocer offered "Kingan's Indiana Hams, best in the world, any size desired." The company was also known for its presliced bacon, a Kingan innovation. The business was sold to Hygrade in 1952 and operated until 1966. In 1967, a massive fire destroyed much of the complex.

August 13, 1958

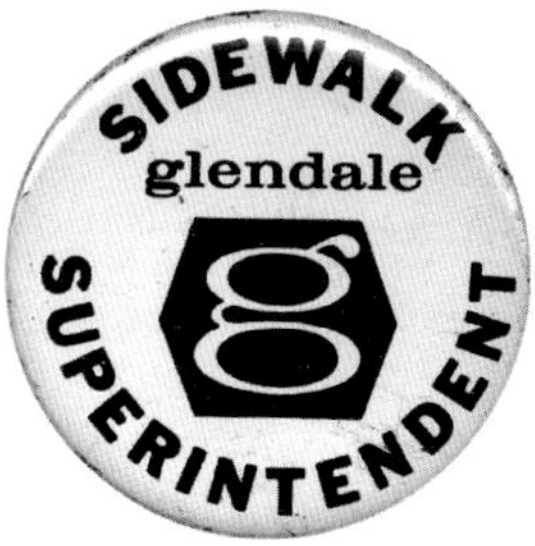

"Sidewalk superintendent" pins were given to bystanders watching the construction of Glendale Mall. *Author's collection.*

By the early 1950s, suburban shopping centers were the newest trend in U.S. retail. Middle-class families who were moving into suburbs wanted conveniently located stores with free and ample parking, as well as access to many stores in one location. On this day in 1958, the first suburban retail center in Indianapolis opened. Glendale Shopping Center attracted attention even before it opened: those who gathered to watch construction were given "sidewalk superintendent" pins with the Glendale logo. The shopping center was an open-air development that offered thirty-seven retail stores in one location, including the very first branch location of the L.S. Ayres department store.

August 14, 1828

Indiana's first state bank failed in 1822; the second opened in November 1834. During the years in between, those doing business in Indianapolis often had to deal with a lack of reliable currency. In a May 1824 issue of the *Indianapolis Gazette*, Isaac Stephens announced that he had just received a shipment of "merchandise suitable for the spring market" and that he was "disposed to exchange them for Cash, Bees-Wax, or Peltry [*sic*]." Caleb Scudder promoted his cabinetmaking business from his "fine shop on the State-House square" and noted that he would "receive good merchantable Pork, Beef and Corn—likewise, Sugar, and cash will not be refused." Two years later, Scudder was still in business, now advertising that he would accept "lumber and many articles of produce." Even professional men participated in the barter system. When Dr. William Ross, experienced in "the diseases incident to this country," opened a practice in Indianapolis in 1828, he informed prospective patients that "owing to the scarcity of the circulating medium, he will take a reasonable share of produce in payment of his bills."

August 15, 1945

"Peace!" exclaimed the huge banner headline of the *Indianapolis Star*. When news reached Indianapolis that Japan had surrendered and that World War II was over, celebrations broke out across the city. Newspaper photographers captured a group of children marching through their neighborhood with drums and American flags, adults splashing in the fountains of Monument Circle and uniformed servicemen about to kiss smiling young women. *Star* reporter Mary Bostwick stationed herself on Monument Circle to observe the crowds who began to gather downtown: "More people kept coming all the time, converging into the Circle from all points of the compass to yell, cheer, blow whistles and ring bells. They thumped on lard cans, oil cans, dishpans and tin washtubs." Governor Ralph Gates announced a two-day statewide holiday, and preparations began for a huge victory parade. On the same front page, however, readers also learned of one of the last great tragedies of the war: the sinking of the USS *Indianapolis* and the death of more than eight hundred of its crew.

August 16, 2008

In 1984, Indianapolis proudly welcomed the Indianapolis Colts to a new indoor, inflatable-dome stadium. Just like the sports figures who play in them, professional sports stadiums age quickly, and so in August 2008, the ribbon-cutting ceremony for the new Lucas Oil Stadium took place not far from where the previous dome had been deflated, deconstructed and hauled

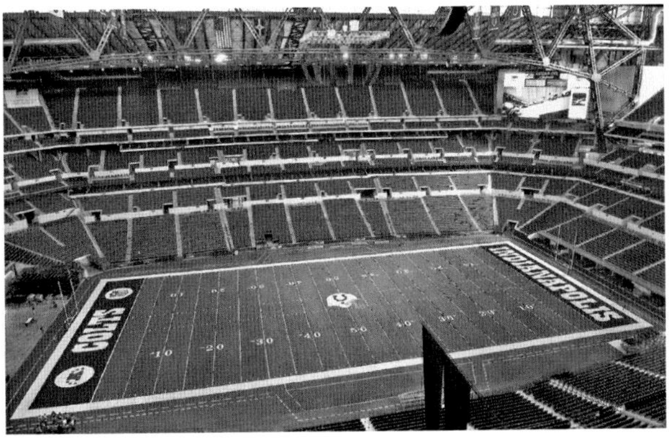

Interior of Lucas Oil Stadium. *Photo by Josh Hallett, Wikimedia Commons.*

away. The new facility could seat more than sixty-seven thousand fans. It featured a retractable roof that could remain open to take advantage of cool fall afternoons and close to fend off snow, rain and preseason summer humidity. The stadium's large outside plazas, expansive indoor public spaces and massive video boards made Lucas Oil Stadium a hit with fans and sports journalists alike. The stadium's distinctive profile is visible from much of downtown Indianapolis.

August 17, 1888

Every morning during the summer of Benjamin Harrison's front-porch campaign for the presidency, a group of his Indianapolis supporters stood waiting at the downtown train station for the arrival of that day's visiting delegations; accompanied by bands and with much ceremony, the local residents and visitors marched to the Harrison home to meet the candidate and hear him speak. In August, as crowds were growing, the Harrison Marching Society officially formed, members continuing their daily support of the candidate until his election. In February 1889, the group reorganized itself as the Columbia Club. From its location on Monument Circle, the

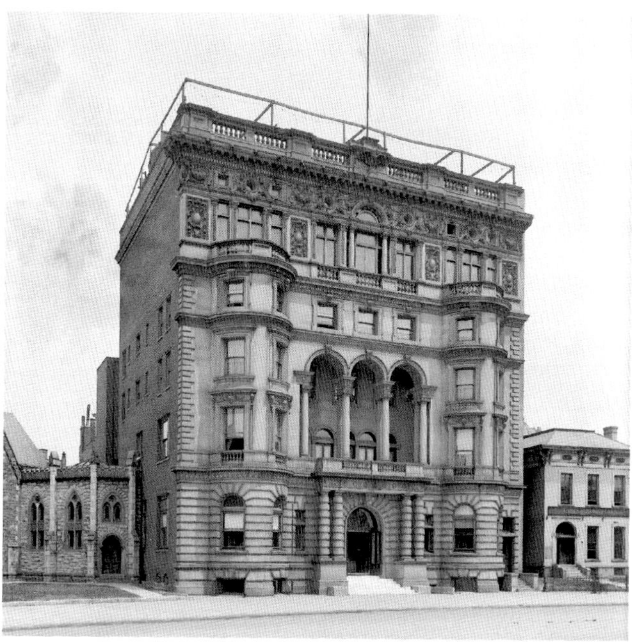

Columbia Club, 1904. *Courtesy of Library of Congress, Prints and Photographs Division.*

club has hosted every Republican president (as candidate or office holder) from Harrison to George W. Bush. Its 1925 headquarters building remains an iconic site in downtown Indianapolis.

August 18, 1988

On the evening of August 17, Republican presidential nominee George H.W. Bush announced his running mate: Senator Dan Quayle. Quayle was born in Indianapolis and grew up in Huntington, Indiana. Trained as a lawyer, he had already served in state government and as a U.S. representative and senator from Indiana when he was chosen for the 1988 Republican ticket. Bush's choice of the young, relatively unknown politician created a media firestorm across the country. On August 18, the *New York Times* ran a series of articles: "The Quayle Question" described the senator as "a conservative of modest accomplishments"; "In Congress Neither Loafer nor Leader" recounted Quayle's reputation "as an amiable legislator of modest intellectual achievement"; "Hometown Remembers No Hint of Great Things" was written from Huntington, where some residents raised an issue that would haunt Quayle for some time—his National Guard service during the Vietnam War. After a memorably difficult vice presidential debate and a long campaign, on January 20, 1989, Dan Quayle became vice president of the United States, serving for four years while media scrutiny continued.

August 19, 1938

The *Indianapolis Star* reported on the dedication of the Patrick Cancer Clinic at Indianapolis's City Hospital. The clinic—the first free-of-charge cancer facility in the nation—was just one small part of the history of City Hospital, which began in 1859 as one building on the extreme northwest edge of the city. Beginning in 1879, Superintendent William Niles Wishard (for whom the hospital was later renamed) adopted modern practices of antisepsis and anesthesia and City Hospital became a surgical facility. The nursing school begun in 1883 was one of the earliest such professional schools in the Midwest. By the end of the twentieth century, Wishard was one of two adult Level 1 Trauma Centers in the state. The hospital's primary mission was to serve the city's poor and indigent, and until the 1940s it was also the only city hospital treating African Americans. Wishard survived more than a century and a half of political conflict over its funding and a physical plant that patched together a series of old and new buildings over a sprawling urban campus. In December 2013, the entirely new Sidney and Lois Eskenazi Hospital opened less than one mile from the original hospital site.

August 20, 1850

When the summer of 1849 passed with no cholera outbreak in the city, Indianapolis residents were relieved. On July 22, 1850, Calvin Fletcher noted in his diary: "Case of the chollera has occured." On July 26, Fletcher recorded "some few cases" among a group of Dutch immigrants. By August 4, several neighbors had fallen ill. Fletcher and his wife, Sarah, visited many of the sick, and Fletcher, who often acted as an unofficial physician, treated some of them. On August 15, Esther Ray, the wife of the former governor and a close neighbor of the Fletchers, died. The next day, returning from Esther's funeral, Fletcher found one of his hired girls, eighteen-year-old Elizabeth Messersmith, ill. By 7:00 p.m., she was "seriously indisposed," and by 2:00 a.m. the next morning, Elizabeth was dead. Four days later, fifteen-year-old Almyra Thompson, the Fletchers' other hired girl, fell ill. Fletcher kept the rest of his family away from the sickroom and cared for Almyra until her death two days later. The epidemic continued in the city through early September; by its end, more than fifty residents had died.

August 21, 1964

On the morning of August 20, the editors of the *Indianapolis Star* sent a reporter and photographer to the Hook's Drugstore on Monument Circle. The next day, the newspaper printed photographs of two hundred teenagers who were standing in line at 9:30 a.m. to buy concert tickets that would not be available until 2:00 p.m. Evidently, Indianapolis was not immune to Beatlemania—the teens were waiting to buy tickets (three dollars each, with a limit of five per person) to see the British group perform at the Indiana State Fair on September 3. American fans of rock-and-roll had heard the group's single "I Want to Hold Your Hand" in 1963, but the Beatles had not yet set foot on U.S. soil. They arrived in America for the first time in February 1964, appeared twice on the *Ed Sullivan Show* and performed in Washington, D.C., and New York City. Their first American concert tour took place in August 1964, when the Beatles performed in twenty-three cities across the country for their screaming fans—including those in Indianapolis.

August 22, 1864

In the summer of 1862, Governor Oliver Morton and his advisors began to worry about support for the Confederacy among Hoosier citizens. Morton, backed by military authorities, began to spy on Democrats who were speaking out against Lincoln and the war—especially a secretive group known as the Knights of the Golden Circle. By the summer of 1864, Morton had received intelligence that members of the Knights planned to seize an arsenal in Indianapolis, free Confederate prisoners at Camp Morton and foment a rebellion. On August 22, the Republican *Indianapolis Daily Journal* reported a military raid on a printing warehouse in the city and the arrest of its owner, local Democratic leader Harrison Dodd, as a leader of the conspiracy. Several alleged co-conspirators were subsequently arrested as well. The trials of the accused, before a military tribunal, began in late September. Dodd was convicted and sentenced to death—but in absentia, as he had escaped from jail during the trial and fled to Canada. After 1866 Supreme Court rulings overturned his verdict, Dodd returned to the United States and settled in Wisconsin.

August 23, 1923

The Hotel Lincoln in downtown Indianapolis featured, among its dining options, a tearoom. "Dainty Lunches!" proclaimed a 1923 ad for the tearoom, which also featured "sodas and sundaes" and "delectable cakes and pastries." Tearooms became popular in the twentieth century as genteel spots for ladies to meet their friends for an elegant lunch or for afternoon tea. The most popular tearoom in Indianapolis opened on the eighth floor of L.S. Ayres & Company in 1929. Women dressed up to eat in the Ayres Tea

Room (as did the male customers); children who were allowed to accompany their mothers were on their best behavior so that they could draw a small gift from the treasure chest at the end of the meal. Models often circulated through the room during lunch, showing the latest fashions from the Crystal Room. Diners enjoyed chicken velvet soup or a molded salad accompanied by a basket of dainty muffins, then an entrée such as chicken pot pie or shrimp Creole and perhaps a slice of lemon pie.

August 24, 1899

The *Indianapolis Patriot Phalanx*, a newspaper devoted to the cause of prohibition, reported on an assembly at which Luella McWhirter, president of the Indiana chapter of the Woman's Christian Temperance Union, had "presided with her usual grace and dignity," presenting the WCTU's goals "in a forceful manner." Luella and her husband, Felix McWhirter, were both active in the prohibition movement in 1890s Indiana—Felix was the Prohibition Party's nominee for mayor of Indianapolis in 1894 and for governor of Indiana in 1904. Husband and wife were also city business leaders as two of the five charter founders of Peoples Deposit Bank, where Luella served as a member of the board of directors (a first in Indiana for a woman). Luella McWhirter went on to co-organize and serve as vice-president of the Women's Franchise League of Indiana (1911–16) and to serve as president of the Indiana Federation of Clubs (1911–13). For more than forty years, she was also the editor of the *Message*, the WCTU's monthly magazine.

August 25, 1943

In February 1942, the United States began relocating Japanese Americans from their homes, many into western internment camps, others to cities across the United States. The Christian Church–Disciples of Christ, headquartered in Indianapolis, was one of the religious groups that spoke out against the government policy and worked to find suitable homes and jobs for affected individuals and families. A small number of Japanese Americans settled in Indianapolis during the war years—apart from the Disciples, few groups offered welcome and assistance. Both the Home Missions Council of the Disciples and the government's War Relocation Authority (WRA) conducted a variety of public relations campaigns in the city on behalf of those who had relocated there. WRA photographer Charles Mace spent two days in Indianapolis photographing some of the resettled citizens. He depicted Marie Kitazumi, who was working as a secretary, buying a war bond. Mary Matsamura was photographed in her waitress's uniform, wearing a pin with two service stars—her husband and brother were both serving in the armed forces of the United States.

August 26, 1956

By the mid-1950s, thousands of Indianapolis residents had purchased new, modern homes in new, green suburbs. The mid-century modern homes featured lots of open space. The living room and dining room were frequently one large room, and how was the modern homemaker to arrange her furniture? Magazines and newspapers offered plenty of suggestions, including the "Multi-Purpose Room" in the Sunday *Star Magazine,* which illustrated how easily living and dining could be "integrated—decoratively speaking." The living area was carpeted; the dining area floor consisted of "strips of black and yellow vinyl with flecks of coral," with a "gleaming brass strip" separating the two areas. Color, the magazine assured readers, was key to the room: yellow walls, avocado green curtains with large black dots and smaller coral dots and a partial metal room divider in the same avocado color. The modern dining furniture was all in black. The true effect of the room was left to readers' imaginations, since the illustration was printed in black-and-white.

August 27, 1969

In the 1920s, Indianapolis vice squads had raided clubs selling illegal liquor and had often uncovered illegal gambling as well. Now the city's vice squad was cracking down on prostitution. A 1967 state law allowed judges to sentence women convicted of the crime to 180 days—unless the male customer involved was willing to testify, in which case the woman could receive a two- to five-year sentence. Men seemed immune from the prescribed punishments: those who had solicited the prostitutes became public servants if they testified, and not one of the local "panderers" had been arrested and charged, although two or three had moved elsewhere. By late August 1969, the head of the vice squad bragged to an *Indianapolis Star* reporter that in the previous six months, the county had jailed three women for two- to five-year sentences and ten women for six-month terms, with forty more women awaiting sentencing. The officer stated that there had been "some 200 known prostitutes in the city a year ago, but today there are only 10 to 20." No verification for the claim was ever offered.

August 28, 1920

On August 19, supporters of women's suffrage finally received the news that Tennessee had voted in favor of the Nineteenth Amendment, which would now become law. "Both Parties Start Fight for Hoosier Women's Vote," read the *Indianapolis News* headline. Marion County officials announced that they were planning to put up sample voting machines across the city to instruct the new voters. Luella McWhirter, a longtime local activist, "declared her delight…and expressed the belief that the woman vote will have a favorable effect in obtaining prohibition enforcement and enactment of legislation in the interest of women and children." On August 28, one hundred women gathered at the Claypool Hotel for a "jollification luncheon" in celebration of the outcome and to pay tribute to their forerunners. Those present included Grace Julian Clarke, Dr. Amelia Keller, McWhirter and many other Indianapolis women who had dedicated the better part of their adult lives to securing the right to vote for women.

August 29, 1826

For the first settlers of Indianapolis, receiving state and national news was a slow and often complicated process. In August 1826, the editor of the *Indianapolis Gazette* printed an apology: the issue was smaller than usual, due to "a disappointment in procuring paper of the usual size from Cincinnati… The distance of Indianapolis from a paper mill is among one of the greatest inconveniences" he was facing. While the *Gazette* was doing its best to provide weekly news, Indianapolis residents were waiting for their mail, carried via the Madison and Indianapolis Mail Stage. The schedule was printed in the *Gazette* so that everyone might be aware of its weekly progress: depart from Indianapolis every Thursday at 7:00 a.m. to arrive in Columbus at 5:00 p.m. on Friday, then depart Columbus the next morning and finally arrive in Madison at 5:00 p.m. on Sunday afternoon. The same four-day schedule was observed from south to north, with the stage leaving Madison Thursday morning and arriving in Indianapolis Sunday afternoon.

August 30, 1916

On this day, the Circle Theater opened on Monument Circle. The building was the city's first dedicated movie theater. In 1928, *The Jazz Singer*, the first "talking picture," made its Indianapolis debut on the Circle's screen. Built at a cost of more than half a million dollars, the Neoclassical Revival building featured an interior with elaborate plaster moldings on ceilings, walls and the proscenium frieze framing the stage. For sixty-five years, the facility functioned as a movie theater and a venue for stage shows. In 1981, in a city full of suburban multi-screen movie theaters and modern venues for stage productions, the Circle Theater closed and its already poor condition deteriorated. After a massive $7 million renovation, the theater reopened in 1984 as the new home of the Indianapolis Symphony Orchestra. The Hilbert Circle Theater once again operates as a center of culture in downtown Indianapolis.

August 31, 1923

By the summer of 1923, the Ku Klux Klan was a significant social and political force in Indiana, both in rural areas and in cities—including Indianapolis, the location of its state headquarters and its newspaper, the *Fiery Cross*. After a highly successful July 4 rally in Kokomo, the Klan's next public display of its power was planned for the capital city. "Klansmen to Have Day at the State Fair," their newspaper announced on August 31. "Strength of Klan to Be Shown All Doubting Thomases—Petty Politicians and Arrogant Police to Find Claims Are Not Fanciful Dreams—Gala Day Planned—Indianapolis to See Biggest Crowd in History." The editors noted that delegations were forming across the state, planning to fill every railroad car and interurban with flag-waving Klansmen and their families. The Klan wanted particularly to show up Mayor Lew Shank, who, along with the city's police chief, would "be given the chance to see the countless staunch and law-abiding Americans who compose the Klan…and realize, if possible, just how little their tyranny will affect this body of resolute Americans banded together to preserve American liberty."

SEPTEMBER

September 1, 1909

In 1909, the newly opened Indianapolis Motor Speedway hosted a variety of races. The five-hundred-mile race that would make the speedway famous had not yet become a yearly tradition, and racing fans were anxious to express their opinions as to the future uses of the new track. In a letter to the editor of the *Indianapolis Star*, city resident Charles W. Walker offered his "Suggestions for the Speedway." "I think something ought to be done," he began, "prohibiting these long auto races. I think that 100 miles should be the limit." Walker went on to suggest the addition of safety features to prevent driver injuries and deaths: "Plow up all the ground for fifty feet on each side of the track, thus giving the driver and his mechanician a chance for their lives" should they crash. "A pile of soft dirt" such as Walker suggested was never implemented, although the speedway has worked to keep safety rules in pace with car technology ever since the first Indianapolis 500—not 100—in 1911, two years after Walker's letter.

September 2, 1947

Americans were elated when World War II ended, but many people also looked at photos of Hiroshima and Nagasaki and began to wonder what kind of force had been unleashed into the world. In September 1947, the editors of the *Indianapolis Star* commented on the work of Dr. H.J. Muller, an Indiana University geneticist who was to lead a group of scientists to Japan to study the effects of nuclear radiation on children who lived in regions close to the bomb sites. "Deformed and abnormal offspring" might be born to the current generation of children, Muller theorized, although he stressed that it was too early to detect genetic mutations. "Civilization itself is in jeopardy," the editors wrote, "if the effects of scientific war, indescribably ghastly in themselves, are projected into postwar years. Destruction of cities is contemplated with horror. Even worse would be the collective doom of peoples threatened with the disaster of abnormality." Muller and his work were caught up in political controversy in the 1950s, but he is considered the founder of the field of radiation genetics.

September 3, 1829

A small settlement with only a few churches, Indianapolis was nevertheless one of the earliest towns in the Midwest to found a Sabbath School program, dating from 1826. Early Sabbath Schools were often not linked to a particular denomination (although all were run by Protestant groups) or congregation, and they provided instruction in basic literacy and mathematics as well as religious precepts. Local schools followed the recommendations of the American Sunday School Union and planted schools in available homes and other buildings. In Indianapolis, by 1829, the local Sabbath School Union was expanding its single school to multiple schools around the county. "Viewing the situation around us," proclaimed the board of directors, "destitute in a great degree of literary or religious instruction for children, whose Sabbaths are generally spent in play, idleness, or something worse," they announced in May that four new schools had begun with two hundred pupils. In September, the *Gazette* described a recent Sabbath School procession through the streets of Baltimore that had drawn five thousand children and expressed the hope that the people of Indianapolis would be "more and more excited on this subject."

September 4, 1919

President Woodrow Wilson returned from France and the conclusion of the Treaty of Versailles to a skeptical nation and significant opposition in

Congress, both to the treaty and to U.S. participation in the League of Nations. Although Wilson was already ill and had suffered a series of small strokes during his time in Europe, he undertook a twenty-two-day cross-country tour to speak in favor of the treaty and the league. His speech at the Indianapolis Coliseum on September 4 was a defense of the League of Nations, which, Wilson claimed, would help to forestall future world conflicts. Arbitration would delay a rush to battle and resolve conflicts, so that war might be avoided. He rejected the claim that joining the league would compromise U.S. sovereignty and concluded his speech by calling on his opponents to offer a better alternative. Wilson's last speech of the tour took place on September 25; he collapsed and returned to Washington, where, on October 2, he suffered a major stroke that kept him incapacitated while the Senate debated and rejected the Treaty of Versailles and U.S. involvement in the League of Nations.

September 5, 1931

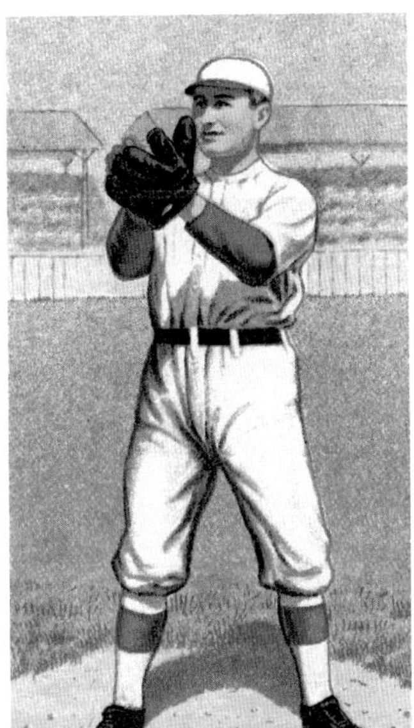

Baseball card of Orville Woodruff, Indianapolis Indians, 1911. *Courtesy of Library of Congress, Prints and Photographs Division.*

Indianapolis residents have been able to enjoy local, professional baseball since 1887. In 1902, the Indianapolis Indians, a charter member of the American Association, played their first season; they continue as the city's resident professional team to this day. In 1939, the team began to affiliate with Major League Baseball. The Indians' first affiliate was the Cincinnati Reds; although the Indians changed affiliations several times over the years, they returned to the Reds three more times, including 1968 through 1983 and 1993 through 1999. One of the team's most successful periods was during the years 1984 to 1992 while affiliated with the Montreal Expos—the Indians won four consecutive playoff championships in 1986 through 1989. Beginning on September 5, 1931, the team played in the near-downtown Perry–then

Victory–then Bush Stadium. In July 1996, the new Victory Field, part of the White River State Park, opened downtown.

September 6, 1999

Beginning in 1999, consumers could walk into the kitchen and housewares section of their local Target store and buy something designed by one of the twentieth century's most famous architects. Michael Graves was born in Indianapolis in 1934 and graduated from Broad Ripple High School. After graduating from Harvard and studying in Italy, he returned to the United States and founded his own architectural firm in 1964. He became known as one of the "New York Five," a group of young architects who were redefining Modernism. By the early 1980s, Graves was designing postmodern buildings with classical references. Over his career, he designed more than 350 buildings, but as the *New York Times* noted in his obituary, he was "perhaps best known for his teakettle and his pepper mill." Graves became interested in bringing high-end design to ordinary consumers; he designed, for a time, for the Italian company Alessi and then introduced his line for Target. Graves's teakettles, toasters, pepper grinders and whisks—along with his other designs with their distinctive blue handles and buttons and knobs—helped establish Target as a discount store with flair.

September 7, 1907

The Saturday *Indianapolis Sun* detailed "five overflowing days" at the Indiana State Fair, beginning Monday morning. The new $100,000 livestock pavilion—"America's largest and best appointed"—would be dedicated Monday morning by the governor of Indiana. In addition to the animals, farm products and farm machinery on display, the fair offered four horse races per day (per fair tradition, trotters and pacers), free shows by trapeze artists and other performers and band concerts, as well as "dairy demonstrations by expert butter makers from Purdue University." On Thursday night, fairgoers could watch Abe Attell and Jimmy Walsh, two "mighty clever fellows," meet for a ten-round boxing match. The *Sun* also reported that the *Eagle* airship had arrived at the fairgrounds and would be offering twice daily flights over the fairgrounds. The fair had become so popular that three special streetcar lines ran directly to the fairgrounds with "facilities for 25,000 people every hour. Fare 5 cents."

September 8, 1888

One of the more unusual newspapers published in Indianapolis was the *Iron Clad Age*, begun on April 1, 1882, by Dr. Jasper Monroe. The front-page banner declared: "A Paper with Few Principles. A Weekly with Few Wants." A typical issue contained a variety of articles not to be found elsewhere: a piece on the "discouraging" decline of the American Secular Union; a front-page letter titled "Agnostics, but Atheists All the Same" ("If ever there was a 'natural-born' atheist, I certainly am one," wrote A.R. Ayres); "Searching the Scriptures as Directed with a Running Commentary as Not Directed," offering a highly critical/satirical look at a biblical passage; a letter concerning "the Christian religion…the invention of the most bloody-minded savages that ever cursed this planet"; and an editorial titled "No Hope for American Citizens—Church Work Entirely Useless." After Dr. Monroe's death in November 1891, the newspaper continued with son Harry and later daughter Lulie as editors until it ceased publication in early 1895.

September 9, 1931

In 1920, Dr. Ada Schweitzer of the Indiana State Board of Health instituted one of the most popular attractions at the Indiana State Fair: the Better Babies Contest. Schweitzer believed in the use of modern science to improve health. One part of her public outreach involved teaching mothers about child rearing and health; she also promoted better breeding—i.e., eugenics. The Better Babies Contest embodied both ideals. Only white, native-born mothers and children were allowed to enter the contest, as Schweitzer, like other eugenicists, believed that African Americans and immigrants were biologically inferior: "We cannot make a silk purse out of a sow's ear, neither can we make a citizen out of an idiot or any person who is not well born." On September 9, 1931, mothers lined up to register their babies, who then went through a health history, mental tests, weighing and measuring and exams by various physicians. At each station, experts filled out the "Standard Score Card for Babies." The baby who scored highest was deemed the year's Best Baby. The contest continued through the 1935 fair, drawing proud family members and general spectators who filed through the contest building to view the babies.

September 10, 1866

"If Andrew Johnson were to-day expected to visit this city as President of the United States, the whole people of this city and State would turn out and welcome him…but he comes here as a partisan to harangue the people for the benefit of the Copperheads and to build up a party composed almost exclusively of men who were disloyal to the Government during the terrible Civil War." The *Indianapolis Daily Journal* made clear its sentiments, shared by Republicans throughout Indianapolis, regarding the visit of President Andrew Johnson to the city. Johnson was on a speaking tour to defend his opposition to the Fourteenth Amendment and to promote his view of conciliation toward the South. Johnson's visit to Indianapolis was little short of a debacle. Governor Oliver Morton was conspicuously absent, and no city officials greeted the president. Johnson was escorted to the Bates House by a small group and a band; when he appeared on the balcony that evening, his words were drowned out by shouts from a largely hostile crowd. Johnson retreated inside. When his supporters tried to conduct a torchlight parade, a riot broke out, and most of the city police force had to be called out to restore order.

September 11, 1885

When a group of veterans from the Mexican War met in Indianapolis in September 1885, they invited poet Sarah T. Bolton to compose and read a poem on the subject of the war. In the early 1850s, Bolton had become known for her support of women's rights and for her (unsuccessful) work with Robert Dale Owen to have women's property rights written into the 1851 constitution. During the same years, however, Bolton became much more widely known for a seven-stanza poem that began: "Voyager upon life's sea, to yourself be true, and where'er your lot may be, paddle your own canoe." "Paddle Your Own Canoe" was set to music and translated into several foreign languages; it made Sarah Bolton a nationally known poet who was frequently called on to read her work at public events. Her literary reputation outlived the public memory of her political work, and when she died in 1893, the *Indianapolis Sun* recorded the "funeral...of Indiana's poetess," which had taken place at Crown Hill Cemetery.

September 12, 1933

Both the *Star* and the *News* carried obituaries of Arthur C. Newby, "pioneer bicycle and automobile man and widely known philanthropist." Newby began his association with bicycles and cars in 1882, working his way up in the Nordyke & Marmon Company. In the 1890s, Newby, along with Edward Fletcher and Charles Test, formed the Indianapolis Chain and Stamping Company, manufacturing Diamond bicycle chains, which captured a huge market hitherto owned by European companies. Newby also helped found the city's Zig-Zag Bicycle Club and built the Newby Oval bicycle race track, which hosted national competitions. In 1900, Newby turned his interest to automobiles, partnering with Test and others to create the National Motor Vehicle Company, which manufactured electric vehicles, and then in 1903 began to build gasoline autos—in particular, high-end racing models. In 1909, Newby was one of the five co-organizers of the Indianapolis Motor Speedway. In later life, he funded the Newby Outpatient Clinic at Riley Hospital for Children and contributed generously to Butler University.

September 13, 2015

In September 2015, the Eiteljorg Museum of American Indians and Western Art marked the tenth anniversary of its *Quest for the West* art show and sale. The event, one of the nation's premier sales of contemporary western art, is just one piece of the museum's innovative programming. The museum began with the private collection of Harrison Eiteljorg, who also helped plan the building that would house his art. The Eiteljorg features stunning outdoor

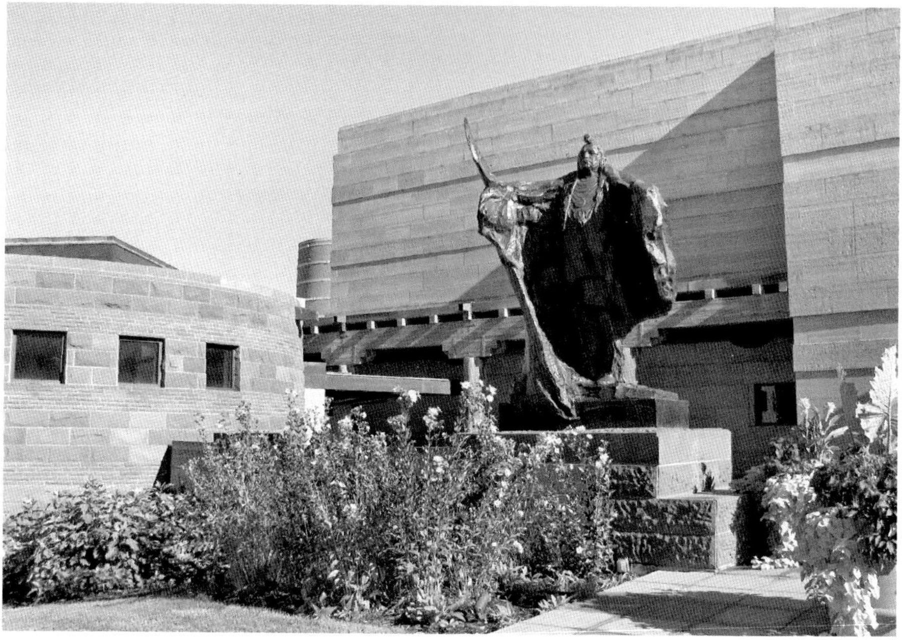

The Greeting, a sculpture by George Carlson, stands at the entrance to the Eiteljorg Museum. *Author's collection.*

sculptures; an ever-growing collection of western art, Native American art and Native American historical artifacts; special exhibits that have included the work of Ansel Adams and Dale Chihuly; and shows such as the Quest and the annual Indian Market. Every holiday season, the museum features *Jingle Rails: The Great Western Adventure*, where children and adults can marvel as seven model trains make their way from Indianapolis to the West through an imaginary landscape.

September 14, 2008

In September 2008, after a ninety-nine-year absence, motorcycle racing returned to the Indianapolis Motor Speedway with the first Indianapolis MotoGP, part of the Grand Prix Motorcycle Racing tour. With a similar track configuration to the Grand Prix auto racing that had taken place at the Speedway, much of the MotoGP race took place on what would be the infield for the Indy 500 (including the infamous Snake Pit). The race was run in the opposite direction of every other race at the Speedway. The course included most of the front straightaway, but not one of the Speedway's famous banked curves was used for MotoGP, which requires its drivers to execute remarkable leans of bike and body into curves far less extreme than those negotiated by Indy racing cars. The race required twenty-seven laps around the 2.59-mile course, with a total race distance of just under 70 miles. Indianapolis is not on the MotoGP 2016 schedule.

September 15, 1937

Marian University is the only institution of higher learning in Indianapolis that can trace its historical origins back to a twenty-four-year-old Austrian nun. Sister Theresa Hackelmeier arrived in Oldenburg, Indiana, in 1851 to found a congregation of the Sisters of St. Francis and teach the German-speaking children of southern Indiana. After the merger of the sisters' school, St. Francis Normal, with a junior college, the sisters began a search for a larger facility. In 1936, the sisters purchased Riverdale, the former estate of James Allison, in Indianapolis; in September 1937, the first classes began at Marian College. In the early years of the college, the Allison mansion housed the administration, classrooms, library and sisters' quarters. By the late 1940s, the college began to expand its physical presence as student enrollment grew. Today's university trains teachers, nurses, doctors of osteopathy and other professionals, as well as offering degrees in the arts, sciences and business.

September 16, 1955

In 1955, the American Automobile Association withdrew as a sanctioning body of auto racing in the United States. Speedway owner Tony Hulman used his influence to bring car owners, drivers and mechanics together to form the United States Auto Club (USAC) as a sanctioning and certifying body for Indy racing and other race car series. USAC headquarters were built close to the Speedway, and from 1958 to 1969, Indianapolis businessman Thomas Binford was USAC president. In the 1970s, USAC separated into divisions for dirt racing, road courses and paved ovals. In

1978, the dissatisfaction of many Indy car owners and drivers with the extent of USAC's control led to the formation of Championship Auto Racing Teams (CART) and a second Indy Car series. For two decades, two sanctioning groups (the Indy Racing League eventually assuming USAC's role for Indy cars) fought it out for dominance, to the detriment of Indy Car racing in general. In the twenty-first century, the Indianapolis 500 and other Indy Car races are reclaiming fan and media support and the commitment of drivers and owners.

September 17, 1945

In September 1945, the U.S. Navy announced—without divulging top-secret details—what had been going on at the ordnance plant in the middle of Indianapolis. Facility commander Captain Warren Gladding told reporters that workers had been producing bombsights for U.S. war planes, adding that "no single worker has ever been taught more than one operation in the complicated manufacture of the bombsight." The plant returned to navy control in September 1945 and remained an important manufacturing facility through the Korean War. In 1956, it became a Naval Avionics facility, working on research and development; in 1977, the plant became the Naval Avionics Center, the center of research and development for all of the armed forces. Naval Avionics developed early versions of the black box for commercial and military aviation, anti-submarine war technology, technology for new generations of bombers and the guidance systems for Tomahawk Cruise Missiles. After more than fifty years of service, the facility was closed in 1995.

September 18, 2000

Indianapolis is much too young to boast an authentic Gothic cathedral, but a building that looks very much like one stands not far north of Monument Circle. From 1927 to 1929, the members of the Valley of Indianapolis Scottish Rite, an affiliated body of Freemasonry, watched their imposing $2.5 million building rise along North Meridian Street. The Scottish Rite Cathedral remains the largest Masonic building in the nation and one of the largest in the world. It is still used by members of the Scottish Rite, but it has become one of the most popular tourist destinations in the city and a favorite location for weddings. The interior is designed around numbers significant to the Masons—each of its ballroom's pillars stands thirty-three feet from the next. The cathedral is famous for its stained-glass windows and its ornate theater. In 2000, with the historic building aging and in need of repairs, members of the Scottish Rite launched a fundraising effort to see the cathedral to its 100th anniversary and beyond.

September 19, 1908

In September 1908, members of the Indiana General Assembly were preparing to be besieged by an army of temperance advocates. With an upcoming vote on a bill that would allow a county local option on the question of being dry or wet, temperance crusaders realized that they were four to six votes short of victory. Local groups across the state planned letter-writing campaigns, petition drives and excursions to Indianapolis. On Saturday, the *Indianapolis Star* reported that by Monday, delegations from several Indiana cities were expected to arrive in the capital to put pressure on their representatives face to face: "Special trains, according to a plan now on foot, will bring large delegations of temperance people from Logansport, Terre Haute, Greencastle and other cities." Temperance advocates haunted the statehouse hallways for days, and after intense debate and days of political maneuvering, the county local option was approved and the bill was signed by the governor on September 26.

September 20, 1879

Long before the Indiana legislature debated a county local option to control the sale of alcohol, temperance debates were raging across the state. Was alcohol a sin to be avoided in every form or was it a personal choice that shouldn't be regulated by the church or the government? For three years, from late 1877 until October 1880, Indianapolis imbibers and their supporters could read the *Journal of Freedom & Right*, a newspaper sympathetic to their beliefs. One issue offered a front-page cartoon about a "temperance howler," a sharp-faced woman with a very long nose, whose "mission [was] to destroy the accursed rum traffic, even if we have to drive every beer-bloated Deutchman and whiskey-guzzling Yankee and Irishman out of the country. Cold water is the thing!" A correspondent wrote that "all who are in favor of personal liberty [should] organize at once for self-protection. Let every town and city organize...against the foolish fanatics. It is the only way they can be kept out of power." The newspaper also featured a liberal offering of advertisements from local saloons, beer gardens and wine merchants.

September 21, 1922

In 1920, brothers Fred and August Duesenberg, who had been manufacturing airplane engines in New Jersey, moved to Indianapolis and began to produce automobiles. Even in a city known for producing fine automobiles, the Duesenberg stood out for its quality, including four-wheel hydraulic brakes, the first to be offered in American cars. Disaster was averted in 1922, when the ironwork for the company's new building collapsed; the structural iron was replaced and the building completed. The company's most famous model was produced after Errett Cord had bought out the Duesenberg brothers as well as the Auburn automobile company. The Duesenberg J premiered in December 1928, combining impeccable engineering with one of the most beautiful automobiles ever designed. Many of the Duesenberg J cars were made for European monarchs, the wealthiest business moguls and the most famous movie stars; the bodies could be individually designed, and the cost often approached $20,000. The Duesenbergs that survive today are the stars of classic car shows; in 2011, a model J coupe sold at auction for more than $10 million.

September 22, 1848

In the late 1840s, the Kansas and Nebraska Territories were filling up, and the territorial and federal governments were beginning to talk about statehood. The territorial charters, however, neither explicitly prohibited nor allowed slavery. The debate over slavery became a debate over "free soil"—would free, white labor build the West or would settlers be allowed to hold slaves? An early advocate for keeping slavery out of the territories was the Indianapolis *Free Soil Banner,* and the newspaper's "Free Soil Polka," printed on the front page of the September 22, 1848 issue, is as good a statement of the movement as any: "The curse of Slavery shall not be the wedding gift of Liberty, our Territories shall be Free; we are the Free Soil Voters. Our country shall not bear the shame, with which the South would load her name, on every hill burns Freedom's flame; we are the Free Soil Voters. Come one, come all, this is the hour when Freemen must make known their power, and Slavery will fall and cower, before the Free Soil Voters."

September 23, 1902

President Theodore Roosevelt would visit Indianapolis for three hours on September 23. State and local officials planned a parade from Union Station to Tomlinson Hall, where the president would speak to veterans of the Spanish-American War. The Indianapolis police made detailed plans—President William McKinley had been assassinated on September 6, 1901, and the new president, who would ride in an open carriage, had to be protected. The crowds were kept back with guide ropes; policemen stood on both sides of the route with their backs to the parade, continuously scanning the crowd; and a large contingent of mounted police accompanied the carriage. The president's visit went

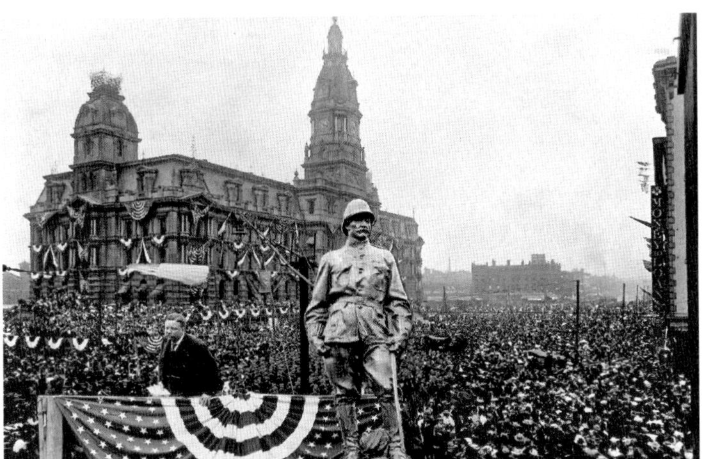

Theodore Roosevelt speaking in front of Tomlinson Hall, 1902. *Courtesy of Library of Congress, Prints and Photographs Division.*

off without incident. Roosevelt spoke to a huge, cheering crowd outside Tomlinson Hall, spoke to the veterans inside, ate lunch at the Columbia Club and departed.

September 24, 1894

Benjamin Thornton and his family lived near Indianapolis Public School No. 4, and that is where his daughter went on the first day of school in 1894. After a few days, the child was sent home with a note from her teacher, conveying a message from the principal: due to overcrowding in the classroom, the girl would be transferred to School No. 24, some distance from her home. School No. 4 was entirely white; School No. 24 was exclusively African American. The Thornton family was African American, and Benjamin was certain that overcrowding was not the real issue. After paying a visit to the superintendent that did not change the school's original decision, Benjamin hired a lawyer. On September 24, the story made the front page of the *Indianapolis Sun*; on September 26, Benjamin and his daughter arrived at the school, she in her best school dress and her father with a court injunction in hand. The superintendent cited "particulars in the case" that allowed for an exception. Benjamin Thornton's daughter remained in her class in Public School No. 4; all other African American children who lived nearby remained in School No. 24.

September 25, 1964

On a September night in 1964, Indianapolis families could go to one of eleven drive-in theaters throughout the city to see two, or sometimes three, movies. The first drive-in theater opened in New Jersey in 1933; by 1958, the number of drive-ins across the country peaked at 4,063. Drive-ins were inexpensive (Indianapolis theaters, like most, charged no admission for children under twelve), many offered playgrounds for children and families could bring their own food and drink. Each vehicle offered private seating, which also made drive-ins popular with dating teenagers. Some drive-ins offered first-run movies after they had played in indoor theaters; others offered "B" grade dramas, sci-fi films, horror movies and slightly salacious movies with suggestive titles. Indianapolis's Twin-Theatair ("6 big features—2 big screens") was showing a Gregory Peck/Anthony Quinn drama combined with a Jack Lemmon comedy on one screen; the other screen offered *Shotgun Wedding* ("Child Brides—See how they live! See how they love!") and *Theodora, Slave Empress*.

September 26, 1873

The Panic of 1873 began when New York's Cooke and Company bank failed; in short succession, several other large East Coast banks failed, and then banks and businesses as far west as Chicago began to close. In the first weeks of the crisis, Indianapolis business owners and residents convinced themselves that the problem was temporary and would not spread to their city. The *Indianapolis Evening Journal* of September 26—with its front page full of the latest ominous news from New York; Washington, D.C.; and Chicago—commented that "in the relation of business to capital invested, the banks of Indianapolis are on as sound a basis as those of any other city in the country…The business of this city is all legitimate, and the money of the banks never goes into the hands of any but legitimate business men." Local business owners were not paying heed to "the silly rumors which were current on the streets." The Panic, however, became a nationwide economic depression that persisted for much of the decade. Statewide, business failures in Indiana went from 82 in 1872 to 362 by 1876; banks and businesses closed all over Indianapolis.

September 27, 1862

Response was swift, from both Northern Republicans and Democrats, to Abraham Lincoln's preliminary Emancipation Proclamation. Democratic Indianapolis newspapers proclaimed that the president was "guilty of a monstrous usurpation" of the rights of Southerners. In contrast, the city's leading Republican paper, the *Indianapolis Daily Journal*, offered a lengthy, pragmatic defense of Lincoln. Abolitionism had taken little root in Indianapolis or in most parts of the state. The editors, rather than effusing at the prospect of freed slaves, instead reminded readers that slavery as an economic institution was essential to the South—end it, and the Confederacy would fall: "How is it that while half of the white men in the North *must* stay at home, not one-fourth in the South need do so, and that all this enormous difference of strength is turned against us in the war? By the one simple fact that the rebels can use their slaves to do the work…The slaves are the laboring life-sustaining element of the rebellion," and emancipation "destroys that strength." As to the rights of Southerners who no longer recognized the Union or the Constitution, they retained "no claim to anything but the penalty of their crimes."

September 28, 1898

In a 2007 interview, Kurt Vonnegut Jr. said that his "dream of America" was a country "with great public schools. I thought we should be the envy of the world with our public schools. And I went to such a public school." Vonnegut was one of many famous alumni of Shortridge High School, the oldest free public high school in Indiana. In 1864, Indianapolis High School opened its doors on the Circle. Superintendent Abram C. Shortridge introduced innovations such as a nine-month school year (up from three and a half months) and a grading system for classes. He also began the unusual practice of hiring female teachers, although his motivation was the cost savings of being able to pay women lower wages. In 1897, when a second high school opened in the city, Indianapolis High School was renamed to honor Shortridge. In September 1898, the *Shortridge Daily Echo* debuted as the first daily student newspaper in the nation; one of its many later editors was Kurt Vonnegut Jr.

September 29, 1880

On September 29, the English Opera House had just opened two days earlier on the Circle in Indianapolis. Actor Lawrence Barrett was to appear in a different play every night for a week to celebrate the theater's opening. This night would feature *The Merchant of Venice*; the next night would offer *Julius Caesar*. Four years later, the first section of the English Hotel was completed; the second section was built in 1896. By the time the hotel was

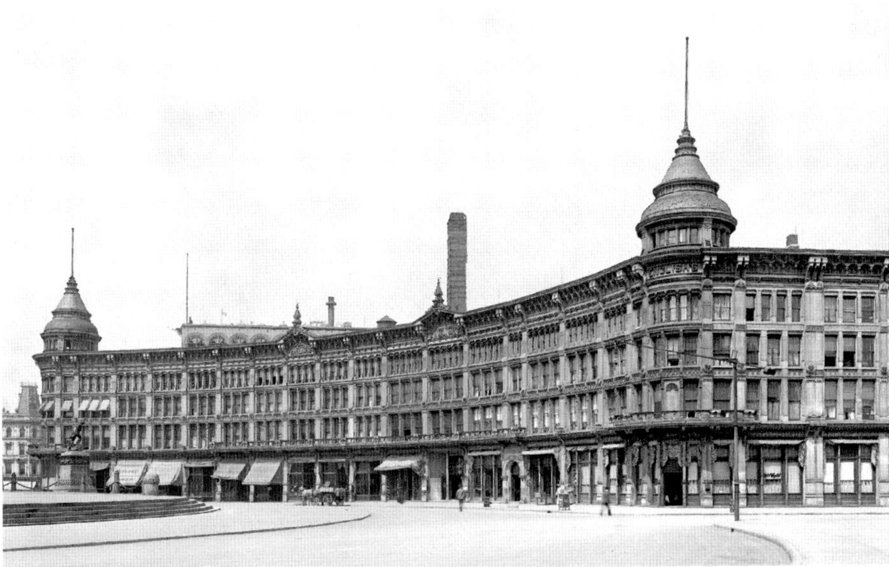

Author's collection.

completed—built around the original opera house— the complex took up one quarter of the Circle. The English offered premier lodging, dining and entertainment in the city until the 1940s. In 1948, the hotel and opera house were razed and a modern J.C. Penney Department Store took their place.

September 30, 1876

An advertisement in the morning's *Indianapolis Journal* announced: "WANTED—IMMEDIATELY—Agents to sell Wooton Desks. Office corner Meridian and Pennsylvania." Indianapolis was home to many furniture manufacturers who could rely on the abundant supply of hardwood in Hoosier forests. In 1870, William Wooton moved to Indianapolis and started a company to manufacture desks. He won a contract to supply local schools with desks but soon began to think on a larger scale. In 1874, he patented the "Wooton's Patent Cabinet Office Secretary"; the massive cabinet desk was shown at the 1876 Centennial Exhibition in Philadelphia, and soon many businessmen and politicians—including Ulysses S. Grant, Joseph Pulitzer, J.P. Morgan and John D. Rockefeller—owned Wootons.

The desk was unique not for its size, which was striking, but its practicality. As one ad summarized: "One hundred and ten compartments, all under one lock and key. A place for everything and everything in its place. Order Reigns Supreme."

OCTOBER

October 1, 1847

In 1832, the Indiana General Assembly approved the charter of a railroad to run from Madison, Indiana, along the Ohio River, north to Indianapolis. Construction of the first southern segment of the railroad began in late 1837; in November 1838, Governor Noah Noble and a group of invited guests made the first-segment, thirty-four-mile trip northward, at a top speed of eight miles per hour. Regular service did not become practical until 1841: the rise from the Ohio River through Madison to North Madison involved a seven-thousand-foot section that rose at a 5.89 percent grade. Pulling the cars up the incline by oxen was not a permanent solution; an 1841 cog-wheel system finally allowed the railroad to run under its own power, but finances ran out that same year. On October 1, 1847, the first locomotive and its cars arrived in the capital city. In January 1848, the Madison & Indianapolis Railroad finally began a regular schedule for the eighty-six-mile trip between the two cities. The southbound train left Indianapolis at 7:30 a.m., Monday through Saturday, and arrived in Madison at 2:30 p.m. The northbound train arrived in Indianapolis at 2:00 p.m.

October 2, 1872

The story of the Sarven carriage wheel, manufactured in Indianapolis, brings together the histories of two immigrants, one an English shoemaker and the other Scottish-born John Muir, who had not yet become a famous naturalist. In 1835, Samuel Fowler Smith migrated to America. He moved to Indianapolis in 1855 and struck up a partnership with Judson Osgood to manufacture wooden lasts and pegs. The partners soon retooled and bought out a St. Louis company making carriage wheels. The Sarven wheel was mass manufactured, but because of its design, the parts fit together with great precision, making the wheel stable and long lasting. In 1866, young immigrant John Muir was hired by the company. Within a few months, Muir's innovative ideas for improving manufacturing processes impressed the owners, but the young man suffered a serious accident that injured his eye. Upon recovery, Muir left the business and headed westward. Smith remained with the company until his death in 1879, when the Woodburn Sarven Wheel Company employed five hundred men and produced $700,000 of product per year.

October 3, 1828

On October 3, a group of men met at a Methodist church in Indianapolis to form the Temperance Society of Marion County, whose purpose was "to discontinue the use of ardent spirits, except as a medicine, both by precept and example." The first meeting yielded seventeen men who agreed to act as officers and members of a committee of correspondence; the group met quarterly and grew quickly. At its November 1829 meeting, the society adopted a series of resolutions based on the premise that "entire abstinence is the only course which promises success in suppressing intemperance." The next month, a statewide temperance organization formed, proclaiming at its first annual meeting that "the customary and fashionable use of ardent spirits is dangerous to the civil institutions of our country." Temperance advocates often told tales of the dangers of alcohol—an early story in Indianapolis concerned the fate of old John Shunk, a patron of the city's first saloon. Drunk at work, "he fell with his head against the kettle and his shoulders in the mouth of the furnace; and he was roasting all night." Found barely alive the next day, he died that evening "roasted brown half way down."

October 4, 1880

The presidential election of 1880 presented Civil War veterans with a challenge. Many veterans had come out of the war voting Republican, maintaining their allegiance to the party of Lincoln, but in 1880, two former Union generals—Democrat Winfield Scott Hancock and Republican James A. Garfield—were running against each other. State and city Republicans stepped up to ensure that veterans would remain loyal to their party. In late September, a large advertisement appeared in the *Indianapolis Journal*: "Grand Reunion of the Boys in Blue at Indianapolis, Oct. 8, 1880. All ex-soldiers, sailors and citizens who favor the election of Garfield & Arthur, good government and prosperity, are invited to attend." The day would include "a grand procession" with another "magnificent torchlight procession" in the evening. On October 4, organizers detailed how visiting veterans would be organized into one-hundred-man companies for the procession; on October 9, the *Journal* declared the day "the grandest reunion ever held in the state" and reported that seventy thousand people had watched the parade of more than six thousand veterans.

October 5, 1895

On this day, Walter Bedell Smith was born in Indianapolis. As a young man, he enlisted in the Indiana National Guard and fought briefly in World War I as an infantry second lieutenant in the army. In February 1942, Smith became secretary of the U.S. Joint Chiefs of Staff and U.S. secretary of the Anglo-American Combined Chiefs of Staff. By September 1943, he had risen to become chief of staff of the European theater and chief of staff to General Dwight Eisenhower. He negotiated and accepted the surrender of Italy in 1943 and the German surrender in 1945. Shortly after the end of the war, he was appointed as the U.S. ambassador to the Soviet Union, which he later wrote about in *My Three Years in Moscow* (1950). During his last years of military service, he was the director of the Central Intelligence Agency from 1951 through 1953. He served as undersecretary of state through 1954 and then, until his death in 1961, served on advisory councils and commissions on a variety of military and national security issues.

October 6, 1959

Wes Montgomery was born in March 1923 in Indianapolis into a musical family of three brothers who were all jazz artists: Wes was one of the defining jazz guitarists of his generation, Monk played double bass and electric bass and Buddy played piano and vibraphone. Wes toured with Lionel Hampton's orchestra from July 1948 to January 1950 but then returned to Indianapolis and played in local clubs during the evening while working in a factory during the day to support his family. At the end of 1957, Wes began to record with his brothers. In 1959, after Cannonball Adderley heard him in an Indianapolis club, he was signed by Riverside Records, moving in 1964 to Verve Records. One of the recordings Wes and his brothers made for Riverside was the 1959 *Wes Montgomery Trio* album, recorded on October 5 and 6. Jazz guitarist and historian Bobby Broom wrote of Montgomery's 1959 recordings that they "ushered in a figure that became one of the most celebrated, if not the most celebrated, on the instrument in Jazz music. Wes introduced a brand new approach to playing the guitar." Montgomery died suddenly at the age of forty-five in 1968; he is still cited as a seminal influence by today's jazz guitarists.

October 7, 1850

In the middle of the nineteenth century, every one of the states that had formed from the Northwest Territory revised its original state constitution. In Indiana, politicians and voters were dissatisfied with the standards governing the General Assembly and believed that the state's legal system was ready for reform. Indiana's Second Constitutional Convention began on October 7, 1850, when 150 delegates gathered in Indianapolis. The new constitution that emerged from months of debate streamlined the legislative process and modernized the courts; it also prevented the state government from incurring debt, a direct response to the disastrous debt incurred by the Internal Improvements debacle of the late 1830s. Even with the reforms, Indiana remained a conservative state and the new constitution reflected that character. Despite the support of influential delegate Robert Dale Owen, women were not given the right to own property. Discrimination against African Americans was not only perpetuated but also increased by Article XIII of the new constitution, with its blunt statement: "No negro or mulatto shall come into or settle in the State."

October 8, 1821

"The sale of lots commenced near our house—a large concourse of people were present," wrote Sarah Fletcher in her diary. The town of Indianapolis had been platted into lots, and on this day the first land sales took place at Matthias Nowland's tavern on Washington Street. Nowland's establishment and the two other taverns in town enjoyed good business for an entire week as buyers bought up lots. Settlers and speculators purchased 314 lots; the partial cash payments due from each buyer totaled $7,119 out of a total sale of $35,596. However, as Gayle Thornbrough and Dorothy Riker indicate in their annotation to Sarah's diary entry for this day, "Of the 314 lots sold, 161 were subsequently either forfeited or relinquished under a relief act of 1826. As speculation investments Indianapolis lots were not a success...By 1844, when the agent of state for the sale of lots closed his books, the entire receipts were less than $100,000."

October 9, 1849

The *Indianapolis Journal* extolled the virtues of the newest innovation in transportation—the plank road. Beginning in 1843, New York, Pennsylvania and neighboring states began to build roads paved with planks of wood covering mud, ruts, stones and stumps. Plank roads were touted as "Farmers' Railroads," which would allow farmers and business owners to make quick day trips to and from their closest markets. By 1845, newspapers in Ohio and Indiana were commenting on the benefits of these new roads; in 1849, the first plank roads appeared in Indiana, in both Fort Wayne and Indianapolis. Built in between the routes of railroads, plank roads were intended to connect rural areas with towns and small towns with one another. Unfortunately, by the time the trend reached Indiana, the limitations of the technology were apparent in the East. Boosters had estimated a ten-year lifespan for plank roads and anticipated that modest tolls would pay for repairs; the reality, with warpage and moisture, was often two years or less, sharply increasing the cost of the roads. One Indianapolis newspaper commented of a deteriorating local road: "It's a hard thing to pay a toll to break your neck."

October 10, 1996

Author Kurt Vonnegut Jr. was born and raised in Indianapolis but as an adult often expressed a conflicted relationship with his hometown. Vonnegut retained fond memories of his school years: "a free primary and secondary education richer and more humane than anything I would get from any of the five universities I attended," recalling particularly his time at Shortridge High School. But he also remembered "a provincial capital" where his architect father had to witness "the systematic replacement of works of art, many of which he helped create, with a bunch of amorphous cinder blocks." Later in his life, in a speech at the Indianapolis Athenaeum in October 1996, Vonnegut offered a reassessment of the revitalized city, where the "artistically talented as was my grandfather Bernard" and the "scientifically gifted as my brother Bernard, need not leave town to find training, encouragement, and inspiration. It was all here for me 73 years ago, and I have come home specifically to express my gratitude." Today, at the center of the city, the Kurt Vonnegut Memorial Library honors the writer "and the principles of free expression, common decency, and peaceful coexistence he advocated."

October 11, 1908

For more than a century, Indianapolis residents could visit the nearest branch of Vonnegut Hardware to find what they needed for their homes or to see the newest innovation—such as the "Searchlight Utility Return Floor Heater," a new type of coal-burning stove demonstrated outside the store all day on October 11, 1908. The company was begun by Clemens Vonnegut, who in 1851 sailed for the United States on a business trip from which he never returned. Vonnegut remained in the country and moved to Indianapolis. In 1858, he opened Vonnegut Hardware Company, which remained an Indianapolis institution until the late 1970s. The one-room store on Washington Street was soon left behind for a series of increasingly larger headquarters. Through the decades, the company also established branch stores throughout the city. Sons Clemens Jr., Franklin and George worked in the family company; Bernard became an architect. Clemens Sr. played an active role in the city's German American community, particularly as a co-founder of the Athenaeum Turners gymnastics society and the German-English Independent School.

October 12, 1910

On October 10, the *Indianapolis Star* reported on a sermon given by Reverend G.R. Kimmel, chastising the teachers and administrators of the city's high schools for allowing students to play card games. "Nine-tenths of all gambling," the minister claimed, could be traced back to card playing, which produced "a fascination that becomes a passion which destroys every noble virtue." A deck of cards was "the devil's chief tool to work ruination." Two days later, the editors of the *Star* offered an alternate view of the matter, based on a new history of Indianapolis written by Jacob Piatt Dunn. The editors noted that Dunn had uncovered similar condemnations of gaming and dancing in the town's earliest years: "The history of the growth of the two forms of amusement into popularity, should indicate to their opponents now the impossibility of banishing pastimes that carry an appeal to a great number of people, young and old."

October 13, 1912

The Sunday *Star*'s "About the Theaters" column announced that the Aborn English Grand Opera Company was returning to Indianapolis for "its annual engagement of eight performances this week" at the Murat Theater. Indianapolis audiences could attend a different grand opera every night, including *La Boheme* and *Carmen*. The Murat Theater is part of the Murat Shrine Temple, built in 1909, and it shares the building's romanticized Middle Eastern–Egyptian style. The temple, with its towers and minaret,

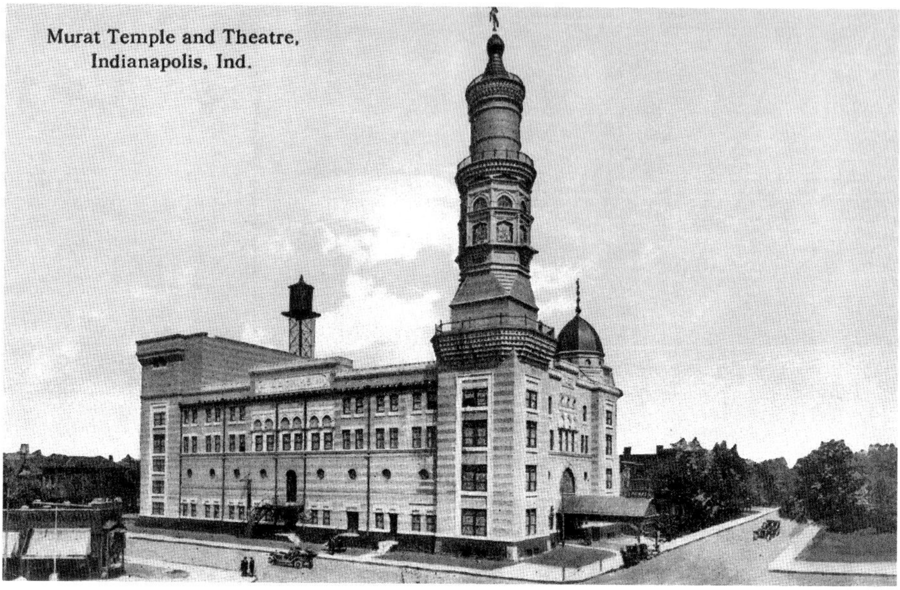

Author's collection.

has been a striking architectural presence since its opening; the theater has been an important venue for theater, music and a variety of events, and it continues that function today.

October 14, 1896

In October 1896, the Grand Army of the Republic met in Indianapolis at Tomlinson Hall. The huge brick building downtown at the corner of Delaware and Market Streets opened in June 1886 and became a venue where famous visitors gave speeches, where large groups such as the GAR held meetings and where Indianapolis residents went to hear famous performers. The building's dedication ceremony had been part of a GAR music festival organized to raise money for a Civil War memorial in Indianapolis (that would become the Soldiers' and Sailors' Monument). Tomlinson Hall was part of downtown Indianapolis until 1958, when the building was destroyed by fire.

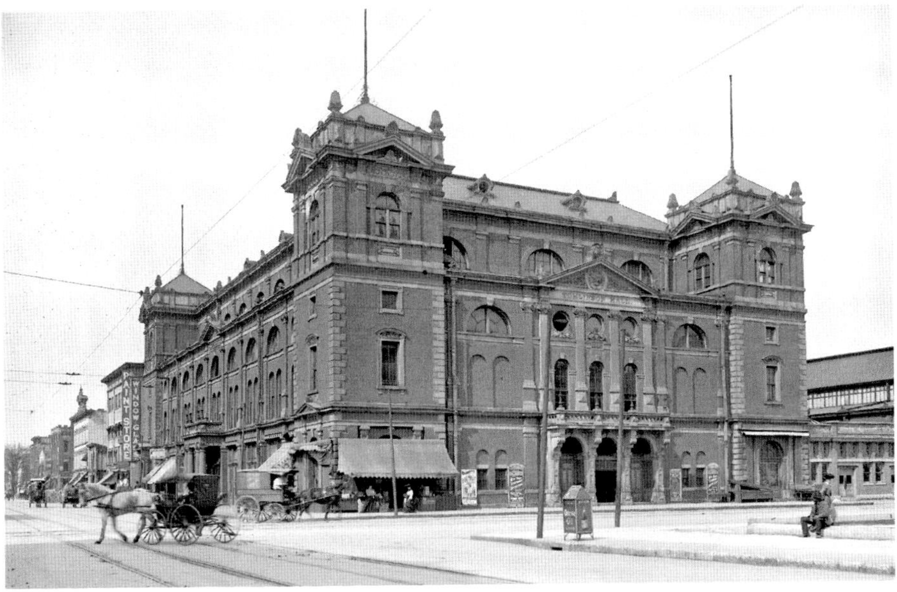

Tomlinson Hall, circa 1900. *Courtesy of Library of Congress, Prints and Photographs Division.*

October 15, 1948

Traveling for his reelection campaign, President Harry Truman spoke at the Indiana War Memorial Plaza. Truman's speech was a defense of policies that had defined Roosevelt's New Deal and his own presidency. The president challenged Republicans on Social Security, education, healthcare and economic policy, concluding his speech with a series of simple declaratives: "This Nation is no wiser than the education of its citizens. This Nation is no stronger than the health of its citizens. This Nation's security begins with the welfare of its citizens. The Democratic Party believes in the people. We believe that the people are entitled to prosperity, to health, to education, to social security. We believe that it is the function of the Government to see to it that people have these advantages." After the speech, the presidential motorcade returned to Union Station. Truman, however, was elsewhere in the city—a young soldier who had worked on the presidential yacht was being inducted into the Masons. Truman and a small security detail drove to the ceremony in an unmarked car; the president made a surprise appearance and then returned to his train.

October 16, 1983

Not long before his death in 1984, "Max, the Deli Man"—Max Shapiro, second-generation owner of Shapiro's Delicatessen—was profiled in the *Indianapolis Star*. In 1905, Russian Jewish immigrants Louis Shapiro and his family settled in Indianapolis and opened a small grocery store in the 800 block of South Meridian Street. The family lived above the store for many years. In the early twentieth century, the south side of Indianapolis was home to a growing community of Jewish immigrants, and the Shapiros enjoyed a thriving business. When the Klan began to threaten in the early 1920s, Louis defiantly changed the name of his store from the American Grocery to Shapiro's. By the mid-1930s, many Jewish families were moving northward in the city. Shapiro's remained and became a deli, serving cold beer with sandwiches of salami or corned beef. Louis retired in 1940; Max ran the business from 1940 until 1984. The fourth generation of the family still offers Shapiro's corned beef and pastrami, latkes with sour cream, cheesecake—Jewish delicatessen food that rivals the best in the nation.

October 17, 1862

By the end of the summer of 1862, the political fortunes of the Indiana Republican Party were failing. A series of Union losses in the eastern theater, opposition to the preliminary Emancipation Proclamation and Lincoln's growing suppression of public dissent all combined in the midterm election to hand both houses of the General Assembly to the Democrats. Editors of Republican newspapers statewide expressed the despair of the party faithful. The Indianapolis *Indiana Daily Journal* bluntly declared: "The terrible inefficiency with which the war has been conducted, has done more than all the President's proclamations to dissatisfy and alienate the people from the Administration. They see their blood spilled, their money wasted, and they see no result at all commensurate with the fearful outlay." Even so, the editors insisted that another cause had decisively "created this defeat. Without it all other influences would have been feeble. The absence of 70,000 Union voters in the army is the overmastering cause of the catastrophe…Our only wonder is that we were not beaten worse."

October 18, 1940

"Dupree's Floor Show Opens Cotton Club Fri., Oct. 18," announced the *Indianapolis Recorder*. Pianist and singer Jack Dupree would headline the revue at the newly remodeled club every Friday night, continuing "indefinitely." The Cotton Club was just one of the jazz and swing clubs in Indianapolis's African American community. In a city where housing, business and education were segregated, music could cross the color line, with white patrons coming to hear great jazz artists playing at the Walker Theater, the Cotton Club and the Sunset Terrace and a few famous black performers taking the stage at Tomlinson Hall. Still, the place to hear blues and jazz in Indianapolis from the 1920s through the 1950s was in one of the clubs along or near Indiana Avenue. Count Basie and Duke Ellington performed, and so did local groups including Buddy Bryant and His Gentlemen of Jam and the Montgomery Brothers. Young musicians flocked to the clubs to learn from seasoned performers—Hoagy Carmichael visited from Bloomington in the 1920s, and in the 1940s, locally born trombonist David Baker began to appear on club stages.

October 19, 1912

In 1912, artist Christian Schrader gave an exhibit of his drawings—what the *Indianapolis Star* called his "memory sketches." Schrader was born in Indianapolis in 1842. He began to sketch in the 1850s but never pursued art as a career. Sometime after his retirement in 1909, he took up art again, producing a collection of finished drawings from sketches done in the 1850s and 1860s. Schrader drew the Indianapolis he remembered from his boyhood. At the time, the town, still contained in the original square mile, was full of buildings that dated from the 1820s and 1830s; Schrader's scenes often looked as though they were from the town's earliest history. Schrader captured the rutted, muddy streets of Indianapolis and the simple wooden fences that surrounded most of the buildings. Schrader produced only 110 drawings and twelve paintings, but his work offers an unmatched glimpse into the earliest history of Indianapolis.

October 20, 1987

It was a quiet time of day at the airport Ramada Inn in Indianapolis, late enough in the morning that most guests had checked out. Only a few staff members were in the lobby when an air force jet smashed into the front of the hotel and exploded. The pilot of the A-7 Corsair had radioed to air traffic control that he was unable to restart his stalled engine. The jet, dropping quickly through cloud cover without instruments, was headed toward an emergency landing at the airport when the pilot lost all control and ejected, hoping that the jet would land in the open space he could see ahead. Instead, the plane landed in the hotel parking lot and slid into the building. Nine employees in the lobby died in the explosion; one man in the parking lot died days later from burns. An investigation by the air force concluded that the engine had failed due to a faulty gear box. Air traffic controllers, the report stated, failed to give the pilot sufficient information on his altitude and remaining distance to the airport, information that might have enabled him to avoid any populated area.

October 21, 1976

The Indiana Pacers played their first National Basketball Association game on this date. In 1967, the team had debuted as a member of the American Basketball Association; in nine seasons, the team reached the finals five times and won the ABA championship three times. Of the four Pacer players whose numbers have been retired in honor of their contributions to the team, three date from this period: George McGinnis, Mel Daniels and Roger Brown. The fourth is the most famous and popular player in the team's history: Reggie Miller, number thirty-one, was drafted onto the NBA team in 1987 and played in a Pacers uniform until his retirement in 2005. Miller regularly galvanized Pacer fans; his rivalries, especially with the New York Knicks, became sports media legend. "You have been the heart and soul of this franchise for eighteen years," team CEO Donnie Walsh told Miller in 2006 when his number was retired in front of a cheering, packed house. The team continues to pursue its first NBA championship from its home in Bankers Life Fieldhouse in downtown Indianapolis.

October 22, 1852

In 1852, the State Board of Agriculture held the first Indiana State Fair. The three-day event, located downtown, attracted thousands of visitors and was so financially successful that for a time the location was moved yearly. In 1868, the fair returned to Indianapolis on a permanent basis to a fairgrounds north of the city limits. The fair promoted agriculture, livestock and farm machinery; the women's division added competitions such as pie baking and quilting. Musical entertainment also became an important part of fair-going. By the turn of the century, when the fair had moved to its home at 38th Street and Fall Creek Parkway, Hoosiers could travel to the fairgrounds on the interurban to hear John Philip Sousa and his band. By the middle of the twentieth century, the high school band competition was in full swing. In the 1960s, fans packed the Coliseum to hear the Beatles and Diana Ross. And fairgoers have always loved to eat—from roasted Indiana sweet corn and grilled pork chops to corn dogs and lemon shake-ups—so much so that the fair now features a yearly Signature Food Contest.

October 23, 1924

On New Year's Eve 1921, Purdue graduate Francis Hamilton made the first radio broadcast in Indianapolis, heard by almost no one, from his garage. Hamilton's first program included a midnight vaudeville show from a local theater (via a telephone receiver) and an interview with Indianapolis mayor Lew Shank who, coming into the garage and staring at the wiring, said into the live microphone, "Do you mean to tell me that people can actually hear me over this damn dingus?" Hamilton soon hooked up with the *Indianapolis News* as a sponsor and moved to a better location. The *Indianapolis Star* quickly launched a competing station, but both stopped broadcasting in 1923. In October 1924, WFBM radio began broadcasting from a downtown studio in the Athletic Club, reporting on the results of the 1924 local and state elections. WFBM and WIRE, on air in 1925, became longtime fixtures in the homes of Indianapolis listeners.

October 24, 1909

Renowned opera singer Marcella Sembrich had embarked on a farewell tour of America and would be performing at the Maennerchor Hall on Sunday, announced the *Indianapolis Star*. The Maennerchor society began in Indianapolis in 1854 as a small male chorus of German immigrants. As the choir grew, it became part of the North American Saengerbund, a national association of German American singing groups, and began to compete in and host singing competitions. Indianapolis residents enjoyed the regular concerts that the choir offered as well as the festivals presenting some of the best choirs in the region and the nation. The Maennerchor acquired its own building in 1907; a year before Sembrich visited Indianapolis, the hall welcomed the National Saengerfest, which brought seventy-five thousand visitors to Indianapolis.

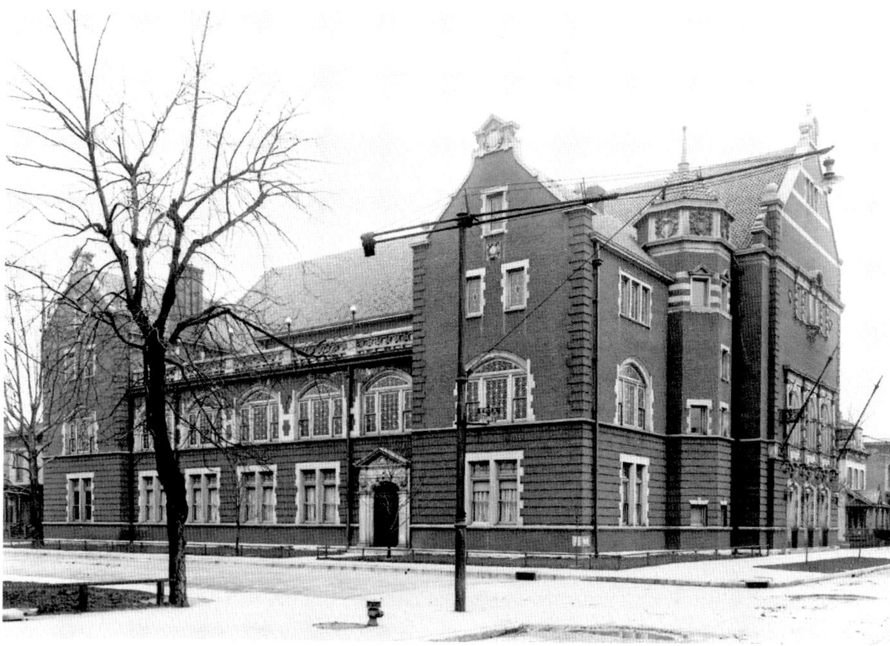

Courtesy of Historic American Buildings Survey, Library of Congress.

October 25, 1905

With Vice-President Charles Fairbanks looking on, the cornerstone of Methodist Hospital was laid at a site on Capitol Avenue just north of Sixteenth Street. The facility opened in 1908 with sixty-five beds; two years later, the hospital board approved the construction of two more pavilions. Methodist's first motorized ambulance, introduced in 1910, was used to carry injured Indy 500 drivers to the hospital. In 1970, the hospital first made use of its helicopter transport system to evacuate badly injured drivers. In 1922, the hospital was one of only two facilities in the nation to work with Eli Lilly & Company to offer insulin to its diabetic patients; in 1990, Methodist was the first Midwest hospital to implant the new insulin pump for the same disease. The hospital was also a pioneer in transplant surgery: the first kidney transplant in Indiana in 1972, the first successful heart transplant at any private hospital in 1982 and in 1987 the state's first artificial heart transplant. In the twenty-first century, the sprawling complex of IU Health Methodist Hospital continues to pioneer technologies such as the da Vinci surgical robot.

October 26, 1965

In the summer of 1965, Sylvia and Jenny Likens's mother was in jail. Their estranged father sent them to board with Gertrude Baniszewski and her children at an agreed-upon sum of twenty dollars per week. When the payment was late one week, Gertrude began to punish the girls, particularly Sylvia. Over the course of three months, Gertrude and her children, along with several neighborhood teenagers, physically abused and tortured Sylvia. When police arrived at the Baniszweski house on East New York Street on October 26, they found Sylvia dead, her malnourished body covered with sores, bruises and burns. The story, complete with the horrific details of how the sixteen-year-old had been repeatedly abused by at least a dozen people—not one of whom had ever attempted to stop the torture or to report it—was a national media sensation. Gertrude and her oldest daughter Paula, seventeen at the time of Sylvia's death, were found guilty of murder. Three teenage boys, including Gertrude's son John, were convicted of manslaughter. Despite a life sentence for first-degree murder, Gertrude was paroled for good behavior in 1985 and lived until 1990.

October 27, 1853

At the London Yearly Meeting of 1853, the assembled members of the Society of Friends decided to send a deputation to leading political officeholders in the United States to plead the case for the abolition of slavery. Delegate John Candler, writing home to his wife in late October, recounted the group's experiences in Indianapolis. Few Hoosiers outside Quaker areas of settlement such as Richmond were abolitionists, and the new state constitution had banned free blacks from migrating to the state. Candler and his companions had few illusions when they visited with Governor Joseph Wright, who "vindicated the policy of Indiana in preventing the influx from other provinces of colored people into the State, accompanied as it is by an annual outlay of money to promote their emigration to Liberia." The group dined with the governor, whom Candler described as "a polite intelligent man," but privately Candler expressed their opinion of his views: "Liberia, however good as a colony, will never lead of itself to the abolition of slavery, or serve as a home for the slaves of the Southern states, if emancipated, and it is a perfect delusion to imagine that it ever can be so."

October 28, 1970

In April 1968, the "American tribal love-rock musical" *Hair* opened on Broadway to considerable controversy. The cast portrayed a group of hippies, the music was late 1960s rock and during the performance, members of the cast could be seen taking drugs and, in one brief scene, could be seen nude. The first touring production of the musical reached Indianapolis in October 1970. The owners of Clowes Hall and the Murat Theater refused to host the musical. City attorneys and police officials informed the show's producer that nude cast members might be arrested under state indecency laws and suggested body stockings for every actor. The show opened on October 19 at the Circle Theater to a packed house. The critic for the *Indianapolis News* wrote that "the production, judged as musical theater, is a roaring success. It may not be to everyone's taste but for those who want it, it's gloriously there." Conservative disapproval continued: "No thinking person can uphold un-American, anti-Christian obscenity in the name of freedom," offered one letter to the *Indianapolis Star*. The musical's run was extended due to demand for tickets.

October 29, 1964

In the early 1960s, the women's rights movement was just beginning to form. Indianapolis had been a conservative city, electing few women to political office. Two local women had served as state representatives beginning in the 1930s; the first female state senator also came from the city in the 1940s. For the most part, Indianapolis women's political involvement was expressed through women's clubs and party auxiliary organizations and through the League of Women Voters. One regular *Star* columnist probably expressed the view of most local men (and many women) regarding women's political involvement with his piece "At 7 or 70, Women Are a Puzzle in Politics": "Men and women often have different viewpoints on political matters… The basis of that different [viewpoints] is curiously interesting…A Chicago housewife may have given the answer when she explained that men usually base their voting on 'business things' and that women are 'more emotional.' That is the charm of women in politics or wherever they are. They remain so refreshingly emotional, so eternally feminine."

October 30, 1835

In 1835, Indianapolis hosted the first Marion County Agricultural Society Fair. The fair was solely committed to improving the quality of the county's livestock through scientific principles. East Coast immigrants to the Midwest often commented on the poor quality of frontier livestock, valued mostly for the ability to survive and thrive in difficult conditions and seldom managed with an eye to improving the breed. The society was organized to address these issues. In late October, Calvin Fletcher, society treasurer, began to fret in the pages of his diary, with "much anxiety for fear our fair would turn out a failure…and prove injurious to the organization of societies in other counties." Attendance at the fair was good, although Fletcher commented on "some fine stock but mostly of the scrub kind." No doubt farmers were drawn by the prizes in hard currency, but the fair had begun to establish standards for horses, cattle, oxen, pigs and sheep, as well as for cheese and butter.

October 31, 1963

Just after 11:00 p.m., a crowd of more than four thousand was watching the final number of the Holiday on Ice show at the Coliseum in the Indianapolis fairgrounds. During the show, a leaking propane tank had been filling a concession area with gas. The first explosion threw spectators, seats and massive pieces of concrete flying. A second explosion caused a fireball that reached the ceiling. Fifty-four people died at the scene and twenty more died of their injuries in subsequent days; four hundred spectators were injured. The fair's cattle barn became a makeshift hospital, and the icy surface of the Coliseum became a temporary morgue. Newspaper photos showed bodies laid out on pieces of plywood across the ice, arms and legs still showing under blankets, while family members filed past, lifting the coverings to identify their loved ones. In August 2011, the fairgrounds were again the site of a terrible accident. In stormy conditions with strong wind gusts, a crowd stood outdoors waiting for the country music group Sugarland to perform. As police, concert organizers and fair officials debated whether to cancel the concert, wind brought the roof structure of the stage crashing down into the crowd. Seven spectators died, and many more were injured.

NOVEMBER

November 1, 1855

North Western Christian University opened its doors on the first day of November 1855. The school consisted of a single building on twenty acres of land, but its goals were ambitious: to offer "every branch of liberal and professional education" and to accept students "without regard to sex, race, or color." The man behind the school was Ovid Butler, who had worked as a schoolteacher before moving to Indianapolis in 1836 to become Calvin Fletcher's law partner. Butler was a devout member of the Disciples of Christ and an abolitionist. After he retired from practicing law due to ill health, he designed his ideal of a college, donated twenty acres of his own land, endowed the school and became its president for its first twenty years. Butler's dream drew students and teachers. In 1875, the college moved to larger quarters in the new suburb of Irvington where, two years later, it was renamed Butler College in honor of its founder.

November 2, 1913

In August 1913, union organizers attempted to unionize the employees of the Indianapolis Traction and Terminal Company, which owned and operated the Indianapolis Street Railway Company. As organizers met with employees, the company hired spies to attend meetings. On the evening of October 31, pro-union workers declared a strike, attacked many of those who were still working and damaged many of the city's streetcars. When sixty-five crews reported for work the next morning, strikers prevented the cars from moving. The stalemate grew more heated and violent when the company brought in workers and strikebreakers from outside Indianapolis and demanded that police fight off the strikers—some officers complied, but many were sympathetic to the strikers. Finally, with the city's streetcars shut down, Governor Samuel Ralston ordered the National Guard to restore order. Ralston met with both sides and negotiated compromises on wages and hours. The strike ended at 6:00 p.m. on November 7; the company at first refused to meet its new obligations, but the Public Service Commission, tasked with arbitration, granted employees higher wages and shorter workdays.

November 3, 1944

For many decades, homemakers across the country relied on the Acme Evans Milling Company of Indianapolis to provide E-Z-Bake Flour for their cakes, cookies, muffins and bread. Acme Evans had its origins in the early history of Indianapolis. Isaac Wilson began Evans Milling in the 1820s; John Carlisle began Acme Milling in 1840. The two companies merged in 1909, and in 1917, after a fire destroyed the old facilities, Acme Evans built a modern concrete-and-steel nine-story plant with reinforced concrete storage bins for its product. Ads for E-Z-Bake Flour promised that it "always gives successful results" and offered the product in a variety of sizes: 3-pound, 10-pound, 20-pound, 48-pound or 98-pound sacks or 196-pound barrels. Like many companies trying to capture the loyalty of home cooks, Acme Evans put out free paperbound cookbooks with recipes featuring its product, including *101 Ways to a Man's Heart: Delicious Prize-Winning Recipes...All Using E-Z-Bake Flour.*

November 4, 1862

When the Civil War broke out, physician Richard Jordan Gatling was living in Indianapolis. From his youth, Gatling had also been an inventor—among his ideas, a machine to sow rice and wheat and a steam-powered plow. During the war, Gatling turned his attention to creating new weaponry, and on this day in 1862 he was issued a patent for the Gatling gun. The Gatling was a multi-barrel machine gun that could fire a large number of rounds very quickly: the first six-barrel model fired 350 rounds per minute, and the second ten-barrel model fired 400 per minute. Dr. Gatling hoped that his invention would allow armies to fight with fewer men and thus reduce casualties; he also expressed the wish that such a powerful weapon would discourage war altogether. Instead, the Gatling gun was used by Union troops during the Civil War, became an important part of the U.S. Army's wars against Native Americans in the West and was standard weaponry during the Spanish-American War.

November 5, 2008

As vote tallies came in for the presidential contest between Barack Obama and John McCain, the state of Indiana remained uncalled for some time, but most people watching were certain of the outcome. Indiana had last voted for a Democratic presidential candidate in 1964, when Lyndon Johnson won the state; after that, Indiana became a reliable "red state" for the Republican Party. Obama and McCain had both campaigned in the state. Obama had visited Indianapolis in early May for a huge rally on the American Legion Mall; he had also spoken at the state fairgrounds in October. When the major television networks finally called the vote in Indiana, something remarkable happened—they called it for Barack Obama. When the vote was analyzed, Obama had captured only fifteen Indiana counties, but those counties held 44 percent of the state's population. He had won 63.8 percent of the vote in Marion County.

November 6, 1991

When the *Indianapolis Star* looked back on the accomplishments of Mayor Bill Hudnut's administration, the editors also gave credit to a group begun years before by Democratic mayor John Barton. The Greater Indianapolis Progress Committee (GIPC) began in 1964 as a volunteer group of civic and business leaders, convened to advise the mayor on furthering the city's economic development. The group recommended a variety of possible improvements, including an urban state university, a major convention center, a reservoir at Eagle Creek and a fully developed interstate system through the city center. Republican mayors Lugar and Hudnut, and their successors, continued to work with the group. GIPC became part of the task force that planned Unigov. The group helped bring public radio and public television to the city and worked with government and neighborhood groups on such projects as the redevelopment of Lockefield Gardens. In recent years, GIPC was involved in the new Eskenazi Health Center that replaced the old city hospital. Today, with the city's Department of Metropolitan Development, it is working on Plan 2020, the bicentennial plan for Indianapolis and Marion County.

November 7, 1870

As northern cities grew in the aftermath of the Civil War, a new concept in urban living emerged: the suburb, where middle- and upper-class families could escape the crowded living conditions of the center city and enjoy life in green, spacious surroundings. Begun in 1870, Irvington was one of the earliest suburbs in Indianapolis. Investors and developers Jacob Julian and Sylvester Johnson bought 320 acres of land four miles east of the city center. They laid out curving streets to conform to the topography and to preserve trees and streams. Middle-class families in Irvington would be free from many of the noises, smells and immoral temptations of the city. Irvington deeds included a clause stating that no "distillery, brewery, soap factory, Pork or slaughter house or any other establishment offensive to the people" would be built and that no homeowner would "sell or suffer any one to sell… any intoxicating beverages except for sacramental medicinal or mechanical purposes strictly." In 1876, Irvington gained regular street rail service into the city, ensuring its growth.

November 8, 1967

Richard G. Lugar was born in Indianapolis and attended city public schools. After serving in the navy, he became a business owner whose first public office was membership on the city's school board from 1964 to 1967. Lugar's pragmatic and thoughtful approach to issues caught the interest of local Republican leaders, who persuaded him to run for mayor. On November 8, 1967, he was elected as mayor of Indianapolis. Lugar and his administration focused on urban renewal as well as consolidation and efficiency of city resources. Lugar became known for his concern with neighborhood development and for working with community leaders; he also broke with conservative Hoosier tradition, actively pursuing and utilizing federal funds for a wide variety of city improvements. Lugar gained national recognition for his urban reforms: in 1968, Indianapolis was named a national Model City, and in 1970, Lugar was elected president of the National League of Cities. Two of Lugar's most enduring contributions to Indianapolis were the creation of Unigov and the founding of the city's first urban university, IUPUI.

November 9, 1947

John Bartlow Martin grew up in Indianapolis and attended Arsenal Tech High School. After graduating from college, he became a journalist with the *Indianapolis Times*. Martin published his first book just before World War II. After his military service was completed, Martin took up his second book, intended as a portrait of Indiana. *Indiana: An Interpretation* was published in 1947 to mixed reaction and reviews, especially from Hoosiers. Martin had cast a journalist's eye on the state, writing a series of stories of its people, both famous and unknown. Martin admired labor organizer Eugene Debs and devoted a long chapter to him. Martin also looked at the darker side of the state's culture and devoted another long chapter to D.C. Stevenson and the Klan. The book received a polite but tepid review from the *Indianapolis Star* in November 1947, with reviewer Eugene Pulliam Jr. writing that it was "interesting and different as books about Indiana go."

November 10, 1918

The Great Influenza Pandemic of 1918–19 killed 675,000 people in the United States and, by best modern estimates, more than 30 million people worldwide. By early fall of 1918, the flu apparently had not yet reached Indianapolis or much of Indiana. On September 19, John Hurty, director of the state Board of Health, proactively telephoned every county health officer for a report. Hurty learned that discrete cases of flu were popping up throughout the state, including among two groups of soldiers being housed within the city of Indianapolis. By early October, 200 cases per day were reported in Indianapolis; on October 8, the mayor prohibited any public gathering of more than 5 people, excepting most businesses and necessary public services. The restrictions remained in place until the end of the month. Statewide, influenza raged, and the *Indianapolis Star* carried daily enumerations of the dead from each county as well as the daily count of new cases—on November 10, 934 new cases were reported statewide. When the disease subsided, Indianapolis had been fortunate, with one of the lowest death rates for any city in the nation.

November 11, 1933

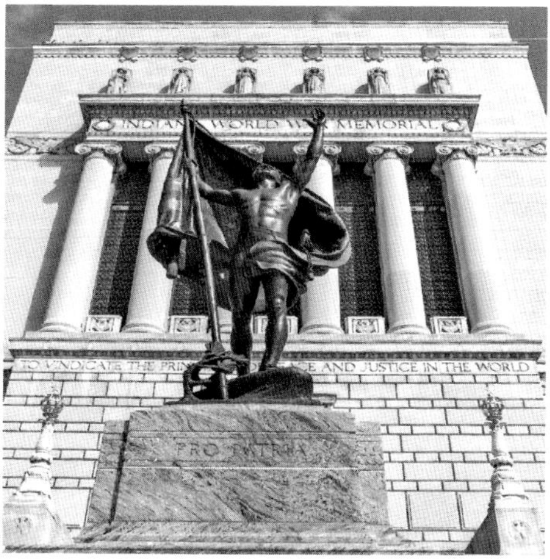

Pro Patria by Henry Hering stands on the south side of the Indiana War Memorial. *Photo by Ronald Waicukauski, Wikimedia Commons.*

When the American Legion selected the city of Indianapolis for its national headquarters in 1919, the city began to plan for a grand plaza that included the Legion building as well as a memorial to the soldiers of World War I. The Indiana World War Memorial was designed in a Neoclassical style and built of Indiana limestone. General John Pershing laid the building's cornerstone on July 4, 1927; the building was dedicated on Veterans' Day, November 11, 1933. The memorial houses a museum of American military history, and the beautiful third-floor Shrine Room is also popular with visitors. At the south entrance to the building stands the striking bronze statue *Pro Patria*. The Memorial Plaza occupies six square city blocks and dominates the cityscape just north of Monument Circle.

November 12, 1986

The Indianapolis Symphony Orchestra (ISO) began in 1930 as a musicians' co-operative under the direction of violinist Ferdinand Schaefer and grew into an important orchestra under its second music director, Russian émigré Fabian Sevitsky. For fifty-seven seasons, the ISO was led by only four music directors: Schaefer, Sevitsky, Izler Solomon and John Nelson. In November 1986, the symphony board announced the fifth music director: Maestro Raymond Leppard, a London native who had become famous in the 1950s and 1960s for his pioneering concerts and recordings of baroque music. Leppard had conducted all over Europe and the United States and was a favorite guest conductor of the ISO. Leppard built on the strengths of the orchestra: its size, which made it perfect for nineteenth-century classical works, as well as its particular sound within its "new" concert hall, the renovated Circle Theater. Under Sevitsky's leadership, the orchestra had toured and recorded; Leppard brought back both those traditions, taking the ISO on two extensive European tours and garnering excellent reviews. Leppard led the ISO until his retirement in 2001, when he became its conductor laureate. In 2003, Leppard became a U.S. citizen, and he continues to reside in Indianapolis.

November 13, 1909

At the turn of the century, Indianapolis could not claim to be a cultural center, but residents enjoyed regular offerings of theater and music. In November 1909, the *Indianapolis Sun* announced the upcoming opening of the new Colonial Theater in downtown Indianapolis. Manager Cecil Owen declared that his "thoroughly modern and attractive playhouse" would offer only the "very best in vaudeville" entertainment. Owen bragged that he had hired vaudeville star Cecilia Loftus (at a "princely salary") for the theater's opening week. Normally, he related, Miss Loftus would only appear in cities such as New York and Chicago, but she had been lured to Indianapolis with the honor of opening a new theater. The *Sun* also offered news from a lower echelon of the city's theatrical offerings: Frank Criswell, "proprietor of a moving picture show," had been arrested for "desecrating the Sabbath by keeping his theater open on Sunday." Criswell, the paper noted, had now been acquitted of the charge by a local jury, and he had promised that a portion of his Sunday receipts would be donated to charity.

November 14, 1957

In 1898, the African American Service Center opened in a small, donated house. The facility, which soon became known as Flanner House, became a center for a wide variety of social services for the African American community in Indianapolis. Flanner House provided a health clinic and a special tuberculosis clinic, care for unmarried mothers and their children, child care for working mothers, health classes run by the Red Cross and an employment service. Throughout the twentieth century, Flanner House continued to expand its physical facilities and its programs. One of its most ambitious undertakings was the Flanner House Homes project begun in 1950, which produced 175 modern homes for African American families at a time when Indianapolis housing was highly segregated and options for black homebuyers were limited. The project attracted national attention: in November 1957, Eleanor Roosevelt visited Flanner House, spending three hours touring the health clinic and some of the homes.

November 15, 1917

The English Hotel had been an elegant fixture on the Circle since 1884; the opera house featured famous singers and theatrical performers. On May 3, 1917, a drama of another kind took place in the hotel lobby. Dan Shay was the manager of the Milwaukee Brewers, in town to play the Indianapolis Indians. After losing an afternoon game, Shay went out on the town. He visited Gertrude Anderson's "manicure parlor" for a two-hour "manicure." Shay and Anderson then went to the English Hotel for dinner. Shay and African American waiter Clarence Euell had begun to exchange words when Shay stood up and shot Euell in the abdomen. The bleeding Euell was put in a chair in the lobby and left by hotel managers until the police arrived, by which time it was too late to save his life. Shay went on trial for second-degree murder. During his trial, which lasted from November 14 to 22, his defense painted a highly racist portrait of a dangerous black man who had threatened a white woman and her companion. Despite conflicting testimony by witnesses and evidence that the defendant had been drunk and belligerent, Shay was found not guilty.

November 16, 1905

The House of 1,000 Candles, published on this date, was one of Meredith Nicholson's most successful books. Nicholson was born in 1866 and moved to Indianapolis with his family in 1872. At age fifteen, he left school, educating himself through voracious reading and teaching himself four foreign languages. In the mid-1880s, he began to publish his poetry in newspapers. After a brief period in Denver trying his hand at business, in 1901 Nicholson returned with his wife and children to Indianapolis and lived there until his death. He published his first novel in 1903 and went on to write twenty more books. He was also known as an essayist in magazines such as the *Atlantic* and *Harper's*. Nicholson's sentimental novels—sometimes romantic, sometimes adventurous and mysterious—were national bestsellers. Nicholson was also active in Democratic politics. In the 1930s, his political connections, especially with Governor Paul McNutt, and his support for Franklin Roosevelt helped to earn him posts as United States minister to Paraguay, Venezuela and Nicaragua. His elegant house still stands on North Delaware Street, now home to the Indiana Humanities Council.

November 17, 1907

In the early twentieth century, Indianapolis public health officials began to notice that infant and child mortality rose during the hot summer months. One factor, they soon realized, was spoiled milk. Pure Milk programs had already appeared across the country in response to the practice of adding formaldehyde to milk as a preservative; in Indianapolis, the Children's Aid Society set out, working with the local board of health and other groups, to have large quantities of milk pasteurized in modern facilities and distributed at stations located throughout the city. Each station was staffed by doctors and nurses. Parents who came for a supply of pure milk could have their babies and children weighed and examined for health issues; nurses also offered advice on nutrition and child care. Local newspapers promoted the program. During the summer of 1909, the *Indianapolis Sun* offered the story of Billy, "a sturdy boy…lively and friendly," who just one year earlier had been "very sick." Billy's mother now fed him pure milk, "making her boy manly and vigorous." In one year, the city's seasonal mortality rate for children under five was reduced by half.

November 18, 1863

At the beginning of the Civil War, the U.S. Sanitary Commission (USSC) was formed as a civilian organization to organize and provide aid to Union soldiers. The USSC funded hospitals, paid doctors and nurses, established training facilities for nurses and shipped clothing and supplies to soldiers. Each Northern state ran its own commission, and one of the most important funding sources was the sanitary fair. Fairs offered goods for sale, raffles of donated items, entertainment and music. During the course of the war, sanitary fairs raised $3 million in support of the troops, and almost all of the work was done by women. The fairs become more elaborate and profitable as the war continued: the 1864 Indianapolis Sanitary Fair included a "fancy dress ball" and theatrical performances by some of the women. The 1865 fair featured a full-length play, prompting one local Methodist church to consider disciplining one of its members, a woman who had been one of the volunteer "stars" of the play. The charge was dismissed after church leaders decided that fundraising for the troops made the activity morally permissible.

November 19, 1829

Transportation into and out from the new state capital was a problem. In late 1829, the *Indiana State Gazette* observed that "for a few months past the roads leading to this place, have been unusually bad for the season. Last week a considerable snow fell, which has disappeared, and the rain which followed it has rendered them still worse than ever." Platting of the National Road across the state had been completed in 1827, but Hoosiers waited well into the 1830s for the road to be complete from Richmond in the east to Terre Haute in the west. Nevertheless, the *State Gazette* also noted that "emigration…still presses onward, and we daily witness wagons and numerous horsemen bending their course to the west…The work now progressing on the National Road, and the prospect of something effectual being done with regard to the road from Lake Michigan, at the ensuing session of the Legislature, has inspired a new confidence in the people, and they go forward, in improving the county, with a more lively zeal than heretofore."

November 20, 1866

In April 1866 in Decatur, Illinois, a group of former Union soldiers formed the Grand Army of the Republic. The veterans' group was organized with local posts and with state-level departments. Members of each department gathered at an annual encampment; every year, the departments also met at a national encampment. The first national gathering took place in Indianapolis in November 1866. The veterans met in Morrison's Opera Hall, filled with regimental and national flags. The evening address was given by Indiana governor Oliver Morton, who had been known for his staunch support of the Union and his aid to soldiers. Morton noted with approval that Union veterans had "returned home to disappoint the predictions of their enemies in every particular. From being good soldiers, they had become the best of citizens." Morton also reminded the men that they would be the ones who would "govern this country for the present generation." The GAR became an important national organization, advocating for veterans' pensions and for aid to needy veterans and their families. The last national encampment of the GAR took place in Indianapolis in 1949.

November 21, 1834

Before the National Bank Act of 1863, banks and their currencies could be transitory entities. Indiana's first "state" bank began in the Indiana Territory, one of two banks chartered in 1814. The Bank of Vincennes/State Bank of Indiana lasted until 1822, failing due to competition from the Bank of the United States, the economic depression of 1818–19 and the malfeasance of some bank directors. The first residents of Indianapolis relied on the branches of the national bank in Cincinnati and Louisville for more than a decade, but then President Andrew Jackson's opposition to a national banking system prompted the state legislature to action. In January 1834, hoping to create a stable state currency and increase the availability of credit, the legislature and the governor created the second State Bank of Indiana. On November 21, the Indianapolis branch, and nine other branches across the state, opened for business.

November 22, 1856

Charles Coulon was an unlikely choice for mayor of Indianapolis, but perhaps that was part of the reason he served in the office for only two weeks. Coulon was a local lawyer who as a young man had been a staunch Democrat. Playing billiards one Sunday with a friend—in a public place—Coulon was arrested and charged with desecrating the Sabbath. After paying the statutory fine, Coulon swore never to support a Democrat again and switched his party allegiance. In 1856, Coulon was serving a term as a local justice of the peace when Henry West, the fifth mayor of Indianapolis, died on November 8 while still in office. The city council unanimously chose Coulon as interim mayor, until such time as a special election could be held. Coulon served as mayor for two weeks until the election on November 22. He returned to serving the rest of his term as justice of the peace, and when that term was up, he returned to his law practice.

November 23, 1972

On Thanksgiving Day 1972, the Mt. Vernon Missionary Baptist Church of Indianapolis served its first free holiday meal, offered to anyone in need. Reverend Mozel Sanders had pastored the congregation since 1959 and had led his church to become a force for change in the neighborhood and the larger African American community. What began as a congregational project in 1972 grew over the decades to become a citywide event. When the meal became too big to prepare and serve at the church, the project moved to two different local motels, then to the cafeteria of Arsenal Technical High

School and finally in the 1990s to Butler University. Volunteers from all over the city joined together to serve food to thousands of people and deliver meals to thousands more off-site. After Mozel Sanders's death in 1988, a foundation begun in his name—whose purpose was to feed the needy on a daily basis—continued the Mozel Sanders memorial Thanksgiving dinner. In 2014, two thousand volunteers worked for three days to provide meals for forty thousand recipients.

November 24, 1963

On November 23, Indianapolis newspapers carried news of the assassination of President John F. Kennedy, the swearing-in of Lyndon Johnson as the new president and the first accounts of suspected killer Lee Harvey Oswald. On November 24, the morning *Star* reported on the president lying in state and carried announcements that the governor had declared thirty days of mourning and that the city of Indianapolis would essentially shut down the next day to watch Kennedy's funeral procession on television. All members of the city merchants' association were closing their stores for the day, IPS was closing all schools and downtown department stores had shuttered their windows filled with bright holiday displays. City reporter Bob Collins walked the downtown, observing the "stunned disbelief" and "numbness" in the faces and voices of people at work and lunch. Later that day, those who were watching the news on television would learn that Lee Harvey Oswald had himself been killed, shot in the basement of Dallas police headquarters by Jack Ruby.

November 25, 1858

The modern holiday of Thanksgiving had a slow start in the nineteenth century, as evidenced by the diaries of Calvin Fletcher. On December 7, 1837, Fletcher wrote: "This is our first Thanksgiving ever held by proclamation of the Governor." Despite Governor Noah Noble's proclamation, the courts were still open in the morning; Fletcher and his family attended church in the afternoon, returned home to dine with friends and spent the evening at a "large and respectable meeting…for the benefit of the poor in which all the churches joined." Fletcher concluded of the day: "All the stores were shut and Indianapolis was in great harmony." By November 1858, the holiday was taking on traditions and becoming more widespread. On November 24, Fletcher recorded a visit to a local farm for two turkeys. The next day, he wrote: "All assembled. Had thanksgiving dinner. Mrs F. [Fletcher's second wife, Kezia Lister] had worked hard to get it up…During this day many of the business houses closed and legislature adjourned. Some 20 or more of the States have set apart this day."

November 26, 1836

C.P. Ferguson grew up in Clark County, Indiana, and became a distinguished citizen and judge of that county. One of his most vivid boyhood memories, however, was a trip to Indianapolis. In August 1836, Ferguson's father was elected to represent Clark County in the state legislature and decided to have his young son with him in the state capital for the opening weeks of the session. Ferguson, traveling in advance of his father, journeyed to Indianapolis with a family friend, Indiana State Supreme Court chief justice Charles Dewey. The two boarded a steamboat in Charlestown, disembarked at Madison overnight and then traveled a full day northward to Columbus via stagecoach. The next morning, their stage to Indianapolis not appearing, they rode to Franklin in a farm wagon and from there boarded "a large covered spring wagon, drawn by four horses." The traveling party, now including another judge and a lawyer bound for the capital, "trudged the balance of the day and into the night through mud and chuck-holes and over corduroy roads," arriving in Indianapolis after dark. "In darkness and in quiet the stage drew up," Ferguson wrote, "and there emerged therefrom and entered the hotel, cold and tired, a supreme judge, an ex–supreme judge, a great lawyer, and a little country boy."

November 27, 1835

The first statehouse in Indianapolis was the Marion County courthouse, and for more than a decade, the state legislature did not meet in its own building. In late November 1835, the *Indianapolis Indiana Journal* announced

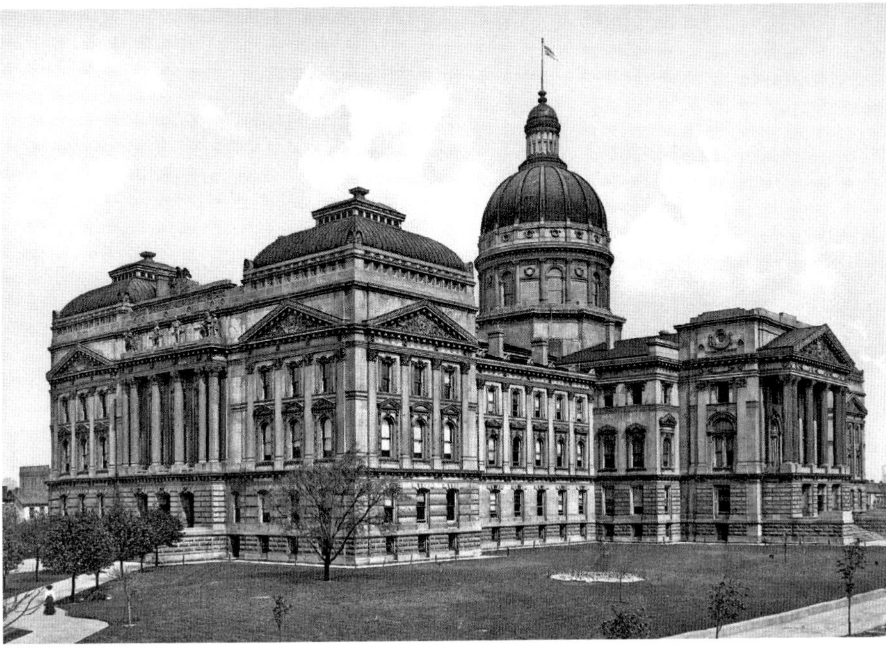

Second Indiana statehouse, 1888. *Courtesy of Library of Congress, Prints and Photographs Division.*

that in two weeks' time, state lawmakers would "meet in the new State-House, which is just being finished, and which, in size and taste, is not equalled by any building in the west." The building was styled after a Greek Doric temple topped by an Italian Renaissance–style dome, albeit with Hoosier economies: the exterior was brick and not marble, and the dome's zinc roof, which was to have been gilded, was left plain. Within thirty years, the building began to fall apart. In 1877, much of the roof was blown off by high winds and the ceiling fell in; nevertheless, a new statehouse was not completed until 1888.

November 28, 1888

"If Chicago only had natural gas it might hope to become as great a city as Indianapolis. It might also, some day, be the home of a president. At present, however, its prospects for the future are mighty discouraging." The editors of the *Indianapolis Sun* were correct: the city was the home of soon-to-be-president Benjamin Harrison, and people could walk the streets of downtown Indianapolis at night under light provided by natural gas. Beginning in early 1886, huge deposits of natural gas were discovered under parts of Ohio and eastern Indiana. Anderson, Muncie, Marion and Kokomo, Indiana, became industrial boomtowns by harnessing the new energy source. In 1887, several Indianapolis companies also successfully drilled for natural gas. When Baroness Alexandra Gripenberg, visiting the United States from Finland, traveled through the city during the summer of 1888, she was impressed with the sight: "In the evenings a real migration of people to the soda shops took place. Then they strolled in the dusk along the streets…As soon as it became dark, a majestic flame resembling a bath-whisk lighted up the city. It was so-called natural gas, which had recently been discovered near the city in enormous quantities."

November 29, 1922

With automobile ownership increasing every year, crime began to take on some new variations. Bank robbers with a high-powered automobile could rob a bank in one town and quickly escape to the next county or the next state. Motorists transporting goods from one place to another could also be stopped on the road and robbed: the term for the new type of robbery was "hi-jacking." In November 1922, the Indianapolis Police Department announced that, by order of the mayor, its officers were fanning out across the city to catch an "alleged ring" of hijackers, "terrorists of the county highways." Closer reading of the article revealed that police were rounding up every bootlegger in the city; the "terrorists" had been stealing from rumrunners who were transporting illegal alcohol from its point of origin to its point of consumption. The police arrested every still-keeper and petty criminal they could locate, with no indication that they had found any ring of terrorists.

November 30, 1913

In November 1913, the *Indianapolis Star* announced a new book of sayings by the fictional rural philosopher Abe Martin. *Back Country Folks* was the latest in a series containing the work of humorist and artist Frank McKinney "Kin" Hubbard. In the 1890s, Hubbard worked as an artist for the *Indianapolis News* and later for the *Sun*. Hubbard always claimed that his lack of formal art training made it difficult for him to produce the variety of illustrations that his editors demanded. Nevertheless, he went back to work for the *News* in 1901 and remained with the newspaper until his death in 1930. Hubbard produced his own style of caricatures for the newspaper, starting with drawings of state and city politicians. In December 1904, the paper introduced Hubbard's Abe Martin, a rural character with a floppy hat and a scraggly beard who always offered a wise quip ("We'd all like t'vote fer th'best man, but he's never a candidate."). Abe Martin was a hit with the paper's readers, especially after Hubbard moved his character south into Brown County, Indiana, adding a whole cast of characters on whom Martin could comment. Kin Hubbard had created a true, if fictional, rural Hoosier humorist.

DECEMBER

December 1, 1899

Even though decades of experience had proven otherwise, in 1899 the Indianapolis Commercial Club partnered with the *Indianapolis News* for a trip from Indianapolis southward to see whether it might be economically feasible to render the White River navigable. The flatboat and its party set out on November 28 from downtown. By the afternoon of December 1, the boat had reached Waverly. "From Pleasant Run to Waverly," reporter Fred Knodle wrote, "the river has a depth ranging anywhere from twenty feet to two, and the only trouble we experienced in navigating was due to

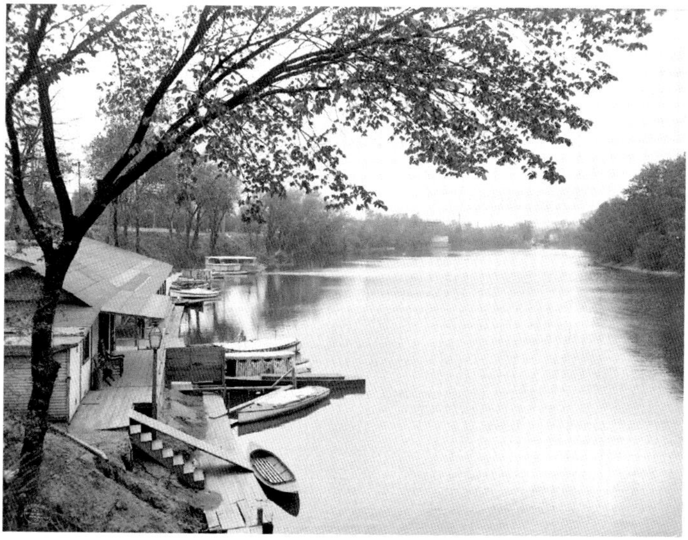

A view along the White River at Broad Ripple, 1907. *Courtesy of Library of Congress, Prints and Photographs Division.*

the numerous labyrinths of snags...There is no railroad here, and if the river were cleared of obstructions, it would be the making of the town." Knodle also admitted that "though Waverly is but eighteen miles by road from Indianapolis, by river it is fifty-five miles." The entire 214-mile trip took twelve days.

December 2, 1924

In the winter of 1924, former U.S. senator Albert Beveridge was invited to the White House for a private dinner with President and Mrs. Coolidge, a chat with the president after dinner and an overnight stay. More than ten years after his time in the Senate ended, Beveridge still traveled in elite political circles. As a young man, Beveridge came to Indianapolis after college to practice law. He became deeply involved in Republican politics and was a sought-after speaker for the party. Beveridge was also active in the city through a variety of organizations. In 1899, his talent and his party connections earned him a seat in the U.S. Senate from the Republican-controlled state legislature. Beveridge served two terms in Washington, becoming a Progressive Republican who believed in using the power of government to order society. He joined Roosevelt's Bull Moose Party in 1912, running unsuccessfully for Indiana governor as that party's nominee. Beveridge never served in public office again. Instead, he turned his time to the study and writing of history. He produced a distinguished four-volume biography of John Marshall and a biography of Abraham Lincoln.

December 3, 1844

In the 1830s, New York farmer William Miller became convinced that Jesus was going to return and end the world during or near the year 1843. By 1840, Miller's message spread via conferences and a biweekly newspaper throughout the East, Midwest and Canada. In early 1843, Miller announced that Jesus would return sometime between March 21 and the same date twelve months later. When nothing happened by the end of March 1844, believers devised a new scenario that changed the date to October 22, 1844. Many so-called Millerites sold their homes and businesses and by early October were sitting in white robes waiting for the end. The "Great Disappointment" caused the movement to fracture, but even then some persisted. The editors of the *Indiana State Sentinel*, having observed Millerites in Indianapolis, were incredulous: "To our great astonishment, we now find the delusion resuming its sway with, if not more general extent, with more extravagance than ever." The world did not end; many Millerites in Indianapolis and elsewhere became part of the newly formed Seventh Day Adventist Church.

December 4, 1910

The Sunday *Star* offered a charmingly illustrated article—with some interesting but questionable advice—on "When the Little Tot Goes to Town," showing a small girl in a fashionable dress and hat accompanied by her mother as they board an interurban car for a trip downtown and lunch together. But the author foresees disaster: a day that is too long and tiring for a child, with a careless mother unprepared to deal with inevitable trouble. The first mistake? Mother feeds the little tot "ice cream and cake, rich pastry or indigestible made dishes highly seasoned." The solution is simple: train the child "to take what you suggest…a sensible, digestible luncheon. Soup and graham bread will win out every time against a chocolate éclair." Another mistake? When the child refuses to go where she should, Mother drags the child by the hand and then lifts her by one arm into the homebound car. What does the author advise? To pick up the child the correct way and *then* compel her to go where Mother wants: "When lifting the body, place a hand under each armpit and raise slowly. It does not require any more time and is certainly more comfortable for both."

December 5, 1933

Hoosiers had been talking about the evils of alcohol since the state began. A century of temperance work culminated in Prohibition, but Indiana upped the ante in 1925, passing the "Bone Dry Law" that made medicinal liquor illegal. In Indianapolis, Reverend Edward Shumaker attacked Governor Ed Jackson and state Attorney General Arthur Gilliom for obtaining alcohol for family members sick with pneumonia and invoked the "Bone Dry Law" against them. But all across the country, Prohibition was already failing; people who wanted to drink alcohol found ways to do so. In Indianapolis, Shumaker was forced to end his crusade when news came out that the "tonic" he had consumed for much of his adult life contained 35 percent alcohol. Prohibition ground on until late 1933; on December 5, the last vote to ratify the Twenty-first Amendment finally came through. Now state officials hurried to establish new taxes and laws, and Governor Paul McNutt had a new source of political patronage: state liquor licenses.

December 6, 1924

"H.P. Wasson & Co. The Christmas Shopping Center," ran the advertisement in the day's *Indianapolis Star*. Nearly all of the items on sale could have gone under a modern Christmas tree: gloves, socks, handkerchiefs, slippers and robes, stationery and women's dresses and fur coats. Wasson's was one of three major department stores that dominated downtown Indianapolis for much of the twentieth century. Hiram Wasson bought an interest in a local dry goods store in 1874; when he became sole owner in 1883, the store changed its name. The Wasson's store most Indianapolis residents remember was actually its third location. Wasson's, like its competitors, expanded into the suburbs in the 1950s, but expansion was not enough to save any of the department stores in the long run. Wasson's closed its downtown store in 1979.

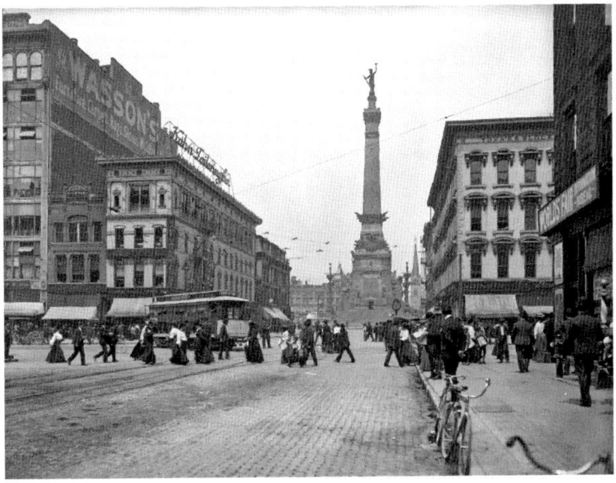

Downtown Indianapolis with Wasson's department store on the left. *Courtesy of Library of Congress, Prints and Photographs Division.*

December 7, 1919

In February 1919, Theodore Roosevelt Jr. and a group of World War I veterans met to form a new veterans' organization; in November 1919, the American Legion held its first national convention, and during that meeting, the members chose Indianapolis as the site for the group's national headquarters. The legion advocated for veterans' benefits and for national security, offered services for veterans and promoted patriotic ideals. Indianapolis community leaders envisioned the legion linked to the memorial the city was planning to the veterans of World War I. The result was War Memorial Plaza in downtown Indianapolis, flanked on one end by the World War Memorial and on the other by American Legion Headquarters.

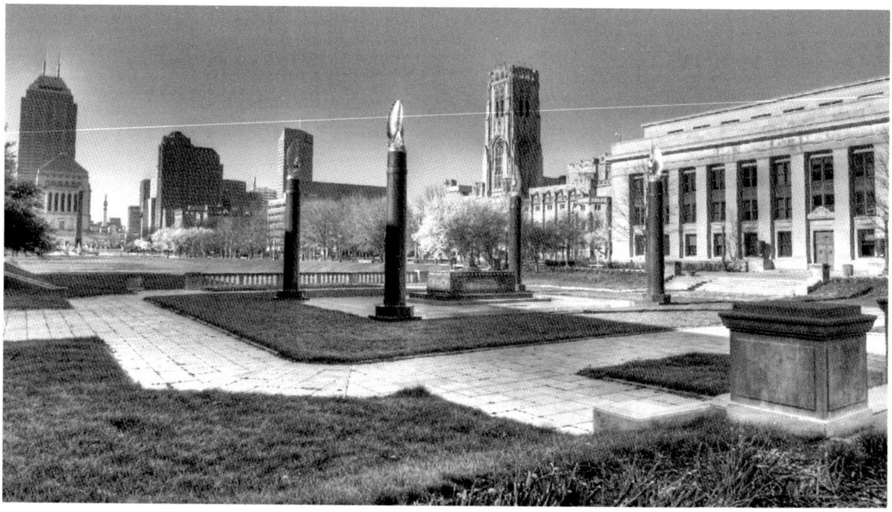

American Legion Headquarters (right) on the War Memorial Plaza. *Photo by Serge Melki, Wikimedia Commons.*

December 8, 1941

The headline story of the *Indianapolis Star* on December 7, 1941, was President Roosevelt's personal message to Japanese emperor Hirohito, in response to reported Japanese military movements in the Pacific. Hoosiers would learn later that day from their radios of the attack on Pearl Harbor. The December

8 morning paper gave details of the attack and the American dead and informed readers that the president would address a joint session of Congress that morning, to be carried on all three major radio networks at 11:30 a.m. Roosevelt's speech confirmed what listeners knew—the country was at war. One of the most immediate and curious effects of the declaration of war in Indiana and in Indianapolis was not military but political. Hoosier Wendell Willkie, the 1940 Republican candidate for president, had been under intense criticism from the isolationist wing of his own party, so much so that his forthcoming speech at the Indianapolis Columbia Club had drawn protests from some members. In the space of a day, local GOP leaders conceded to a *Star* reporter, Willkie had become "a party hero."

December 9, 1958

In 1945, an Army Intelligence officer named John Birch was killed while on assignment in China. In December 1958, a group of eleven Indianapolis residents chose to honor what they saw as his sacrifice against the spread of Communism and name their new society after him. The John Birch Society was led by retired candy manufacturer Robert Welch Jr. Welch had been convinced for years that a massive Communist conspiracy had infiltrated U.S. society, especially politics—President Dwight Eisenhower and Supreme Court chief justice Earl Warren were Communists or at the least Communist sympathizers, he believed. The society grew quickly, claiming 100,000 members by the early 1960s. The group organized itself in small 20- to 30-member cells and operated as much as possible in secret. Members believed that 40 to 60 percent of the nation was controlled by Communists, and they looked for the philosophy everywhere, teaching their children to report anything suspicious in their classrooms. The society still operates out of its headquarters in Appleton, Wisconsin—now with a website and an online newsletter.

December 10, 1864

It took some time for the December 10 military court verdict to reach the public in Indianapolis. Lambdin Milligan, Stephen Horsey and Andrew

Humphreys had been found guilty of treason against the United States and sentenced to die by firing squad. Earlier that year, the three men, along with three co-conspirators, had been arrested for plotting to seize weapons from the Indianapolis arsenal, free Confederate prisoners at Camp Morton and instigate an insurrection. Harrison Dodd, the first man to be tried, had escaped from jail and fled to Canada. Two other men had turned state's evidence. By December 28, rumors were coming from Cincinnati and Chicago newspapers that the defendants had been convicted and sentenced and that the verdicts "now only await the signature of the President to be carried into execution." In fact, lawyers were already appealing to the president for pardons, but the matter was undecided when Lincoln was assassinated. Instead, the appeals wound through the court system, reaching the U.S. Supreme Court as the *Ex Parte Milligan* case, in which the court found that civilians could not be tried by a military court where and when civilian courts were in full operation.

December 11, 1924

The *Indianapolis Star* encouraged "Mr. & Mrs. Indianapolis" to visit the new Christamore House, being finished on the west side of Indianapolis. Christamore had begun in 1905 when friends and fellow Butler University graduates Anna Stover and Edith Surbey, inspired by Chicago's Hull House, decided to start a settlement house in Indianapolis. Stover and Surbey gathered other young women who were teachers and social reformers and—backed by the city's Charity Organization Society, the Indianapolis Free Kindergarten Association and the head of the Indianapolis Public Library—rented a five-room house in an area filled with factory workers and their families. Christamore offered a free neighborhood kindergarten, a library and clubs for older children, as well as a Mothers' Club for women and the services of a trained nurse. In the early 1920s, as the neighborhood around it changed, Christamore moved westward, in search of larger facilities and an area with a predominantly white clientele, as it, like almost all other social services in Indianapolis at the time, was strictly segregated.

December 12, 1909

The new automotive test track known as the Indianapolis Motor Speedway was ready for two days of trials, and the *Indianapolis Star* devoted much of its front page to the news that had captured the "interest of the automobile world." "Famous drivers," the paper announced, "will try to break all world's records from: 28 1.5 for a mile to 1:06:53:49 for 100 miles, a rate of 89.70 miles an hour." Race car drivers were spending much of the week at the track preparing their cars for "the speed trials that will show the mettle of the giant steel steeds" Lewis Strang had arrived in Indianapolis with his two-hundred-horsepower Fiat, "holder of many world records and reputed as the fastest car ever built." Driver Hughie Hughes, after inspecting the track's long straightaways and the banked turns, predicted that he would break the quarter-mile record with a new record of 7 seconds. Strang, Hughes and other drivers did break records at the trials, although many of the teams complained that the excessive cold handicapped the operation of their cars.

December 13, 1963

In 1850, the Tremont House, a roadhouse and bar, opened for business on South Meridian Street. For many years, its upstairs front room was used by railroad passengers from nearby Union Station. During the Civil War, tunnels from the bar to Union Station were part of the city's Underground Railroad network. For a period after the war, the upstairs was subdivided into twenty-three rooms and operated as a brothel. Through various owners and under a variety of names, with customers unknown and infamous (including the Brady and Dillinger gangs), the bar continued to do business. Just prior to Prohibition, it was Moore's Beer Tavern; during Prohibition, Moore's Restaurant operated in the former bar (and made beer in the basement). In December 1963, the Yeagy family took possession of the business, renamed their bar the Slippery Noodle Inn and made the inn the "Home of the Blues in Indiana," using what was once the livery stable as the music room. The Slippery Noodle Inn is now the oldest surviving commercial building in the city of Indianapolis.

December 14, 1822

A few of the earliest residents of Indianapolis were convinced that the small town, destined to be the state capital, should be officially incorporated. But most of the residents, like so many Hoosiers who came after them, thought their current situation was good enough—especially when the proposed change meant new taxes. The editors of the *Indianapolis Gazette* agreed with the majority, warning readers that "a petition was got up some weeks since, for the purpose of being presented to the legislature, praying a special act of incorporation of this town…Is it reasonable? Is it consonant with the wishes of a majority of the inhabitants…it is not." Taxes were "already sufficient," and the petition was the work of "a few special favorites" in town who had tried to sneak the issue into the legislature. Nine-tenths of the people in town, the editors added, were opposed to the plan. When incorporation was needed, then "the citizens will step forward, in their own persons, and present a petition *above board.*"

December 15, 1921

Indianapolis Star reporter Mary Bostwick had been trying for some time to get an interview with city mayor Lew Shank, but to no avail. So when she heard about the mayor's new proposal for the police force, she offered a satirical report: "Mr. Shank," she wrote, "is going to make the Indianapolis cops go to school, on account of some of their spelling not being all it should be in some cases, and their not being up on the date when Alexander swam the Hellespont and such historical matters." Bostwick noted that she had covered the police beat and knew many of the beat cops and their officers—she volunteered herself as an assistant professor. She offered to teach them spelling because she remembered the old story about the cop who found a dead horse on Massachusetts Avenue but dragged the horse over to East Street before he wrote up his report because he couldn't spell "Massachusetts." She could also teach grammar: "I would ask some such sentence as this 'I seen the guy when he clumb out of the canal at Washington and Meridian Street.' What's the matter with the sentence? Well, the answer is—the canal doesn't go to Washington and Meridian Street."

December 16, 1911

The *Indianapolis Star* noted that on the previous day Governor Thomas R. Marshall and five other governors had stood "with bared heads about the chair of James Whitcomb Riley…in semi-silent homage to the 'greatest of Hoosiers,' as they termed him." Riley, known during his lifetime and long after as "the Hoosier Poet," was one of the most famous residents of the city and the state. Riley began writing poetry in the 1870s and publishing it in newspapers. Unable to break through into national magazines, in the 1880s he toured with recitations of his poetry, much of it written in an exaggerated dialect. Riley's sentimental poems of childhood and rural life, combined with his delivery style, garnered public acclaim. Beginning in the 1890s, collections of his poetry were published in small, illustrated volumes, and his fame and wealth grew. In 1912, the state of Indiana began to celebrate Riley Day on the poet's birthday (and continued to do so until 1968). When Riley died in July 1916, he was the second person to be honored with a public viewing of his body in the statehouse—the first had been President Abraham Lincoln.

December 17, 1883

Jasper Monroe, free thinker and publisher of the *Indianapolis Iron Clad Age*, offered up his own version of holiday cheer in a December column. Under the title "Infidel Festivals," Monroe related the proposal of a fellow non-believer from Boston that non-Christians "turn the religious holidays to 'freethought uses.'" The solution to so much Jesus during the month of December was to pick an "infidel martyr" who could be celebrated instead. Monroe suggested Giordano Bruno, the sixteenth-century Italian friar, philosopher and scientist who had been burned at the stake for his heretical theology. Bruno had become a symbol of free thinking to subsequent generations, and so Monroe proposed "pitting an infidel martyr against the christian martyr—Bruno against Jesus." Monroe liked this "new idea of martyr-worship during the closing and opening of the old and new years… [we] can play Bruno while the devout play Jesus. No harm can come from this innocent employment of the imagination, while we have the real cooked goose and turkey and doughnuts before us—not one bit."

December 18, 1966

A few days before the release of *The Sand Pebbles*, a Los Angeles newspaper printed an interview with star Steve McQueen, described as the American ideal of the "rugged individualist" who "triumphs against all sorts of adversity." McQueen was born in Beech Grove, a town within Indianapolis limits, in March 1930. After an unstable and difficult childhood, McQueen joined the U.S. Marines. He took up acting in the 1950s and became a household name starring in the television western *Wanted—Dead or Alive*. He was one of the top movie stars of the 1960s and 1970s, with *The Great Escape* (1963) and his famous escape attempt through the German countryside on a Triumph motorcycle, westerns like *Nevada Smith* (1966), dramas such as *The Sand Pebbles* and crime dramas, particularly *Bullitt* (1968) with its own iconic chase scene, this one through the streets of San Francisco, with McQueen driving a Mustang. McQueen became the epitome of the "cool," tough bad boy turned hero—so much so that after his death, a pair of his sunglasses sold at auction in 2006 for $70,000; one of his motorcycles at the same auction brought $276,000.

December 19, 1867

The war was over, and Indiana had seen its borders invaded only once by Confederate troops. John Hunt Morgan and his raiders, followed closely by Union troops and state militia, had wreaked considerable damage and loss on hundreds of southern Indiana businesses and farms. On December 19, 1867, the Morgan Raid Commission, authorized by the state legislature, finished its hearings in the statehouse and tallied citizens' claims. The total was just over $479,000; claims allowed totaled $412,000, with $330,000 of damages by Confederate troops, $47,000 by Union troops and the remaining $35,000 by state militia. Few Hoosiers ever saw payment of their claims. The state legislature proved unwilling to pay for damages done by Southern troops; U.S. government officials required documentation of losses and, in many instances, receipts. When farmers tried to point out that Union troops who had ridden through their farms and commandeered fresh horses gave them no time to ask for receipts, the U.S. Quartermaster General's office stood firm and the claims went unpaid.

December 20, 1937

In December 1937, writer and social critic W.E.B. DuBois criticized the Madame C.J. Walker Company, writing in his column for the *Pittsburgh Courier* that he was dismayed to hear that the company, after its founder's death, was now primarily in "the hands of white capitalists." DuBois went on to lament that Walker Manufacturing, like so many other black-owned businesses, was based "on the usual exploitation of labor." It might instead have been "a co-operative enterprise," which could have grown into "a socialistic mass movement." In the December 20 issue of the same newspaper, Freeman Ransom, manager and attorney for the company, replied: "There is not now or has there ever been one share of stock" in Walker Manufacturing "owned by any white man." The company was still wholly owned by the Walker family, Ransom added. A series of letters, public and private, ensued between the two men. Ransom demanded a public retraction from DuBois and threatened a suit for libel; in January 1938, DuBois retracted his claim regarding the company's ownership. The two men continued to disagree on larger issues: DuBois remained committed to his socialist ideals, while Ransom believed that African Americans could achieve progress within existing economic structures.

December 21, 1928

In 1928, a group of forty-one local businessmen came to the aid of Butler College, which was trying to upgrade its athletic facilities. The significant and lasting result was Butler Fieldhouse, dedicated on December 21. The Bulldogs played their first game in the unfinished arena on March 7, beating Notre Dame in overtime 21–13. The fieldhouse, through a lease agreement with the IHSAA, also become home to the state championship in boys' high school basketball, an arrangement that lasted from 1928 to 1971. As the popularity of high school and college basketball grew into Hoosier Hysteria, the Butler arena became a symbol of the state's love for the game. In 1966, the building was renamed for Butler's longtime athletic director and basketball coach Tony Hinkle. In 1986, the movie *Hoosiers*, a paean to 1950s Indiana basketball, filmed the final game won by the fictional team from Hickory High at Hinkle Fieldhouse and featured Indiana sports broadcasting icons Tom Carnegie and Hilliard Gates as the game announcers.

December 22, 1921

Only two shopping days until Christmas, and L.S. Ayres & Company knew its male customers—all those husbands, sons and boyfriends who dreaded shopping and still hadn't bought the women in their lives a single gift. "MEN!" began the eye-catching ad in large type, "we're all alike—we all feel lost when it comes to buying a gift for a woman." Ayres offered "a REAL Way Out…It's safe to buy a woman's gift in a woman's favorite store! It's twice as safe if you have the assistance of a clever, talented, sympathetic woman when you shop." The store had trained "a dozen or so of our cleverest, most agreeable, tactful young women" to come to the aid of desperate male shoppers. The women were ready "to shop WITH you, to shop FOR you"; men needed only to bring their shopping list "to a commodious private office on the street floor" where nobody else could discover their dilemma. And just to be certain of success, the advertisement concluded: "Women—Be Sure the Men See This Announcement!"

December 23, 1837

Indianapolis Whigs took their politics seriously. A few days before Christmas, the *Indiana Journal* announced the forthcoming "Whig Celebration" to "take place on Christmas Day and evening." The celebration would "commence by the forming of a Procession in front of Browning's tavern about 2 o'clock, which will march to some suitable place where several speeches will be made. Our fellow-citizens of the country are respectfully invited to be present." Skeptical readers might assume that those in attendance at the speeches had made use of Browning's tavern earlier in the afternoon, but Whigs were made of stern stuff. New Year's Day 1838 was set "as the time for a Whig county meeting. The main object of the meeting will be to appoint Delegates to the Whig State Convention, which will meet in January. We hope our friends in the country will feel the importance of a well attended meeting, and come up to assist in its deliberations."

December 24, 2012

The year 2011 was a low one for Indianapolis Colts fans. Their quarterback, Peyton Manning, was out for the season; the team won two games and lost fourteen. After the season ended, the team released Manning to play elsewhere. Colts' management also began to clean house, and fans saw many of their favorite players depart. The only good news was that the Colts' record gave them the first pick in the first round of the 2012 NFL draft and the chance to acquire a young quarterback who was widely considered to be a future NFL star. Andrew Luck had been projected as the top pick in the 2011 draft, but he returned to Stanford to graduate with a degree in architectural design. Luck was intelligent and affable in interviews, as well as being a gifted quarterback who won the respect of teammates with his tough, physical play and overall attitude. By the end of his first season with the Colts, Luck had set the rookie single-game passing yards record (433) and the rookie season record for passing yards (4,374). The team had turned itself around: "Playoffs? Playoffs!" announced the December 24 *Indianapolis Star.* The Colts made it to the first round of the playoffs but lost to the Baltimore Ravens.

December 25, 1829

Indiana's constitution outlawed slavery and indentured servitude, but several court cases during the 1820s and 1830s showed that the status of slaves who journeyed from the South into Indiana could be unclear. On the afternoon of Christmas Day 1829, Calvin Fletcher appeared in court on behalf of a black woman and her three children who had arrived in Indianapolis with their owner, Virginian William Sewell. The woman fled from Sewell, claiming her freedom in Indiana. Fletcher wrote that the courtroom "was full. Most of the members of the legislature were present. Great excitement among the people of the county. Their sympathies were alive for the woman & childrin [*sic*] while the members of the legislature & some few who in our own place yet countenance the horrid traffic were almost clamorous for the pretended owner." Evidence was given on behalf of both sides, and the trial "closed about 8 o'clock at night." The next day, the judge rendered his verdict: "A man abandoning a Slave state with his Slaves for the purpose of settling in a free state… the moment that his slaves & himself reached a free state they were free."

December 26, 1927

After the death of Madame C.J. Walker, her daughter A'Lelia became director of the family company. It was she who planned the Madame C.J. Walker Building, which opened in late 1917 at the intersection of Indiana Avenue and West Street in Indianapolis. The building housed company headquarters; the manufacturing facility where three thousand workers made the famous hair and beauty products; the "home" salon in a line of beauty salons across the country; professional offices for African American doctors, lawyers and others; and a ballroom and theater. On December 26, the Madame Walker Theater opened with a Hollywood film starring Ronald Coleman and the music of Reginald DuValle's Blackbyrds Orchestra. Freeman B. Ransom, the Walker company's general manager, offered a dedication of the building "to those who toil; those who think; those who love good music; good pictures, high class entertainment…to all races." DuValle and the Blackbyrds, along with hundreds of other orchestras, jazz and blues combos and soloists, would perform at the Walker Theater and create its reputation as a musical destination in Indianapolis.

December 27, 1900

Perhaps the failure of prohibition can be attributed in part to the zeal with which temperance reformers pursued their goals. At the end of 1900, Mrs. J.R. Wood wrote to the temperance newspaper the *Patriot Phalanx* with a proposal of action for the coming year. Each local temperance group should choose one or more of the major Protestant denominations, make a list of every local congregation associated with that group and then investigate "whether they use unfermented wine, or whether they depend on the sweet wine of commerce to use at the holy communion." "Many churches," she claimed, "offer alcoholic wine, not knowing it contains alcohol. They buy it for pure grape juice." Temperance advocates could teach members how to prepare their own grape juice. "Think, dear sisters," Mrs. Wood concluded, "if one cursed with an inherited appetite should get the first taste of alcohol at their first communion and go from our Lord's table down to destruction! Are we guiltless if we do not do all in our power to put away this great evil from the church."

December 28, 2011

What to do on a cold December day when Christmas was over but New Year's Eve parties were three days away? For Indianapolis residents in 2011, the answer was easy: check off another day on the countdown to Super Bowl XLVI at Lucas Oil Stadium. The *Indianapolis Star* offered its readers a story per day about the preparations; December 28's article was about the Chase Near Eastside Legacy Center. The $11 million community center on the campus of Tech High School was part of the city's Super Bowl Host Committee's Legacy Project, an attempt to extend the benefits of hosting the event outside the core of the city's downtown. The center was set to open two days after the big game and offer fitness and wellness classes to the community, as well as functioning as a community center. Today the center continues to offer classes six days a week and host a variety of community groups.

December 29, 1888

In his annual report for 1888, the Indiana state superintendent of schools raised the issue of compulsory education. Massachusetts was the first state to initiate compulsory schooling in 1852, and several other states followed in the next decades. Indiana legislators and their constituents were still deeply divided on the issue. The editors of the *Indianapolis Journal* took up the superintendent's recommendations. His report estimated that 25 percent of enrolled pupils attended school on a regular basis and less than half of eligible students were even enrolled. No matter what the exact numbers, the editors noted, there were too many ignorant, uneducated children in Indiana. A republican society "cannot knowingly tolerate the growth of illiteracy" among its youngest citizens and future voters. The editors of the Indianapolis newspaper the *People* offered the opposing viewpoint:

compulsory education was "tyrannical to the last degree," taking away parents' right to decide for their children. "This thing of sticking one's nose into another person's business should not be encouraged by law…To Helen Blazes with your compulsory education law, say we."

December 30, 1848

Gold was discovered at Sutter's Mill, California, in January 1848. By June, people throughout the West were headed to the gold fields. Midwesterners were skeptical of the news until President James Polk gave a December speech confirming the find. The rush was on, and the Indianapolis *Locomotive* commented on "the excitement [that] prevails in every city and town in the Union. We are deluged with communications and personal inquiries as to the best, shortest and cheapest routes of getting to California." The editors provided a detailed description of the three major routes to California, including travel time, average cost and the particular difficulties of each journey. "We do hope," the editors concluded, "all who contemplate going to this country will make an early start…We should not be surprised if California was as thickly settled in three years from this time as Indiana is now." By the end of 1849, 100,000 people had come to California in search of gold.

December 31, 1823

New Year's Eve in Indianapolis began well but ended badly. Calvin Fletcher recorded in his diary that Thomas Carter, the owner of a log tavern just north of Washington Street, was offering "a theatrical performance…by Mr. & Mrs. Smith *perporting* to be directly from N.Y. Theater." The actors—"both not less than 50 years of age!" according to Fletcher—were to perform two short plays, *Jealous Lovers* and *The Doctor's Courtship*, preceded by music from two local fiddlers. Mrs. Smith began by singing "The Star-Spangled Banner" and then offered up her signature performance: one of the fiddlers broke into a lively tune and Mrs. Smith began to dance a hornpipe—after eggs were scattered on the stage and after she had been blindfolded. The dance had scarcely begun when tavern owner Carter interrupted. As a strict Baptist (although not a "dry" Baptist), Carter allowed only hymn tunes in his establishment. The Smiths opted to end the dance and proceed with the first play, but they proved less than convincing as two young lovers. The audience began to jeer, the Smiths left the stage and the New Year's Eve celebration in Indianapolis came to an abrupt end.

SELECT BIBLIOGRAPHY

Indianapolis newspapers online at NewspaperArchive, http://www.newspaperarchive.com (accessed through Indiana University–Bloomington libraries); IUPUI Digital Collections, http://www2.ulib.iupui.edu/digitalscholarship.collections; Chronicling America: Historic American Newspapers, http://chroniclingamerica.loc.gov; the *Indianapolis Star* and *Indianapolis News* (1925 onward) on microfilm.

Articles from *Indiana Magazine of History*. 111 volumes, 1905–2015. http://scholarworks.iu.edu/journals/index.php/imh.

Bodenhamer, David J., and Robert G. Barrows, eds. *The Encyclopedia of Indianapolis*. Bloomington: Indiana University Press, 1994.

Candler, John. *A Friendly Mission: John Candler's Letters from America, 1853–1854*. Indianapolis: Indiana Historical Society, 1951.

Carmony, Donald F. *Indiana, 1816–1850: The Pioneer Era*. Indianapolis: Indiana Historical Bureau and Indiana Historical Society, 1998.

Dunn, Jacob Piatt. *Greater Indianapolis: The History, the Industries, the Institutions, and the People of a City of Homes*. 2 vols. Chicago: Lewis Publishing Company, 1910.

Leary, Edward A. *Indianapolis: The Story of a City*. Indianapolis, IN: Bobbs-Merrill Company, 1971.

Lilly, Eli, ed. *Schliemann in Indianapolis*. Indianapolis: Indiana Historical Society, 1961.

Madison, James H. *Hoosiers: A New History of Indiana*. Bloomington: Indiana University Press and Indiana Historical Society Press, 2014.

———. *Indiana Through Tradition and Change: A History of the Hoosier State and Its People, 1920–1945*. Indianapolis: Indiana Historical Society, 1982.

McCord, Shirley, comp. *Travel Accounts of Indiana, 1679–1961: A Collection of Observations by Wayfaring Foreigners, Itinerants, and Peripatetic Hoosiers*. Indianapolis: Indiana Historical Bureau, 1970.

Nation, Richard F., and Stephen E. Towne, eds. *Indiana's War: The Civil War in Documents*. Athens: Ohio University Press, 2009.

Nowland, John H.B. *Early Reminiscences of Indianapolis*. Indianapolis, IN: Sentinel Book and Job Printing House, 1870.

Philips, Clifton J. *Indiana in Transition: The Emergence of an Industrial Commonwealth, 1880–1920*. Indianapolis: Indiana Historical Bureau and Indiana Historical Society, 1968.

Scott, John. *The Indiana Gazetteer, or Topographical Dictionary*. 1826. Repr., Indianapolis: Indiana Historical Society, 1954.

Tenuth, Jeffrey. *Indianapolis: A Circle City History*. Charleston, SC: Arcadia Publishing, 2005.

Thornbrough, Emma Lou. *Indiana in the Civil War Era, 1850–1880*. Indianapolis: Indiana Historical Bureau and Indiana Historical Society, 1965.

Thornbrough, Gayle, Dorothy L. Riker and Paula Corpuz, eds. *The Diary of Calvin Fletcher*. 9 vols. Indianapolis: Indiana Historical Society, 1972–83.

Williams, David Leander. *Indianapolis Jazz: The Masters, Legends and Legacy of Indiana Avenue*. Charleston, SC: The History Press, 2014.

Winslow, Hattie Lou, and Joseph R.H. Moore. *Camp Morton, 1861–1865: Indianapolis Prison Camp*. Indianapolis: Indiana Historical Society, 1995.

ABOUT THE AUTHOR

Dawn Bakken is the associate editor of the *Indiana Magazine of History*, a scholarly history journal published by the Department of History at Indiana University–Bloomington. She received her PhD in religious studies and American studies from IU–Bloomington, where she has also taught courses in religious studies. Her family moved to Indianapolis when she was six years old, and she grew up on the city's west side.

Visit us at
www.historypress.net

This title is also available as an e-book